MARION BARRY

BRITISH AMERICAN
PUBLISHING

MARION BARRY
THE POLITICS OF RACE

JONATHAN I. Z. AGRONSKY

British American Publishing

Library of Congress Cataloging-in-Publication Data

Agronsky, Jonathan I. Z., 1946–
    Marion Barry : the politics of race / Jonathan I.Z. Agronsky.
        p.   cm.
    1. Barry, Marion, 1936–   . 2. Washington (D.C.)—Politics and
government—1967–   3. Mayors—Washington (D.C.)—Biography.
    I. Title.
F201.3.B37A37   1991
975.3'04'092—dc20
[B]   90-38496
                                                                   CIP

For Bonnie, who was always there for me.

"The griefs we cause ourselves cut deepest of all."

— Sophocles

CONTENTS

PREFACE

I was initially moved to write this book by the anger I felt toward Marion Barry, some of his top lieutenants, and cronies because of what I saw as the great and unnecessary harm they were inflicting on the people, reputation and treasury of the nation's capital—especially during Barry's final years in power. But as I delved into Barry's life and talked with some of those who worked with him, struggled alongside him in the civil rights movement, loved him or hated him during his three decades in the public eye, or who sat on the jury of his drug and perjury trial, I felt saddened. For an indelible picture emerged of a bold, gifted, charismatic leader who had done much for his constituents, particularly those who were most vulnerable, yet who had ultimately betrayed both them and himself.

As I sifted through the documentary record of Barry's life, I also was amazed at the skill, frequency, and seeming ease with which Barry, until the very end, was able to use his minority status to extract concessions from the white establishment, emerge unscathed from repeated allegations of wrongdoing, and, perhaps most significantly, hold onto power long past his usefulness. I was also struck by the intensity of some black Washingtonians' anger at what they saw as an attempt by white federal officials to do judicially what Barry's local political rivals, black and white, seemed unable to do politically—unseat the mayor.

Barry's personal story is, as everyone's, unique; his political story is not. Politicans have used the lever of race to grab and hold onto power since men first discovered differences among themselves. Who in this country can forget, for example, the Willie Horton television ads exploiting white voters' fears of black criminals that helped George Bush win the Oval Office in November 1988? But while it is important to note that many others in positions of power also have exploited racial prejudice

xi

and fears for political ends, Barry alone must live with the ironic legacy of having increased racial tensions in a city he once hoped to racially unite.

I hope that by looking in some detail at Marion Barry's life to date, rather than just the pathetic last chapter of his political career, when he had become, in his own words, powerless over his addictions, the reader will find in his story something useful, perhaps even redemptive, if only a parable about the need for honesty, integrity and, dare I say it, moderation— not just in our leaders, but in ourselves.

Washington, D.C., February 1991

Part One: Getting Caught

1

THE SETUP

The Lincoln Town Car, midnight blue with spoked wheels, tinted-glass windows, and triple phone antennae jutting from the trunk, pulled smartly out of the parking lot of the District Building. Lights on to meet the gathering dusk, it moved steadily away from Washington's crumbling Beaux-Arts seat of government and headed east on Pennsylvania, the avenue of the Presidents. Inside the car on the unusually temperate winter evening of Thursday, January 18, 1990, Washington, D.C., mayor Marion S. Barry, Jr., all 6' 1", 210 pounds of him, sank back into the plush leather seat for the short ride to the Martin Luther King Memorial Library.

The mammoth steel, glass, and tan brick box in downtown Washington had been named after a man who was, among other things, Barry's mentor during his early days in the civil rights movement. Now the 53-year-old mayor was to appear at a housing lottery in the library's basement auditorium, along with city housing director David Dennison and D.C. Council member Frank Smith. Smith had initiated the popular lotteries of houses seized by the city from tax-delinquent owners. The trio would take turns plucking from a rotating drum the names of 10 low- and moderate-income District residents who would win a chance to buy, with a down payment as low as $250, a piece of the American Dream.

Attending the housing lottery, organized under the city's Homestead Exemption Act, was only one way in which the controversial political boss of the nation's capital paid his political debts to the "left out, kicked out or just plain kicked," as Barry sometimes referred to D.C.'s less fortunate residents. The housing lottery, of course, could help only those with the economic resources to exploit it. But over the years, as both a community activist and an elected official, Barry also had

3

tried to help less-affluent residents with federally and city-funded antipoverty programs and with jobs. By Barry's dozenth year in office, the city government had swelled to more than 48,000 employees, making it the largest in the land, on a per capita basis, and perhaps more importantly, the best hedge against unemployment—including the mayor's—the District had ever enjoyed.

The concern Barry had shown for Washington's neediest had translated into votes—enough to win mandates in the 1982 and 1986 mayoral races (middle-class whites had put him over the top in 1978). His 1986 reelection victory had come despite allegations of executive drug use and womanizing, and such chronic and highly visible problems as soaring city budget deficits, a dramatic increase in drug-related homicides, and the conviction of top city officials on corruption charges.

Barry's remarkable staying power was based on a simple political reality: in some quarters of the city the mayor's machismo, his narcissistic preoccupation with his own deeds and pronouncements, his womanizing, even his reported drug use, were not only acceptable, they were perceived as admirable. At least Barry, a former southern poor boy, was enjoying the good life and doing what some of the city's disadvantaged residents would if they only could: defying the white power brokers and the media controlled by them.

"Why was he accepted in the black community?" asks Rich Adams, a veteran black producer at Washington's WUSA-TV, rhetorically. "Here's a guy, he may be a crook, he may be a slime, he may be doing all this [controversial] stuff, but by God, he's manipulated the system and he's made those [white] folks dance to his tune. And for a lot of people, that's more important than any of his moral failings."

Barry had shrewdly exploited such attitudes, along with the fear some black Washingtonians felt that if he were removed from office, the city's mostly affluent white minority, acting on a secret if vaguely defined "plan," would bring in one of their own to govern, thereby setting back the progress blacks had made under Barry. No one ever explained just how D.C.'s white minority would accomplish this.

But during the previous year Barry's support, even among some of his most faithful constituents, had shrunk following news reports that he had paid several visits to Charles Lewis, a former D.C. employment services department employee and Virgin Islands native, at the Ramada Inn Central near downtown Washington. Barry's ties to Lewis were later probed by a federal grand jury after D.C. police found traces of cocaine in Lewis's hotel room. Although Barry vigorously denied that he had used drugs with Lewis—complaining that he was being "tried, convicted and doing time" [sic] by the city's white-controlled media for "things that are not true, guilt by association"—the so-called Ramada Inn incident had made Barry's subsequent attendance at ceremonies such as the D.C. housing lottery politically imperative.

The Ramada Inn incident triggered a wider grand jury probe, initiated by U.S. Attorney for the District of Columbia Jay Stephens, into the alleged misuse of more than $250,000 in city funds by nearly 50 D.C. employees and consultants hired by the city. The employees, and their ultimate boss, Marion Barry, had traveled to the U.S. Virgin Islands, ostensibly to advise its government on revamping its personnel system but actually to spend a good deal of time partying, shopping, playing tennis, or taking boat rides at taxpayers' expense. Barry's old friend Charles Lewis had co-managed the project for the Virgin Islands.

Prosecutor Stephens was also investigating an alleged drug ring inside the city government. According to the *Washington Times*, the wider investigation involved high-ranking D.C. officials, including department heads, who were not only using drugs on the job but procuring them for use by other city employees. The *Times* said the city officials used cocaine distribution channels established by Rayful Edmond III, a deadly black Robin Hood of the slums who was convicted in December 1989 of operating a continuing criminal enterprise and sentenced to life in prison without possibility of parole. (D.C. law enforcement officials reportedly have tied 30 drug-related murders to Edmond "enforcers," including one homicide with which Edmond himself is charged.) The paper said

Stephens also was investigating possible contract fraud and the trading of city contracts for drugs or sexual favors.

Because of these mounting scandals, eight months before the September 1990 Democratic mayoral primary Washington's incumbent mayor already was running, and running hard. He was showing up regularly at black churches and antidrug rallies, at school assemblies, old-age homes, even at funerals. Earlier in the day on January 18, Barry had attended a memorial service for Sammy Unger, a black high school athlete slain by a suspected drug dealer. The popular 18-year-old senior, a football and basketball star at Washington's McKinley High School, had been gunned down on a sidewalk near the school, becoming the city's 17th homicide victim of the year (483 people would die in the city by year's end, setting a grim new record). Barry wanted the community to know he was concerned about the bloodshed, so widespread that for two years running the nation's capital was also the country's murder capital.

At around 7 P.M., as the mayor's limousine dipped into the underground parking lot of the King library, at 901 G Street, NW, a mile farther uptown, in Room 727 of the Vista International Hotel at 1400 M Street, NW, two attractive black women were discussing Barry. The younger woman, wearing a tight-fitting leather skirt, vest, and long-sleeved blouse on her trim figure, was FBI Special Agent Wanda King. For the purpose of the sting, she was masquerading as the proprietress of a Los Angeles cosmetology school, and a friend of Rasheeda Moore's. The other, dressed in a long jacket, slacks, and cloth head wrap paid for by the U.S. Government, was 38-year-old former model Hazel Diane "Rasheeda" Moore. Tall and light-skinned, with photogenic features and a once-shapely body going to fat, Moore had been Barry's lover. Now she was being dangled as bait in an elaborately orchestrated sting operation to catch the mayor buying and using illegal drugs.

Planned for months, the sting was finally falling into place. The man who launched it, Jay Stephens, knew that an undercover operation was probably the only way he would ever catch Barry in the act of breaking the law. The short, mustachioed,

morally driven 43-year-old, white Harvard Law School graduate had been appointed by President Ronald Reagan to replace
another Reagan appointee, Joseph diGenova, in February 1988.
Stephens knew that as the *Washington Post* reported, during
diGenova's five-year tenure as U.S. Attorney for the District
of Columbia, FBI agents dispatched by him had "sorted through
the mayor's American Express bills, staked out his house,
examined his signature on city contracts, analyzed his bank
accounts, checked his tax returns, verified his campaign
contributions, even subpoenaed two pairs of shoes he denied
receiving from a city contractor," yet, said the *Post*, the G-
men still had failed to "break through what they called Barry's
'insulation,' the barrier of friendship, power and racial pride
that surrounded the former civil rights leader."

Stephens had seen how wide and deep that protective barrier
ran by following the mayor's misadventures.

In December 1981, for instance, Barry reportedly had attended a drug-filled Christmas party at a 14th Street, NW, nude
dancing club called "This Is It?" where he allegedly used
cocaine. D.C. Police investigated, but Barry escaped arrest.
In fact, the only visible result of the investigation was the
reassignment of the black police inspector who had initiated
it. The quashing of the investigation had not surprised
Stephens or anyone else familiar with Barry's politicization
of the D.C. police department, where he reserved for himself
the power not only to appoint the chief but also to approve
promotion of top commanders.

In 1984 diGenova had come closest to nailing Barry when
the mayor was questioned—twice—by a federal grand jury
about his alleged cocaine use with former D.C. Public Works
Department employee and convicted cocaine dealer Karen
Johnson. Johnson, the mayor's first publicly acknowledged
paramour, chose jail rather than testify against Barry, to whom
she reportedly had sold cocaine some 20 or 30 times. After
spending eight months in D.C. Jail for contempt of court,
Johnson later told federal investigators that two of Barry's
friends—D.C. minority contractors John Clyburn and Roy
Littlejohn—had paid her $25,000 in hush money—an allegation
the mayor's friends denied and diGenova could not prove.

Although diGenova had failed to indict or even arrest Barry
in five years of trying, he had bagged two of the mayor's top
lieutenants, deputy mayors Ivanhoe Donaldson and Alphonse
Hill, and several lesser officials, on corruption charges. But
whenever diGenova had focused his investigations on Barry
himself, the mayor had a standard response: the white prosecutor was intent on removing him from power simply because
he was a strong black leader.

In 1987 Barry had declared "war" on diGenova, accusing
him of "abusing the subpoena power in a way I have not
witnessed in forty years" by rounding up some of Barry's
friends and associates as potential witnesses in a probe of
alleged contract peddling. The mayor demanded in a civil suit
that the U.S. Justice Department investigate diGenova, alleging
that he had tried to discredit Barry by leaking information about
the probe to the news media. Then Barry sued both diGenova
and the U.S. Justice Department for alleged "prosecutorial
abuse." However, U.S. District Court Chief Judge Aubrey E.
Robinson, Jr., a black man, rejected the complaint as unfounded. Still, Barry scored some propaganda points with his
highly publicized suit.

Barry's remarkable ability to use his public utterances not
only to escape arrest but, in may instances, to put his accusers
on the defensive, had become his political trademark: no matter
what allegations were leveled at him by, in his word, the
"barracudas" of the media, no matter how many close subordinates were picked off by federal prosecutors, the mayor had
managed repeatedly to avoid the legal, moral, and political
consequences of his actions and rise like the legendary phoenix
from the ashes of his apparent ruin.

Having watched Barry's amazing political act from the sidelines since the mid-1970s, when he had served as an assistant
special prosecutor during the Watergate investigation, Jay
Stephens knew that to bring down the mayor legally he would
have to do what Joseph diGenova could not: find a way either
to penetrate or circumvent Barry's formidable wall of protection. He would need to find a close friend or associate of the
mayor, or even a former lover, who would be vulnerable to

persuasion by the government, had a reason to seek revenge, or perhaps believed the only way to save the mayor from himself was to arrest him.

Rasheeda Moore met all three criteria.

Moore, a D.C. native whose mother was a church organist, first caught Barry's eye in December 1977, when she graced the cover of *Essence* magazine. In that provocative photograph Moore wore cornrows and gold leaflet barrettes in her hair and a sultry, open-mouthed smile. After seeing Moore's picture, Barry called her in New York City and tried to persuade her to come to D.C. as his guest. Moore refused the invitation. She wanted to pursue her promising modeling career. But that ended abruptly only four years later when she ignored her agent's advice and flew to London to rendezvous with her lover, a reputed international drug trafficker. Moore testified at Barry's trial that her lover was arrested for allegedly smuggling $18 million of heroin on the same day her plane touched down at London's Heathrow Airport. (She said that she was arrested, too, but was released after being questioned.)

When Moore returned to New York, she said, she was blackballed as a model. Her career in a shambles, Moore fell on hard times—she gained weight, became a crack addict, gave birth to three illegitimate children with two different fathers, both reputed drug dealers.

Barry finally had met Moore in 1986 at a birthday party for Robert Johnson, founder of the Washington-based Black Entertainment Television network and at that time a fund-raiser for Barry and a close political ally. During the stormy and sporadic relationship that ensued, Moore struggled with her conscience, telling Barry at one point she wanted to stop seeing him because she felt their drug-filled extramarital affair—carried on not only in Washington but in other U.S. cities and in the U.S. Virgin Islands—was immoral. He had persuaded Moore that "divine providence" had brought them together. To make sure she'd stick around, Barry had allegedly let it be known that he wanted funding approved for "Project Me," a summer youth program Moore had designed with her sister, Mertine, and a friend, Carol Bland Jackson. The trio received nearly $180,000 from the city over the next two years to teach modeling skills to black teenage girls. Their initial no-bid contract asking for more than $60,000 had been approved by the city's notoriously slow-moving bureaucracy in a matter of days.

But then Barry had allegedly threatened to cut off the funding for "Project Me" in May 1988 after Moore had refused to give him oral sex in a D.C. hotel room. ("If you give up on me, you lose everything that comes with me," is how Moore says he couched his request. The funding was later cut, she said.) Later Barry had allegedly slapped his mistress to the floor during a love spat at another D.C. hotel and secretly had begun seeing Rose Marie "Maria" McCarthy, a woman Moore had introduced him to. (Moore knew nothing about "Aunt Bettye," "Miss T," Grace Shell, and the mayor's many other actual or would-be trysting partners.) So Moore had finally broken off the relationship. She moved to California in May 1989. The mayor had neither seen nor spoken to Moore for at least four months when she suddenly popped back into his life with a vengeance on January 18, 1990.

Between 6:00 and 6:25 P.M., as FBI agents listened in, Moore called Barry at his office 11 times, only to learn from Barry's secretary that the mayor had left. Did her former lover sense the trap she was helping set for him? Was he still angry at her? Was this opportunity finally to redeem herself—in her own eyes, in the eyes of the law (Moore was facing possible felony charges in Washington and drunk-driving charges in Los Angeles if she refused to cooperate), and in the eyes of the Lord (she said she had experienced a religious reawakening while living on the West Coast)—going to be wasted, like too many other opportunities in her life?

Maybe not.

"He took your number with him," the mayor's secretary said on Moore's final call.

At this point doing the right thing was very important to Moore, whom one law enforcement official described as "on a crusade" to get Barry arrested once she made up her mind to cooperate. According to the official, Moore wanted to rescue the mayor from his addiction and saw such a move as the only possible way to do that. But she also was trying to rebuild her own life. By the time she volunteered to play her greatest role, a role that would make "Rasheeda Moore" a household name worldwide, the once-stunning model who had captivated countless men was a cocaine addict and alcoholic living in a public shelter in Los Angeles. An unwed mother, she regularly spent her children's welfare money on drugs. Less than three weeks earlier, on New Year's Day, Moore had landed in the Los Angeles city jail for driving under the influence.

That routine traffic bust had provided the break FBI agents from the Washington field office and detectives from the D.C. police internal affairs division were waiting for: the Los Angeles police, responding to an FBI bulletin, had notified the Washington field office they were holding Moore, who had dropped out of sight several weeks earlier after initially refusing to participate in a sting against Barry. Two Washington-based FBI agents had flown to L.A. in early January and made Moore an offer she could not refuse: in return for her cooperation in the proposed sting operation against Barry, federal prosecutors in the District would agree not to prosecute her for lies she admitted telling a federal grand jury in D.C. and for possessing cocaine on numerous occasions, and Los Angeles prosecutors would agree to drop the drunk-driving charges.

A week before the sting, Moore was flown back to D.C. along with her three children. Since then the Bureau had picked up the tab for all their expenses at Washington hotels. Bureau generosity was understandable. Moore was, after all, the only person who had ever agreed to play the turncoat's role. On the night of the sting, FBI agents were babysitting her children.

Watching Rasheeda Moore through the viewfinder of a miniature video camera in Vista room 726, next to hers, was FBI Special Agent Ronald Stern, head of a combined sting team that also included FBI special agents Wanda King (operational name "Wanda Moore"); Peter Wubbenhorst, and Robert Core; D.C. police internal affairs division detectives Al Arrington (the sole black D.C. police member) and Jim Pawlik; and Assistant U.S. Attorney Daniel Bernstein—a highly unusual team member who was there to provide on-the-spot legal advice as to what constituted drug possession and to help the law enforcement officers avoid any possible charge that they had entrapped their target. They had gathered at the Vista, in Ronald Stern's words, to give Marion Barry "an opportunity to violate the law."

In a rare move, FBI Director William Sessions had personally reviewed the sting plan and signed off on it. U.S. Attorney General Dick Thornburgh, the nation's highest lawman, had verbally approved the operation but later balked when Stern allegedly proposed going after Barry a few days earlier, on Martin Luther King, Jr.'s, birthday. "No," Thornburgh had said, according to a Justice Department source. "I don't want a goddamn riot on my hands!" (Thornburgh apparently relented when the date was moved back.)

Conspicuously absent from the planning group was D.C. police chief Isaac Fulwood, Jr., a Barry appointee who reportedly was kept out of the loop for fear that he would tip off the mayor. A high-ranking police department source told the *Washington Times*: "The chief didn't know about it, and neither did the director of the IAD [Internal Affairs Division, David Faison]."

The principal architect of the sting, 35-year-old case agent Ronald Stern, was tall, handsome, athletic, with blow-dried hair that he parted in the middle and a neatly trimmed mustache—the epitome of a young G-man of the 1990s. Using a beautiful woman as a lure, Stern had snared Barry's crack-smoking buddy, convicted drug dealer and ex-city employee Charles Lewis, in a March 1989 drug sting in the U.S. Virgin Islands. Lewis, seeking a deal with the government, subsequently had provided grand jury testimony linking the mayor not only to drug use but also to possible drug distribution, obstruction of justice, and perjury charges. Lewis had also identified Rasheeda Moore from a photograph taken during a June 1986 visit Moore and Barry had made to the Virgin Islands, and he told Stern and Al Arrington that he had seen Barry and Moore—whom Lewis knew only by the initials "R.C."—smoking crack together. Stern put it all together and came up with the plan to use Moore as the sting bait. Arrington won the woman's trust, and the team was ready to move.

Less than a week after the undercover operation was approved, Stern's team had secured the hotel rooms, set up the surveillance equipment, put the elusive human lure in place, and drafted a detailed plan that, if properly followed, would secure an arrest while avoiding any possible entrapment charge. Nevertheless, the young case agent knew that, despite his preparations, like dozens of his FBI predecessors who had stalked Barry, unless he got lucky, he too would be left clutching air rather than a suspect.

In a highly sensitive case involving a well-known public figure who had openly flaunted his defiance of the white U.S. Attorney for the District of Columbia and of public opinion for nearly a decade without suffering any apparent consequences, such an outcome was a distinct possibility. The fact that Rasheeda Moore was neither a professional actress nor a cop added another risk to the operation. She was also a junkie, participating in an operation that initially had repelled her. Finally, she had been Barry's lover—a powerful human tie that did not make Moore exactly the ideal weapon for hunting game as big as the mayor of D.C.

And what about Barry? Hizzoner was anything but predictable. Frequently he would turn up hours late for important meetings or not show up at all. The mayor was no super sleuth, but he had shown an uncanny ability to sniff out potential trouble, and an extraordinary facility for dancing out of it once he had gotten himself into it. Moreover, ever since the Ramada Inn incident a year earlier, Barry had curbed his provocative behavior to a degree and become more cautious. Lately he had avoided visiting friends in hotels. Maybe he would refuse to take the bait. Maybe he would not return the calls. Maybe the operation, which already had consumed thousands of man hours and hundreds of thousands of dollars, would fizzle out a great dud, along with Stern's promising FBI career.

At around 6:25 P.M. on January 18 such speculations suddenly became irrelevant. The telephone in Room 727 of the Vista International Hotel began to ring. As Rasheeda Moore picked up the receiver, Stern and his team listened intently over their headsets: was this the call they all were waiting for?

"Helloo," said Moore in a cheerful sing-song.

"Miss Moore, please," said a man in a pleasant baritone, slightly slurring his words.

"Hi!"

"Hey, darlin', what brings ya t'Washington?"

"I been here visiting for a couple days, takin' care o' some business—"

"Visitin' who?"

"My family—who do ya think?"

"How long ya been here?"

"Just got in yesterday."

"Oh, yeah? So, who's with you?"

"I have a friend of mine with me."

"Some man?"

"No!"

"What is it, if not a man, a woman?"

"Yeah, female; she's from California."

"Yeah? So, how long you gonna be up there?"

"I'm probably gonna be here—cause she's takin' care of the expenses and everything, she's here tryin' t'take care o'some business, something I wanta talk t'you a little bit about—we probably be here until tomorrow, and then we might be movin' into New York to finalize something."

"Is she there now?"

"Yeah, uh-huh."

"Because I'm goin' to go by the [Martin Luther King] library in a few minutes to draw some names for the Homestead Exemption."

"For the what?"

"Homestead Exemption."

"Homestead Exemption, uh-huh."

"And I can come by the hotel and we can meet downstairs, and have a drink and talk."

"Oh, okay, or you can just come on upstairs," Moore purred.

"I don't wanna do that."

"No?"

"No. Too many Nosey Rosies around nowadays."

Barry had, in fact, pledged publicly to avoid meetings in hotel rooms following the Ramada Inn incident.

"Really?"

"Yeah, yeah. I mean, what I'd like t'do is have the initial meetin' down there and then maybe we'll decide t'go up after that, but I don't—"

"Oh, okay—"

"But I don't wanna go up there first."

"No problem, okay."

"But I would like t'see you while you're here."

"Oh, yeah, okay," she laughed coquettishly. "So what, you'll call me first?"

"Yeah, yeah."

"Okay."

"Make love to ya."

"Huh?"

"Make love to ya."

"Oh, come on, please—let's talk about that when I see you!"

"All right!" Barry laughed.

"God, you know, give it a break here, I haven't even talked to you in—"

"We all need a break, it's been too long."

"Yeah, I'll talk to ya in a whiz."

"I'll tell ya what, we'll be finished in about a half hour," the mayor said.

"Okay, I'll be here waitin' for ya," Moore said huskily.

"Bye-bye."

At the end of the two-minute conversation, the mayor proceeded to the housing lottery at the King library. Meanwhile, in Room 726 at the Vista, Ronald Stern huddled with his colleagues. Despite the presence of lawyer Bernstein to advise them on legal issues and a detailed operation plan an inch thick, they now faced a practical problem: the target of their operation was balking at coming to the room. They needed to think of a way to lure him there without actually trying to coax or persuade him—actions that could potentially be construed in court as constituting entrapment. The sting would hold up legally only if they could get Barry to come voluntarily to the room where they had hidden three tiny video cameras and several microphones to record his every word and deed.

The proposed solution was relatively simple. It might not work, but the team had nothing to lose by trying. When Barry emerged from the King library and called Moore a second time from his limousine, at approximately 7:25 P.M., they were ready with their ploy.

"Hello."

"Uh, Miss Moore, please."

"Hi, how ya doing?"

"Hey, darlin', y'all ready t'come downstairs?"

"Umm, I was just eating, gosh," said Moore, chewing loudly and clinking silverware near the receiver as if to emphasize her message. "I just ordered room service."

"I told ya I was comin' by there!" the mayor protested.

"I know!"

"Why you do that?" he demanded

"Because I was starving," said Moore. "Cause, I mean, you know, well, anyway, why don't you just come on up?"

"I really don't wanna do that."

"Huh?"

"All right," the mayor finally conceded, "but [only] for a few minutes."

"Okay."

"I don't like these hotel rooms."

"Huh?"

"I don't like t'go into hotel rooms."

"Why, what's the matter?"

"Nosey. Anyway, I come up for a few minutes."

"Okay."

"How long you think you're gonna be there?"

"I mean, I'm just eatin' some crab and some soup."

"Okay, yeah, I'll be there in 'bout five minutes."

"Okay."

"All right."

"And you have my room number?"

''727?''

''Yeah.''

''All right.''

''Okay, bye-bye.''

As the mayor signed off, his limousine sped east on H Street, NW, past the combined National Museum of American Art and National Portrait Gallery. Barry looked out the two-way glass at the 133-year-old replica of the Greek Parthenon, which is one of hundreds of tax-exempt buildings in Washington owned by the United States Government. Uncle Sam also controls more than 40 percent of the District's 61 square miles of territory—an arrangement that costs the city billions in lost tax revenues each year and one reason many D.C. residents feel they are living in America's ''last colony.''

After passing the museum's colorful ceramic statue of a red-shirted cowboy in gold chaps riding a blue bucking bronco, the mayor's official car turned left onto 7th Street, NW, the edge of Chinatown, then moved past the gilded red Chinese Friendship Archway built by Chinatown merchants in honor of Washington's sister city, Beijing. Heading north, the limo passed the recently completed Tech World office and hotel complex, a part of the megadevelopment that had surged in downtown Washington during Barry's tenure.

Three blocks past the Friendship Archway, the mayor's car passed a cluster of white metal trailers serving as emergency shelters for the homeless. Barry had opposed the 1984 voters' initiative that had added scores of such utilitarian eyesores to the urban landscape. The initiative had resulted in a law guaranteeing shelter to anyone who asked for it, a policy that had cost D.C. taxpayers $35 million in 1989 alone and further strained a social welfare system that was already hopelessly overburdened.

The Town Car turned left onto L Street, NW, and traced the southern edge of the Shaw neighborhood. Passing a huge vacant lot on the north side of L slated for development, and some delapidated townhouses farther down the street, the limousine went by some ladies of the night standing on the corner of 10th and L and slowed for a yield sign where the letter street merges with Massachusetts, one of the city's grand avenues.

A block later it eased into the flow of traffic around Thomas Circle, named after Union Major General George H. Thomas. The Rock of Chickamauga, spurring on his trusty steed, guards the southern tip of the 14th Street corridor, a tawdry strip of fast-food outlets, liquor stores, and pawn shops that had been trashed during the 1968 riot following the murder of the Reverend Martin Luther King, Jr. Twenty-two years later, despite the efforts of black leaders, including Marion Barry, to rebuild the riot-torn corridor, shells of burnt-out buildings and boarded-up storefronts still dot 14th Street. Drugs and warm, willing bodies are still sold openly 24 hours a day to customers willing to risk an overdose, an arrest, or a case of deadly AIDS.

The streetwalkers and winos, junkies and pimps, whom Barry's limousine passed in the early evening hours of January 18 were a pathetic lot who seemed tragically intent on destroying themselves. As events of the night would reveal, the mayor was heading for his own destruction—in the person of his foxy former mistress, Rasheeda Moore. He had been surprised when she phoned him out of the blue and invited him to her hotel. Such delicious opportunities don't fall into a man's lap—even the lap of a powerful man like Marion Barry—every day. When they did, at least in the past few years, Barry usually tried to exploit them.

To Washington's free-wheeling mayor the potential pleasures of such clandestine encounters apparently outweighed the potential risks. Or did they? Only Marion Barry could answer that question. However, one thing is certain: by the time Moore called Barry from the Vista Hotel, the mayor had dodged many well-aimed bullets fired by the U.S. attorney's office and the media and still twice been reelected to the District's highest office. So, on this night, he may truly have believed, as he had told *Los Angeles Times* reporter Bella Stumbo less than two weeks before the sting, that he was "invincible."

2

THE STING

As the mayor's limousine pulled off M Street, NW, into the driveway of the Vista International Hotel and stopped beneath its twin crimson canopies, seven floors up more than a dozen people, including two emergency medical technicians from the D.C. fire department, waited anxiously to see what Marion Barry would do next. Despite his telephoned agreement to meet Rasheeda Moore in her room, the mayor still could insist she meet him in the lobby, a move that would prevent the sting. Barry also could pull a "reverse sting" when he got to Moore's room, by calling his police bodyguards on his walkie-talkie and asking them to arrest Moore or FBI Special Agent Wanda King—if either woman offered him drugs.

Such an unlikely move by the mayor was anticipated by the investigators and appeared in the inch-thick guidelines for the sting, along with instructions on how to deal with, in one sting member's words, "every eventuality." The guidelines, and the presence of Assistant U.S. Attorney Daniel Bernstein, gave the operation a basis in law and a semblance of control; but each of the veteran lawmen assembled in Vista's room 726 knew that something could—most likely would—happen during the sting that no one could anticipate. They knew the success or failure of the operation now rested largely with the mayor.

At approximately 7:34 P.M. an agent signaled Ronald Stern that the mayor had just entered the hotel lobby and was walking toward the elevator with his bodyguard. The adrenalin began to pump in every member of the sting team: Barry had taken the bait after all.

At 7:35 a knock announced the mayor's arrival outside room 727.

Rasheeda Moore answered the door.

19

"Hi, how you doing?" asked Barry, as he sauntered into the luxuriously appointed $188-a-night room overlooking the hotel's dramatic 12-story atrium and landscaped lobby. The room had its own refrigerator bar, bathroom phone, complimentary toiletries, and remote bedside controls for lighting and cable television. In these opulent surroundings, Barry extended his hand to the lover he hadn't seen in more than six months.

"How you doing?" Moore responded, seizing the mayor's hand and shaking it.

Placing his walkie-talkie on a narrow wooden desk that stood against the wall, Barry introduced himself to "Wanda Moore," the operational name taken by FBI agent Wanda King. Then he walked over to Rasheeda.

"Hey, stranger," he said, embracing her. "Good to see you again."

"Good to see you, too," said Moore.

"Why don't I just let you two catch up on some old times," said King, who donned her white leather shoulder bag and headed for the door. "I'm going to see what trouble I can get into downstairs."

The mayor suggested they all meet later in the lobby for a drink. He sat down on the bed next to Moore and, just seconds after the undercover agent left, reached out and touched his ex-lover's breast.

"Shame on you," said Moore.

"What? I didn't do anything," said the mayor in mock innocence.

"Yes, you are!" she laughed. "Shame on you, you haven't changed much."

Barry got up and removed his jacket, revealing a white, long-sleeved shirt with cufflinks, suspenders, as well as a paunch.

"You've gained a little weight," Moore teased.

"A little bit," admitted Barry, patting his belly. "I got to lose about 10 pounds." He hung his jacket on a closet doorknob, turned to Moore, and asked her a question that would be endlessly debated at his trial. "You been good?"

"Huh?"

"You been good?" he asked again. Then he answered his own question. "Of course not."

"What do you mean, 'of course not'?" chided Moore, laughing. She had told Ronald Stern that Barry might use the expression, by which she said he meant, "Have you stayed off drugs?" "Have I been good—what about you?" she asked the mayor.

Ignoring Moore's response, Barry disappeared into the bathroom.

Moore paced nervously back and forth at the foot of the bed, poured some Hennessey—the mayor's favorite libation—into a highball glass, sipped the burning amber liquid, loosened and refastened her broad, black leather belt, primped in the mirror, glanced at the television and otherwise acted the high-strung amateur star of what soon would become the world's most infamous home video.

A few minutes later Barry emerged, possibly having been videotaped for posterity while moving his bowels. One of three miniature surveillance cameras was hidden in a ceiling vent in the bathroom, a place where the mayor often had used drugs in the past—ironically, to escape detection. A second camera peered through a wall behind and to the right of the king-sized bed. A third camera provided a waist-level view across the front of the bed and showed the entrance to the bathroom and the door leading to the hotel hallway. The solid-state low-light cameras were practically undetectable since they used pinhole lenses, which could peer through a pencil-sized hole six inches behind the opening in the wall or air vent in which they were placed.

When he returned to the bedroom and living room area, Barry poured himself the first of three shots of cognac he would down during the 83 minutes he would spend in the room. He and Moore sat on the bed, watching television and chatting amiably like the old friends and lovers they were.

"So, how's California—where are you, in Los Angeles?" asked Barry.

"You know where I am, calling me—"

"When?" demanded Barry.

"Tried to call you, last time I tried to call you."

"When? I going to be in California, first of February," the mayor said. He held a master's degree in chemistry and had waxed eloquent on many a public occasion—including his nominating speech for the Reverend Jesse Jackson at the 1984 Democratic National Convention—but when he got behind closed doors with friends, Barry often reverted to the grammar and lingo of the street.

"You'll be there?"

"Mmm-hmm."

"Near Burbank?"

"Compton. I'll be going to Compton."

"That's not that far. What are you doing in Compton?"

"For a meeting of the National Conference of Black Mayors." Barry had twice been president of this organization.

"That's where they're meeting this year?"

"Mmm-hmm."

From their relaxed demeanor and mundane conversation, Barry and Moore could have been a husband and wife on a trip together rather than a pair of drug-addicted, middle-aged, estranged lovers. But then Moore asked him about Maria McCarthy, the former girlfriend of Moore's who had come between them.

"She called me...about this bank deal," said Barry about the 50-year-old Chicago native. McCarthy had lived in the Washington area from 1969 to 1988 and later moved to Greensboro, North Carolina, where she worked for her family's accounting firm. After being introduced to McCarthy by Moore, Barry had allegedly carried on a drug-filled romance with her, visiting McCarthy at her Silver Spring townhouse on a number of occasions. "You know, she's got two brothers who are accountants down in Greensboro," he said.

Then the mayor decided to tease Moore or, was his brain so messed up by drugs that he literally couldn't remember?

"What's her last name?" he asked.

"Who?" asked Moore.

"Maria."

"Oh, give me a break," she laughed.

"No, serious," the mayor insisted.

"Give me a break," Moore repeated.

"I'm serious."

"You should be ashamed," Moore laughed.

"What, I'm serious, baby!"

"McCarthy," Moore finally answered.

"Oh, McCarthy, yeah." Barry laughed. "I can't remember her name, shit." But he could remember that McCarthy's brothers were accountants down in Greensboro.

"What's my last name?" demanded Moore.

"Moore," responded Barry, prompting yet another nervous giggle from his paramour.

"What's my first name?" she asked.

"Uh..." Barry stalled.

"Maheeda?" Moore asked playfully.

"No, Rasheeda, Rasheeda."

"Geez, I don't believe you," said Moore.

"Your real name, your real name is something else," said Barry. Indeed, he would rename her before the night ended.

Then Moore reminded Barry again that he had not returned dozens of calls she placed to him from California where she had been living for the past eight months.

"I was really upset with you when I called you," she said. "And, remember, you told me you would work with me, try to help me find a place to stay—I told you I had some problems in California?

"I can't [get] caught in these situations, I can't help out," Barry replied. Then, slugging the cognac, he stated the obvious: "You must have made it. You did all right." Then he changed the subject. "Where did you get all these watches and things from?" he asked, eyeing Moore's jewelry.

"The guy I'm dating now," said Moore.

"You got his nose open, huh?" Barry asked, implying that she had supplied him with cocaine.

"Mmm-hmm," said Moore.

Barry touched her breast again.

"Stop!" she laughed, removing his hand.

"Can we make love before you leave, before you leave town?" Barry asked. "It would be a good idea just for old time sake, you know, catch up."

In room 726 some of the sting team members fought to keep from laughing. One of them later characterized Barry's line as "corny."

"No," answer Moore, " 'cause I got—"

Moore laughed again as she parried yet another mayoral hand thrust. Then she reminded him that the best things in life aren't always free: "You owe me a watch anyway."

"I do?"

"Mmm-hmm."

"I'll find you one before you leave here," Barry promised.

"You will?"

"Uh-hum." If that's all the woman wanted, he could enjoy her and buy her a timepiece and that would be that.

"You're kidding. Oh, wow."

"When are you-all leavin'?" Barry asked. He remembered that Moore had told him on the phone that she was heading for New York sometime the following day. That meant if he was going to score, he had to do it tonight.

"Hey, I'm looking for a job," replied Moore. Then she drifted off into vagueness, finally focusing on a missing button on the mayor's trousers, probably so she wouldn't have to answer with any specificity. "What's this, what happened?"

"I don't know," said Barry. "It popped off somewhere. You know these cleaners, they...burn buttons up and tear them off."

"Well, you should have enough clout to be able to get them to put a button—"

"No, I think it was weak, and I didn't notice when it came off."

"Oh, okay."

"You know, sometime today."

"Mmm-hmm."

"It might have come off when I was, you know, going to the bathroom or something."

As seconds and minutes ticked off, the inanities continued, leading the sting team to wonder if Barry was ever going to get back to the subject of drugs, or if any of his seduction lines would be fresh. So far Barry had made it clear that he wanted to sleep with Moore, not "get her nose open," as he had put it. The mayor, in fact, kept bringing up the subject of sex, over and over again, even reminding Moore that she once had told him that, as a young model, another beautiful young woman had tried to seduce her.

"I didn't make love to anyone," Moore insisted. "It was a situation. You got a lot of nerve, telling me I did something like that."

"Well, you know, what's wrong?" asked Barry. "People do that kind of stuff."

"Do you?" demanded Moore.

"Ah, twos and threes if I can," the 53-year-old mayor bragged. But, he admitted, "not any more. I used to. That was a long time ago."

There was, in fact, documentary evidence of a mayoral threesome. And if Moore was unaware of it, tens of thousands of mostly white upscale Washingtonians who subscribed to *Regardie's* magazine were not. In December 1988, the same month the Ramada Inn incident made world headlines, *Regardie's* had published a story by Mark Feldstein which contained excerpts from the diary of former Barry mistress Karen Johnson. Johnson gave the mayor a B − or C + in bed but complained that toward the end of their relationship in the mid-1980s Barry had seemed more interested in getting coked up and watching her and another woman have sex while he masturbated, than in making love to her.

But on this mid-January day in 1990, Barry assured Moore that, for him at least, such drug-abetted carnalities were strictly a thing of the past.

"I've been so goddamn good, baby, I tell you, I even surprised myself. No, no, don't [do] no women, and none of that kind of stuff."

The mayor was exaggerating his virtue: according to testimony at his drug and perjury trial, Barry had gotten together sometime during the three weeks preceding the sting with Bettye Smith (a.k.a. "Aunt Bettye"), another old friend who was visiting D.C. from Chattanooga, to snort cocaine and catch up on old times. Smith had once been the assistant secretary of the District and later worked for W.R. Lazard & Company, the city's chief financial advisor on multi-million dollar bond issues. Barry was also planning on visiting another old friend and casual cocaine user, Doris Crenshaw, at the Washington Hilton later in the evening.

"That's good, that's good," encouraged Moore, hoping that Barry would get off the sex kick and get down to the business of getting high so she could get out of this hotel room and on with the new, drug-free life she hoped to build with her three children and her Los Angeles boyfriend, to whom she recently had become engaged. But the mayor would not play along.

"So, why don't you come over here?" Barry suggested, as he leaned back on the bed.

"To what?" asked Moore. As if she didn't know.

"Make love."

Moore burst out laughing.

"I'm not gonna just make love to you!" she protested. "I mean, come on!"

"We ought to do it now," Barry insisted.

"No" said Moore.

"What's your girlfriend's name?" asked Barry, referring to the FBI agent.

"Well, this is her room," said Moore, reading his mind. "I mean, [what if] she walked in here, she got the key and stuff, [what if] she walked in here?"

"Well...before she left, she said, we can, catch up on old times," Barry reminded her.

"No way!" scolded Moore. "You know better than that." She shifted a little farther away from Barry on the bed.

"I'll catch you somewhere tomorrow, then," said the undaunted Lothario. "We'll go over to Don's house."

The mayor meant R. Donahue Peebles, a black developer and former Barry administration official who reportedly was

negotiating a $34 million office building lease-purchase agree-
ment with the city. According to Moore's trial testimony, she
had enjoyed several drug-filled assignations with Barry at
Peebles's house near Dupont Circle in Northwest Washington.

"How is he doing?" asked Moore, hoping to get Barry
focused on something other than her body. "Did he get
married to the girl?"

"No, fuck no," Barry replied. "He's been trying to get rid
of her. [But] then he took her to St. Martin for Christmas."

Barry was familiar with such romantic getaways. In June 1986
he had taken Moore to St. Thomas, in the U.S. Virgin Islands.
According to Charles Lewis's trial testimony, Barry and Moore
had snorted cocaine and smoked marijuana in their room at
the Luxurious Frenchmen's Reef Hotel and on a chartered
sailboat during a day cruise. They had gotten so heavily into
their amorous activities on the deck of the boat, said another
witness at Barry's trial, that he felt compelled to avert his eyes
out of embarrassment. The trip Barry and Moore had taken
to St. Thomas had marked a high point in their illicit relationship, a wild, intoxicated ride into the dark sunset of addiction.
Unlike Moore, however, who had gotten at least a partial
handle on her drug problem, the mayor still seemed firmly
in the grip of his. And while cocaine seemed to turn the
middle-aged mayor into a raging satyr, it now left Moore cold,
uninterested in sex.

Moore poured them both more cognac.

Barry still seemed to have just one thing on his mind.

"I can't caress your breast?" he asked like a hurt child, when
Moore once again deflected a mayoral pass.

"I'm serious!" Moore pushed him away.

"I can't caress your breast?" the mayor repeated.

"No, come on!" said Moore, like a schoolgirl stuck with a
horny date. To put things in perspective she reminded Barry
that on more than one occasion he had inappropriately let his
raging libido do the talking for both of them. "You know, I
think about the situation with Carol," Moore said.

Moore was referring to her former business partner, Carol
Bland Jackson, a comely black woman in her mid-thirties who

would testify at Barry's trial that he had "made sexual advances" toward her at a party that Moore had also attended.

"Carol who?" Barry asked.

"Carol that I was working with," replied Moore.

"What Carol?" Barry asked again.

"Carol Bland. Every time I think about it, I get—"

"I didn't bother that woman," Barry contended.

"Yes, you did. Out on the patio that day."

According to Jackson's trial testimony, Barry had tried unsuccessfully to seduce her at an apartment in the Tiber Island complex in Southwest Washington in June 1986. Jackson said that she, Moore, Barry and three others had gone there to snort cocaine after the annual Potomac Riverfest cruise for D.C. government employees.

"Oh, come on," said the mayor, as if he had been doing only what any other man would do, given the opportunity.

"And Maria [McCarthy]," said Moore. With the sting team— eventually, the whole world—watching and listening, Moore wanted to get her licks in, to let everyone know what a two-timer Barry was.

The mayor, however, was not about to let himself be judged.

"Maria, my ass," he said. Then, perhaps realizing he was not going to score tonight after all, Barry turned to an instrument that never failed to give him pleasure. He picked up the receiver of the bedside telephone and dialed a number as Moore continued her attack.

"And all the other women who—"

"Oh my Lord!" countered Barry, rising to the argument. "All the men you've fucked—gimme a break!"

Moore disengaged herself from the groping mayor, rose from the bed, laughed nervously.

"I—"

"One in this very Vista Hotel at night, some strange motherfucker," continued the mayor. He referred to a previous meeting with Moore at the hotel in May, 1988.

"Don't even try that," said Moore. "Who are you talking about?"

"That, that—[Barry on phone] 2182 please—that strange guy that was hanging out down there [in the hotel lobby]," retorted Barry. He had her going. He'd turned the tables.

"I did not," said Moore, who could have embarrassed Barry by mentioning what else had allegedly happened on their previous rendezvous at the Vista—his veiled threat to cut "Project Me's" funding if she refused his request for a sexual favor. "That was Maria's friend," she reminded Barry. "I told you that night."

"You told me you gave him some pussy," said Barry, who had not forgotten what he came to the Vista for—on both occasions.

"No way, I did not," insisted Moore.

"Hey, doll, what's happening?" Barry said to Doris Crenshaw, on the phone. The Montgomery, Alabama, financial consultant was in town and had called Barry earlier in the day. Then Barry cupped his hand over the mouthpiece and turned to Moore. He wasn't about to let her off the hook so easily about her alleged promiscuity. She, after all, had started the discussion by accusing him of embarrassing her in front of her business partner and friend. "Out at Budget Inn, you remember that?"

"Maria lied about that," snapped Moore. "Maria was always lying on me, trying to make me look like I was just, that size next to her."

She held up her thumb and forefinger to show Barry how small.

Barry ignored her. "Is it, is it okay for me to come?" he asked Crenshaw. "Huh? Hmm? Bush what? Bush whack? Over where? Where? What's up, what he doing down there? Oh, what's the deal? Uh-huh. Okay, I'll be there. Stopped to see a friend of mine who is visiting here. Oh yeah? No problem, you want, what do you want, some jello? Well, no, you know, but I'll keep it in the family, you know what I mean. I'll see if I can find some. ... I'll call you back later." Barry turned to Moore. "You know, let's not—"

"What you doing to me?" Moore demanded. She still was focusing on the mayor's promiscuity allegation.

"Let's not regurgitate all that," suggested Barry, reaching out to massage Moore's neck and shoulder. "Let's just...think about the good thing we had."

"Okay, yeah," said Moore.

"See, I think our shit start going downhill when you moved off of Taylor Street," said Barry, referring to Moore's mother's home in Northwest Washington, where Moore had lived briefly before moving in with her sister. "We were...having a good time...enjoying each other's company."

"You're right," said Moore. Then she shifted the conversation back to Maria McCarthy, and drugs.

"Living with my sister, I couldn't take it and that's why I was hanging at Maria's house all the time."

"Yeah," acknowledged Barry.

"Then I started getting heavier," said Moore. She was not referring to her weight.

"On that stuff," relied Barry. "When you were on Taylor Street, you were more moderate."

"Well," Moore laughed, "you don't know that."

"Well, I got the impression you were moderate," said Barry. "I didn't see the same kind of person that I saw [when you lived] over on 16th Street."

"I know," allowed Moore. "I mean I made a lot of changes in my life at that time. . . I remember when I resigned my job, and Vernon Hawkins said to me, 'You know, you're about two steps from being homeless,' and I'm like—don't do that!" She pushed Barry's wandering hand away.

"Well, I love you still," Barry reassured her. "Even [if] I don't treat you right. But you don't treat me right, either. Once in love, always in love."

"Really?"

"It's true. You know."

"So, what are you doing tonight?" asked Moore.

"I don't know," said Barry. "I got to stop up the Hilton to see a friend of mine for a minute. A couple [I know] is in town but, uh, I hadn't planned too much—why, what you got in mind?"

Moore had to think of a way to bring up drugs without being the first to suggest they indulge. The lawmen and the lawyer monitoring the operation had warned her that such an action on her part might lead to an entrapment defense by Barry.

"I don't care," Moore said, sounding as bored as a school girl on a rainy Saturday. "Let's do something."

"Hmm?"

"I don't have anything to do except Wanda is around, but—"

"What you want to do?" asked Barry.

"I don't care," Moore repeated. She had been coached well: no coaxing, coercing, or even suggesting that they do drugs. "What do you want to do?"

"Be with you!"

Barry then tried to touch her again.

"Why can't you just learn to be warm and c—"

"I try to be," said the mayor.

"Instead of just jumping into a—"

" 'Cause you...keep pushing—"

"No, because you want to go right to it and should just, you know, just be—"

Barry pulled Moore down onto the bed.

"No, no, no, not to that extreme!" Moore protested, laughing. She was quiet for a moment as they hugged and kissed. "Just be warm. You always want, you always—"

"I like your dress," Barry said, touching Moore again.

"No, I'm not going to do that. I'm not!" asserted Moore.

Barry released the woman and lay back on the bed with his arms spread. He began snapping his fingers. She perched on the edge of the mattress.

" 'I'm not going to do that. I can't. I would,' " he mocked.

"What?"

"I would do it, but—"

Moore laughed. "I can't just jump into it. You're sick. So what are you going to do? Let's do something." Perhaps if she punched that button enough times...

"Do what?" Barry replied innocently. He was not about to be drawn into an admission that he wanted to do drugs. Too many Nosey Rosies around. The room could be bugged for all he knew.

"I don't know," Moore said for the third time. "I just want to get out of here, and I don't want to go home to my mother's house—babysitting for the night. I'm taking advantage of being free."

"Your friend mess around?" Barry suddenly asked about Wanda King, the undercover agent in the leather miniskirt and vest whom Moore had described as a friend from California.

Moore jumped on the mayor's query, which had come 20 minutes into his visit. Ignoring its sexual connotations, she replied: "Yeah. Sometimes. She doesn't do a lot. She toots more than she'll do anything else."

Moore referred to snorting cocaine powder.

"Mmmh," Barry grunted noncommittally.

"Like Johnann," said Moore, keeping the drug conversation going by referring to another girlfriend. "Johnann only toots; Johnann would never want to, you know, freebase [smoke crack]."

"Don't have anything," said Barry, seeming to refer directly to drugs for the first time. "What about you?"

"What? Any what?" Moore demurred. "I hate that [free-basing]. I mean, I would have had something. I had something early, you know, yesterday," she lied. "But I didn't have much money. I'm going to get some money."

"That couple still live across the street from you?" Barry asked. He was referring to Lydia Pearson and her boyfriend, Ron Manning, who, according to trial testimony, had sold drugs to Moore and Barry on numerous occasions. "What was their name?"

"Who, Lydia?"

"Yeah," said Barry.

"Lydia. Yeah, she went into...that rehab place...Second Genesis."

"Oh, yeah?"

"But I think she's back now, so I don't know."

"What's the guy's name?" asked Barry.

"Ron."

"Ron, oh yeah," Barry chuckled, "they came through pretty good at times."

"So what, you want to do something?" asked Moore. She really had Barry going now, talking about drugs. "I've been doing it off and on in California."

"Not, not tonight, naw," replied Barry.

"It's different in California," said Moore, not letting the subject drop.

"What's different? Better?" asked Barry.

"Well, one time I had this person in California I get it from," said Moore, "and it was good, you know; but he got busted so now I get it on the street, and it wasn't that great."

"Mmm-hmm."

"Wanda...said she was going to try to pick some up from somebody she know," said Moore, rising from the bed to pour herself another glass of cognac. "She got some friends here... that went to Howard, and she supposed to be trying to make some connections with some people. 'Cause I told her, I said, 'We got [to] do something, I'm bored.' "

Moore finally had made clear what she meant by "do something": get high on cocaine. But then she fell into her jealousy routine again, while describing the personality of her Los Angeles friend, the FBI undercover agent. "She's, she's...not like Maria [McCarthy]. She's not really...as outgoing."

"Well, you're the one that introduced me to Maria," Barry shot back. "So don't complain, all right?"

"I introduced you to her?"

"Yeah, so don't complain."

"I know," Moore finally admitted.

" 'She's a lot different, you'll like her!' " Barry mocked.

"But you know what?" Moore asked rhetorically, "I never thought that was going to turn out like that. That's how naive I am."

Barry chuckled. "I knew she was doing something, but, uh—"

"You never really talked about that then," complained Moore.

"Yeah," confirmed Barry.

"But what do you mean? You knew she was into—"

"What?" Barry asked.

"Freebasing, hitting?"

Once again, Moore had transformed sex talk into drug talk.

"No." Barry wouldn't let it happen.

"Oh, you mean she was—"

"Into wanting to give me some pussy, excuse the expression," said the mayor.

"You know, you think that about any woman," retorted Moore, rejoining the macho mayor on the bed.

"No, no, bullshit!" said Barry. "I know better."

Barry picked up the hotel phone again. Might as well feed one of his habits if she wasn't going to give him anything.

"Who you calling now?" Moore demanded. She wanted Barry's sole and undivided attention. The clock was ticking on her mission.

Barry ignored her. "Any calls?" he asked his message service.

"Look at you, you're a trip!" Moore laughed.

Barry ignored her, taking his messages. Then he brought up sex again. "We had some good times—remember down [at the] L'Enfant [Plaza Hotel], on the balcony?"

According to trial testimony, Barry and Moore had spent two Fourth of July holidays (1986 and 1987) at the plush Southwest Washington hotel, drinking, snorting coke, and watching the fireworks.

"You always talk about that," laughed Moore. "You said it was one of the best."

Barry phoned former advisory neighborhood commissioner Danny Butler, another one of his fast-lane friends, and told him "A friend of mine is in town and . . . we were talking about, uh, doing something." Apparently, the mayor used the same euphemism Moore did to describe drugs. While talking to Butler, he occasionally reached across the bed to stroke Moore's thigh. "Boy, I tell you," he said into the receiver, "I'm the luckiest man in the world. The Lord's on my side."

"Listen to you with 'the Lord's on your side,'" scoffed Moore. She laughed but clearly didn't like this light talk of God.

"He is on my side," Barry insisted.

"He's been on your side for years," Moore reminded him.

"That's right," agreed Barry.

"I been trying to tell you He's on your side," said Moore.

"A lot of people are visiting [D.C.] right now," Barry told Butler, "so I'm trying to make my little courtesy calls."

"You so busy!" Moore teased.

Barry leaned over to touch her. "My little baby here, she's just giving me a hard time," he complained to Butler. "I can't give her to you—shit!" he laughed. "Give her to you? Shit. Fuck yourself, man!"

"Watch your mouth," snapped Moore.

"I'm sorry, I'll be nice, I won't curse," promised Barry.

"I told you about that, you know."

"I'm telling you, I won't curse again, goddamit!" the mayor laughed. "Yeah, I won't curse again. What you got to drink, man?" Barry asked Butler. "Nothing? I don't want any of that damn rum, I'll tell you that. Well, I'm going to run up the street here."

Suddenly Barry's walkie-talkie, still sitting on the desk, crackled.

"Radio 906 to 908," said one of Barry's bodyguards, announcing the mayor's code. Moore brought the black, antennaed device to Barry.

"Uh, 908, 906," said Barry into the walkie-talkie.

The bodyguard informed the mayor that Barry's chief of staff, Maudine Cooper, had called his limousine. Barry went back to the phone. "Yeah, let me call my office here," he said to Moore. Then he picked up the phone again to talk to Butler. "Uh, I'm going up to the Hilton in a few minutes and, uh, if I don't work out something with my buddy here, I'll uh, maybe get her to take a taxi over to your place. All right. I'll call you, though. Good night." He turned to Moore. "You ever met my buddy, Danny Butler?"

"Oh, Danny—over there in Northeast?"

"Yeah."

"Short Danny?" said Moore.

"That's right," said Barry.

"With gray hair?" added Moore.

"That's right," said Barry, then, apparently getting back to gonadal matters, he added, "You, you killed him that day. You wore him, you—"

"I what? I've never been with that guy!" protested Moore.

"No, I don't mean personally," corrected Barry.

"Oh, yeah, we got—"

"Rolling all night. Yeah, Lord."

"Yeah, we got high together—I mean, no, don't even try it. What are you making me this kind of person I'm not?"

Moore's posturing was too much for Barry: "Come on now, give me a break."

"Oh, okay," said Moore. "Oooh, that's a beautiful horse, God!" she said, responding with childlike innocence to the star of *The Black Stallion Returns*, a movie playing on Washington's Channel 20. Moore had been watching the tube since before Barry arrived. The instrument would stay on, providing a banal and homey backdrop to the sting. "I want to get my body like that, like a stallion. [But] I don't know if [it will happen] in this life."

"Yeah, that is a pretty horse, isn't it?" said Barry. Then he called his short, gray-haired friend Danny Butler back.

"Hey, man," he said, "I tell you who the person is—Miss R, you don't remember her? That came by your place? Yeah, up drinking all night?" He laughed. "Yeah, we were just chatting about that a little bit, you know? How much fun she had, you know? Yeah, she's just here for a day or so, on some business thing.... Almost as good as goddamn new money. You know, just like French wine gets better."

He leaned over and tried to kiss Moore on the mouth. Instead he got a peck on the top of his head from the laughing, elusive woman. The mayor sat back on the bed and asked Butler to dial Maudine Cooper's number because "I don't want to call my [official] number from this hotel. You never know what Nosey Rosies might be listening in on the line."

Moore got up and paced.

"You really look good, baby," said Barry as he waited for Cooper to come on the line. Then he turned his attention to political business.

"I may want to do Channel 9 [WUSA-TV in Washington],"
he told Cooper in his fourth phone call since entering the room
a half-hour earlier, 'if I can get [veteran black WUSA-TV
reporter] Bruce [Johnson], if I can get Bruce to do it."

Moore sat down in a chair facing the bed and watched Barry,
who was discussing his plan to announce his candidacy for
an unprecedented fourth term in office on live television three
days later, on Sunday, January 21—a plan he would never
realize.

"Tell him we'll think about it," Barry said about another
reporter's request for an interview. "You know, by tomorrow
we'll decide. Okay." He hung up the phone. "Want to go
to Danny's?" he asked Moore, who had resumed her nervous
pacing.

Moore stalled by asking if Butler still lived in the same place;
then she sat back down on the bed near Barry, who lay back
with his arms spread.

"Come hug me," the mayor begged like a sad little boy.
"Hug me. May I have a hug?"

"Hugga, hugga, hugga," said Moore, lying down on top
of him. Barry's hands began moving from her back to more
intimate reaches. "Uh-uh," she scolded. "You ain't gonna
take it so fast. I have been away from you for a long time."

They sat up and moved apart. Barry took out a handkerchief
and wiped his face.

"Okay. You got to get used to me again, huh?" he asked.

"Yeah, come on."

"You keep sniffing," observed Barry. "You been doing
something today?"

"A little bit, why?" Moore lied.

"When you do it, a few minutes ago?"

"No, it was earlier," Moore lied again. Then she reminded
Barry that Wanda was downstairs in the lobby, trying to score.
The FBI agent actually was in the next room, watching the
official video show along with her fellow G-men.

"Let's go downstairs," suggested Barry, "talk to her. I'm
going up the Hilton. Uh, I may get a tab [a small package of
cocaine powder], but it won't be nothing, you know."

Thirty-four minutes into the sting the mayor finally had indicated he might want to buy some drugs. Moore wasn't about to let Barry leave the room now. She began talking about the fictitious cosmetology school that she had said King ran in Los Angeles and how they all might benefit from a D.C. connection.

"I was thinking," said Moore, ingenuously, "maybe we can pull something together, you know, maybe try to present something?" She was referring to a new modeling skills and self-esteem program for D.C. teenagers she had supposedly put together with "Wanda Moore."

It was the first time since she'd answered the door that she showed any real inventiveness in her acting role.

Barry, who remembered how badly things had turned out with "Project Me," the last time he had tried to mix business with pleasure with Moore, refused to take the bait this time.

"We'll try to talk about it," he said, "I don't know, darling."

Unfazed, Moore continued her pretend plea for a mayoral favor: "We have the dropout program. We have the image building. We got the cosmetology covered...come on, I'm trying to make some money. You're here, you're playing games. ... I'm—trying to make some money, okay?"

"Come on," replied Barry.

"Thank God," said Moore, as if Barry had just signed a city check to her instead of responding noncommittally. "I got three children I have to take care of."

"What the fuck is Eugene doing out there with 'em," asked Barry about the reputed father of at least one of Moore's children; he had been arrested on drug charges in Los Angeles.

"You know Eugene, he comes and—"

"Is he in jail?"

"No, uh."

"You say he got arrested."

"He was. That's why I went out to California, but he's okay now."

"Did he get some time?"

"Uh-uh."

"You got any fake credit cards?" teased Barry, who knew Moore had been busted for credit card fraud during her college days.

"No way!"

"You used to have 'em."

"I know I used to have 'em. I'm not doing none of that stuff. I'm as straight as a arrow."

"Almost straight."

"Almost straight?" Moore laughed. But she was saved from uttering any more cliches or untruths by the ringing phone, which she ran to answer. "Hello, yeah, I figured that was you," said Moore matter-of-factly, disguising her relief. "No, I'm coming down to the uh, downstairs. Oh, you going to come on back up? What? They don't have a bar open down there?"

"That's right, they don't," offered Barry, not realizing he was helping close the trap on himself. "All the [lobby] bars are gone now." Then he sealed his fate: "Tell her to come up."

The two former lovers filled in the time waiting for the drugs with more cognac and small talk—about Danny Butler, about Moore's brother and sister, about alleged cosmetologist Wanda Moore.

"She called to see if the coast was clear," said Barry. That's pretty cool."

"Yeah," agreed Moore.

"Well, she knows you're in love with me," offered Barry, as if explaining why such a warning call would be necessary. "Shit, she knows that. A woman can tell. They got intuition. Shit, you been talking. I bet you told her all about me."

Of course, she had, but not in the way he hoped.

"The coast is clear, darlin'," Barry teased as King walked into the room a few minutes later.

"Okay," laughed King. Then she immediately led Rasheeda Moore into the bathroom.

Barry poured some cognac and lay back on the bed.

The mayor's former lover emerged a few moments later, alone.

"She got something, but we got to pay her for it," Moore announced, sitting down on the corner of the bed."

"How much?" Barry asked.

"At least 50 or 60. See, she does 30s only."

Moore referred to small cellophane packets of crack cocaine sold on the street.

"Got any change?" asked Barry. He handed her a $100 bill.

"I'll make it," said Moore. "Wait a minute." She went back into the bathroom.

Barry leaned forward on the edge of the bed and looked in the mirror. He rubbed his hair, pursed his lips, stuck out his tongue as if to inspect it, cleared his throat, checked his watch, lay back on the bed again, the epitome of anxiousness. It was drug-feeding time.

When Moore emerged from the bathroom a second time, sat down beside Barry, and showed him two $30 packets of crack, Barry surprised her. "I don't smoke no more, honey," he said. Apparently, he had been expecting cocaine powder.

"You don't smoke no more?"

"No," said Barry.

Moore returned to the bathroom with the drugs, consulted with the agent, then reemerged to announce, "I got something. ... I'm gonna do some [crack]. [But] she don't have any powder."

Special Agent King came out of the bathroom and faced the sting target and the "cooperating witness," as the FBI referred to Moore.

"Hey, I'm gonna go and, uh, catch you in a few seconds," she announced; then she abruptly left the room, closing the door behind her. At that moment, as far as King knew, the sting had failed because of Barry's refusal to take the bait.

Moore turned to the mayor. This was the moment of truth— for her and everyone else involved in the politically and legally risky undertaking. If the mayor left at this point, he would abort the sting. The fact that he had provided Moore money to buy drugs would provide scant legal basis for a possession charge. Moore knew she could not in any way coerce or coax Barry either to buy or use the drugs. But she had to give it one last try, to see if her old trysting, tooting and smoking buddy really could just say no so easily. "Okay," she said to Barry, "why don't we just go?"

"Hmm? Say what?" asked Barry from his perch on the bed.

"You're not smoking now?" asked Moore.

"What did you get?" Barry countered.

"I didn't get anything," said Moore.

"Go get some. Go get it," Barry said.

Moore rushed into the hall. "Wanda!" she called.

Barry got up from the bed, stepped up to the mirror, adjusted his tie. Did he sense the noose he had just placed around his own neck?

The two women returned to the room.

"Let me have a 20 [dollar bill]," Moore said to Barry. "I'm gonna get a 20 [dollar packet of crack]."

Barry gave a bill to Moore, who again disappeared into the bathroom with King. He continued primping in front of the mirror while the ladies were gone.

Moore came out a moment later, sat down next to the mayor on the bed, showed the mayor what she'd bought.

"That's a 30," she said, handing Barry a packet of crack. "It's actually a 40, but I'm going to give it back—"

"You got a pipe?" Barry asked. Time to get down to business.

"Yeah," laughed Moore. She had done it. She had gotten the mayor to buy crack cocaine on camera and now he was going to smoke it too. The sting, finally, was working. "Shit, wait," she said, jumping up from the bed.

"You all right?" asked King as nonchalantly as she could. Was the cooperating witness about to back out? Was she feeling guilty? Was she going to expose King and blow this whole operation just when it was about to work?

"Huh?" replied the distracted ex-model.

"You all right?" King repeated. Maybe Moore was simply nervous. Understandable, under the circumstances.

"Yeah," said Moore. "So, if you can get some—if you can get some powder."

"But it'll take about an hour," the much-relieved undercover agent replied.

"Yeah, okay," said Moore.

"Well, let me go downstairs," said King, who promptly left the room.

"Where's your pipe?" the mayor asked Moore again as soon as the other woman was gone.

Moore produced what crackheads call a straight shooter, a hollow, transparent glass cylinder with wire mesh on one end to hold the drugs. Barry got up from the bed, went over to the desk with a packet of crack, put the pipe down under the lamp, fumbled with the pipe and the drugs.

"How this work?" asked the mayor, who, according to witnesses at his trial, not only had smoked crack from various devices but had assembled makeshift pipes from glassware and tinfoil, and even processed cocaine powder into rocks of crack by heating it over a flame and mixing it with baking soda and water.

"What?" asked Moore incredulously as she joined him at the desk.

"I, I don't know how this work," said Barry. Was he playing for those ubiquitous Nosey Rosies who might just be listening in? "I never done it before."

"That's what we used to do all the time," countered Moore. "What are you talking about?"

Obviously the woman didn't understand. "I'm new," said Barry. "We never done that before. Give me a break."

"Put [the drugs] in there," she said, as if speaking to an infant. "Let me give you a lighter."

"You do it," said Barry, handing her the pipe.

"No," said Moore. "I'm not doing nothing."

"No, no, nope, nope, nope," said Barry.

"Huh?"

"No, you do it," replied Barry, emphatically.

"I thought you bought this 'cause you wanted to take a hit," said Moore.

"Nah, nah, you do it," said Barry. If the woman took the first drag, it probably meant she was not setting him up. He was testing her.

"What is this anyway?" demanded Moore. What was the man trying to do, spoil the whole operation?

"Uh-uh," said Barry, again refusing to take the pipe from Moore. "You do it."

Moore led the mayor into the bathroom, where she knew he would feel safer.

"Okay, I'll do it," she assured him. "Come on. You know, you put it up like this." She demonstrated how to smoke the straight shooter. "What do you mean you never did it like this?"

The pipe and the conversation went round and round several more times before the couple emerged from the bathroom and stood near the desk again. The crack sat on the desk next to the lamp. Barry picked it up and inspected it. Moore, who held the pipe, took some crack and put it in the straight shooter. Then, as Barry pressed her again to be the first to smoke, she finally gave him a semi-credible reason why she didn't want to. "It'll make me too hyper," she explained. "I get really hyper."

The mayor still wasn't convinced. "Just go on and do a piece," he insisted as they stood together near the desk.

"I'm not going to. I'm going to wait," said Moore, who held the loaded crack pipe.

"Can't wait," said Barry. "Go on, do a piece."

"No, 'cause it gets—"

"Bullshit!" exclaimed Barry. "Now, come on."

"I get too hyper," Moore pleaded.

"Why don't you do one piece?" the mayor demanded again. Moore stuck to her explanation.

"I been tooting it with her [the agent], I told you," she lied. "I thought I was getting it for you, so I'm gonna wait. You kiddin'? Shit! . . . I got to deal with Wanda. She's paying all these expenses over here, and I'm going to be going through some changes with her."

"What kind of changes?" asked Barry as he leaned over the desktop, carefully arranging the crack in the straight shooter.

While he was preoccupied, Moore walked over to the side of the bed and moved a chair that was blocking one camera's view. No sense going this far and not catching the big moment on tape.

"Lately, when I do this stuff, I get hyper as heck," Moore repeated. "I mean, [it makes me] just too nervous, too hyper.

I be looking at the floor and, oh, I don't know, and I can't bring my [thoughts] back together right away.''

It must have been easy for Barry to believe the hyper part. Moore had been pacing like a caged tigress since the FBI agent had left them alone with the drugs.

"Well, well, you always done that," said Barry, finally putting the drug-loaded straight shooter to his lips at 8:26 P.M., 51 minutes after entering the room.

A visibly shaken Moore poured herself another shot of Hennessey and paced, watching Barry from the corner of her eye. The mayor, standing in front of the mirror, held the crack pipe to his lips with both hands, leaned his head back so the drugs wouldn't spill, lit the pipe with a cigarette lighter, took a deep drag on the pipe, held the crack smoke in his lungs for 10 seconds, exhaled whitish smoke into the atmosphere. Then he immediately took another hit.

"Huh? I always did that?" Moore rambled nervously. "You've got to be kidding. I always did it. I've been tooting a lot and I've been doing that, too, but I don't—how is it?" she asked as Barry exhaled a second time. "How is it?"

"Mmm," Barry grunted as he finished exhaling.

"Where's the rest?" asked Moore. "Where's the rest of it?" Perhaps she wanted to make sure he was holding some when the lawmen arrived. Then Moore blurted, as if she couldn't believe that she'd succeeded in her mission. "You did it? Good. Oh, Maria, Maria!"

At the mayor's trial, Kenneth Mundy would describe this outburst as Moore's "war cry," alleging that Moore had set Barry up as revenge for his having slept with Maria McCarthy.

Barry grabbed his glass of cognac off the room-service table where he had left it and quickly downed it. "Let's go downstairs," he suggested.

"Okay, um, let me put all this away," said Moore, sticking the straight shooter in one of the drawers as Barry put on his jacket. She began tidying up the desk, trying to give the FBI agents and police in the adjoining rooms time to enter. "I don't want to take it [the drugs] downstairs. Damn, where's the key? You okay?"

"Mmm-hmm," mumbled Barry.

"Are you?" asked Moore, who had seen Barry become paranoid enough to hide in bathrooms or closets when he got high, thinking that he was being followed.

"[What are you] talking about?" Barry replied.

"You wanta take another one [hit on the pipe]?" asked Moore, trying to keep the mayor in the room as long as she could. Things could get messy if he went out into the hall and his armed police bodyguards tried to defend him from the agents. She didn't know that the bodyguards were about to be neutralized by the FBI.

"Nah, you're crazy," said Barry, grabbing his walkie-talkie from a bedside table. "Let's go downstairs and meet your friend. Come on."

Clearly the sooner the mayor left the hotel room, the better he would feel, the better his chance to enjoy his surreptitious high.

"She [King] said she was coming back up in a few minutes," said Moore, stalling for time.

"Let's have a drink with her downstairs," Barry repeated.

"She went down to make some calls. You don't want to wait?"

"No," Barry said emphatically. This was getting to be ridiculous. "Nine-oh-eight, 907," the mayor said into the instrument as he stood at the door, waiting for Moore. He was calling his bodyguard to let him know he was on his way to the lobby.

"Nine-oh-seven back," squawked the reply.

It was the last friendly voice Barry would hear for a while. Suddenly, the door connecting rooms 726 and 727 burst open and half a dozen lawmen charged into the room—some actually vaulting the bed to get at Barry before he could leave.

"Police! FBI! You're under arrest!" they shouted as the startled mayor turned to face those wildmen, who wore blue windbreakers with "POLICE" or "F.B.I." emblazoned on the back in bright yellow letters.

Moore ducked into the bathroom.

"All right," said Barry as the lawmen surrounded him. "No problem."

"Don't move!" one of the agents shouted.

"I gotcha," said Barry, who offered no resistance.

"Where is she? Where is she?" shouted one of the agents.

"Take her! Take her!" shouted another as they cornered the frantic woman in the bathroom.

"We're special agents from the FBI and Metropolitan Police Internal Affairs Division," Ronald Stern told Barry as other lawmen dealt with Moore. "You are under arrest for possession and use of illegal narcotics."

"Turn around, ma'am," shouted an agent standing near Moore. "Turn around. Face the wall! Face the wall! Face the wall!"

"Spread your legs!" ordered FBI Special Agent Peter Wubbenhorst. He was trying to make Moore look like a suspect.

"Huh?" said Moore.

"Spread your legs," the G-man repeated.

"Okay, Mr. Mayor, we'd like you to put your hands on the wall," said case agent Stern as his men led Barry away from the door to lean spreadeagled against the wall next to the bed.

"I don't have any," said Barry, referring to the drugs.

"Please put your hands on the wall," Stern repeated.

"I understand," said Barry.

"When you calm down, we'll let you go," Wubbenhorst told Moore.

"That was a good setup, wasn't it?" said Barry, having quickly realized what had happened to him. Then, as agents patted him down, he again claimed: "I didn't have anything."

"Oh! Oh! Where's Wanda? Where's Wanda?" shouted Moore, hysterically. She was still into her role.

"I didn't have anything. I didn't, I didn't do anything," said Barry. He would repeat this mendacious assertion half a dozen times in the next few minutes.

"Mr. Mayor, keep your hands out," said Stern, who stood behind Barry. "We're going to slip your coat off for you."

The mayor allowed his jacket to be removed, then leaned against the wall in his shirtsleeves.

"We're going to have some people, EMT people, take a look at you," said D.C. police internal affairs division Detective Sergeant James Pawlik, a large, friendly man with a thick black mustache. "Make sure you're not gonna pass out or anything."

"Pass out from what?" said Barry. He did not know, after all, that he had been videotaped smoking crack. "I didn't have anything. She, she did that," he lied.

"Let's bring the woman, let's get the woman out of here," said Pawlik.

"No, she, she did that," insisted Barry.

"Take her to a car and get her out of here!" ordered Wubbenhorst, an affable veteran FBI special agent in his early forties.

"Goddamn, I shouldn't have come up here," said Barry. I'll be damned."

"Just take it easy," said Stern.

"How can I . . . get tricked in this shit like this, man?"

"Take it easy," said Stern.

"How'd I get tricked into this stuff?" Barry repeated.

"Just stay cool," advised Albert Arrington. The balding, bearded D.C. police internal affairs division detective sergeant was the only black man on the main sting team.

"Let's get the woman out," said Pawlik.

"She's out," said Arrington.

"She's gone, took her down to the car," said Wubbenhorst.

"I'll be damned," said Barry. "Got set up."

"Okay, just stand still," said Arrington.

"Goddamn set up like that," said Barry, who was still leaning on the wall, flanked by Stern and Arrington.

"Before we do anything, Mr. Mayor, I want to, I want to read you your rights," said Stern.

"What, what, what am I arrested for?"

"Just listen," said Arrington. "We already told you that you're arrested for violations of narcotics laws of the District of Columbia."

Stern tried again to read Barry his rights. "Pay attention to what I'm going to—"

"That, that was a setup," said Barry, ignoring the G-man.

"Okay, I understand," said Stern. "Pay attention to what I'm going to read you."

"That was a setup, goddammit. It was a fucking setup," complained the mayor.

"Listen to your rights now," advised Arrington.

"Mr. Mayor—" said Stern.

"Goddamn, I shouldn't have come up here," said Barry.

"Before we ask you any questions," Stern read from a Miranda card, "you must understand your rights."

"I know," replied Barry. He'd been arrested enough times— during his civil rights days, and later—to know the procedure.

"You have the right to remain silent," read Stern. "Anything you say can be used against you in court."

"I'll be goddamn!" Barry repeated.

"Listen," counseled Arrington.

Stern tried again: "You have the right to—"

"Yeah, I know all that," Barry interrupted.

"—talk with a lawyer for advice," Stern continued.

"Piss me off!" interjected Barry.

"Before we ask you any questions," Stern went on, "you may have a lawyer with you—"

"Damn, got a setup!" said Barry, the litany of his angry repetitions forming an almost comical counterpoint to Stern's reading the required legal warnings to a criminal suspect.

"If you cannot afford a lawyer," Stern intoned, "one will be appointed for you before any questioning, if you wish. If you decide to answer questions now without a lawyer present—"

"Shit!" said Barry.

"—you will still have the right to stop answering at any time."

"I'll be goddamn," muttered the suspect.

Stern continued: "You also have the right to stop answering—"

"Bitch set me up," repeated Barry.

"—at any time, until you talk to a lawyer," said Stern.

"She set me up," repeated Barry. "I'll be goddamn."

"Sir? Mr. Mayor?" inquired Stern. He could see how stoned and angry Barry was, but he had to give the suspect his legal warnings, especially in an opertion this sensitive, an operation Stern knew was being recorded.

"I know," said Barry.

"Do you understand your rights?" Stern asked patiently.

"Yeah, set me up like that, said Barry. "I be—"

Arrington tried his hand: "You understand your right—"

"Yeah, man," interrupted the mayor. "Get me set—"

"Okay," said Arrington.

"Got me set up," muttered Barry. "Ain't that a bitch?"

At this point Barry was apparently sober enough to ask if the agents had audiotaped his phone calls from the room and even wondered if they had videotaped his hotel room visit. They declined to answer, but Barry guessed out loud that he had been the target of what he called an "elaborate goddamn trap." He added: "I should have stayed down the mother-fucking stairs like I decided to."

As the sting team members and their target waited for the government car with blacked-out windows to arrive at the Vista parking garage to take the well-known suspect out the back (to "provide a maximum of decorum under the circum-stances," according to Special Agent Wubbenhorst), Case Agent Stern removed from Barry's right front pants pocket a bank card, some business cards, notes, and blank checks. Stern turned the items over to FBI special agent Frank Steele, the evidence custodian for the sting. In a cursory search of Barry's suit jacket, Steele found breath mints, a pair of plastic combs, a photograph of potholes, along with a note on same from an angry constituent, and other assorted items, but no crack pipe or drugs.

Sting team leaders also notified Jay Stephens and D.C. police chief Isaac Fulwood, Jr., of the bust. Stephens would ask a federal judge to authorize a court order to take blood, urine, and hair samples from the suspect, and to release Barry on his recognizance after being booked. Fulwood was briefed on the arrest and assured that the mayor would be given every courtesy and consideration possible and that his safety would be maintained at all times while in federal custody. The city's head cop was told that out of deference to Barry the mayor would be booked at FBI headquarters rather than the central cellblock at 300 Indiana Avenue, NW, where criminal suspects are normally processed.

During the next half hour, as Barry waited to be transported to FBI headquarters in downtown Washington, he was checked over by D.C. Fire Department paramedics. However, before the medical men measured the mayor's vital signs, FBI special agent Robert Core told Barry, revealingly, "We know about your past cardiac history with narcotics, so we're just going to make sure that you're physically sound and you're not suffering any kind of health problems."

"I feel fine," insisted the feisty and unrepentant sting target, "except I'm pissed off!"

But in examining the mayor the paramedics found a markedly elevated blood pressure of 238 over 144 and a "sinus rhythm, first-degree, A-B block" in the mayor's heartbeat—the latter indicating a minor timing abnormality that, according to heart specialist Joel Schulman, could have been either a temporary condition related to the obvious stress Barry was under or the effect of the drugs, or it could have reflected a chronic cardiac problem. Because the mayor did not complain of any accompanying chest pains or difficulty in breathing, however, on the night of the sting the paramedics dismissed their findings as "insignificant" and ceded to Barry's decision to decline any further medical treatment or testing or a free trip to the hospital.

"No," said the mayor. "I'm going to take a chance on it [his health being okay]."

Special Agent Core and D.C. police detectives Pawlik and Arrington asked Barry how he was feeling several more times during the half-hour wait to depart the room, assuring him the paramedics were nearby. Their solicitations appeared sincere, but they also were aware of Barry's previous hospitalizations for what his office had termed "flareups of a hiatal hernia" (at least three of which were investigated by D.C. police as possible cocaine overdoses). They were trying to prevent a potential catastrophe that could have resulted from providing the mayor with 93 percent pure crack cocaine and allowing him to smoke it. And they were following orders from higher up: the last thing the white U.S. attorney needed, after all, was a dead black mayor on his hands. If Barry died, the riot Attorney General Thornburgh had predicted for Martin Luther King's birthday would surely have exploded now.

During the wait, Barry asked to call his lawyer and his wife but was refused permission. He was told he could call them from FBI headquarters. He was, however, allowed to sit on the bed, even though his hands remained handcuffed behind his back for more than a quarter of an hour. In this uncomfortable position, Barry asked Pawlik if federal prosecutors (that is, Jay Stephens) knew he had been arrested.

"Yes, we told them," said the D.C. police detective, who then added, spontaneously, "We didn't really want this to happen."

"I didn't want this to happen either," retorted Barry.

Then the mayor finally took at least partial responsibility for the mess he was in. "If I had followed my fucking instincts tonight, I'd have been all right," he said. "I should have stayed downstairs. Bitch kept insisting coming up here. Goddammit, I should have known better. I should have known better." He sighed. "Oh, boy." Then Barry turned to FBI special agent Robert Core. "What's your charge again?" he asked. Time to organize himself, fight this thing. Logically, if possible.

"Possession," Core replied.

"Possession?" Barry scoffed. "With what, intent to use?" he laughed. "That little bit, that little speck?"

The macho mayor had returned.

A few moments later Pawlik asked Barry, "What do you think about all this?"

"I'm pissed off," replied Barry, who appeared to be sobering up rapidly. "I should have followed my goddamn instinct and not come up here. Simple as that. And in fact, I was just getting ready to leave too, goddamit." Finally Barry asked about Moore: "Is she under arrest or is she part of this scheme?"

"We, we can't advise you of anything about what, uh, anyone else has been arrested for," said Pawlik, apologetically.

"Motherfucking setup," whispered Barry, almost to himself.

"Two minutes, we'll go," Stern announced. "We got a service elevator and, uh, we'll have a car. Leave as discreetly as possible, in the garage, get you in there."

"You-all going to, you-all going to alert the press about this?" asked Barry. With mayoral blood in the water, he knew the barracudas would be moving in for the kill.

"I'm sorry?" said Stern.

"Going to tell the press about it?"

"We do not tell the press about anything we do," said Stern. "They find out through their usual channels. But you know we can't prevent that."

"Yeah," Barry sighed. Then he asked for the fourth time, "So what's the charge?"

"Possession of drugs," said Pawlik.

"Possession?" Barry scoffed. "Where the possessions? Shit." The former street dude chuckled. "That bitch, I tell you . . . . She was slick, though. I should have known better. When she wouldn't do it first, I should have known something was up."

"You knew eventually it was going to happen, I think, didn't you?" asked Pawlik. "Did you suspect some day it was going to happen?"

"I don't know," the mayor answered quietly. "I guess you-all been checking on me for a long time, huh?"

"Obviously," replied Pawlik.

"I guess you-all figured that I couldn't resist that lady," said Barry. "I should have stayed my ass downstairs like I wanted to."

"It's a traumatic experience," offered Arrington, who then quoted from the Old Testament: "But this too will pass."

"Sometimes it's better," said Pawlik, as they all waited for word that the car had arrived. "Sometimes it's for the good, really, health-wise. You know—consider it that way."

"Oh, you're assuming I got a problem." Barry laughed.

"Yes, sir. Respectfully, I say that."

"Okay, I understand that," said Barry. "What's that based on—other information you have?"

"Well—"

Pawlik was saved from having to reveal what he knew by Arrington, who explained to Barry how he would be taken down to the parking garage in the service elevator.

"This is as traumatic for us as it is for you, I think," said Pawlik, who clearly was moved by the mayor's circumstances.

"Well, I know I wish it had not happened," Barry responded. "But I guess life goes on that way."

"Yeah," said Pawlik. "Well, we have to be strong enough to get over it."

A moment later agent Core slipped the handcuffed mayor's shoes back onto his feet. Pawlik asked Barry if he was still feeling okay.

"I'm more mad than anything else," said Barry.

"Well, I, I would be mad, too, I guess," said the police detective. But then he added: "When it's all over with, it'll be better for everybody."

"You think so?" said Barry. He wasn't so sure himself.

The mayor was taken down the hotel service elevator and hustled into a blue Chevrolet Suburban for the 12-block ride to FBI headquarters at 9th Street and Pennsylvania Avenue, NW. At the J. Edgar Hoover building, squat and ugly as its namesake, Barry was fingerprinted and photographed, then ordered to urinate in a Dixie cup and allow hair and blood samples to be taken, which later would test positive for the presence of marijuana, cocaine and alcohol. He then phoned his third wife, Effi, a statuesque mulatto from Toledo, Ohio, who once had worked as a health inspector for the city. Effi Barry apparently notified D.C. Corporation Counsel Herbert O. Reid, Sr., the mayor's former lawyer and a longtime mentor and father figure, because Reid came downtown.

At 12:40 A.M. the FBI's Chevy stopped in front of a two-story red brick colonial with white pillars in the Hillcrest Heights neighborhood of Southeast Washington. Barry, Reid, and several G-men emerged. Sporting a lopsided grin, the mayor was led by Ronald Stern past supporters, reporters, and the just plain curious into the house where he lived with Effi and their nine-year-old son, Christopher. A shotgun-toting bodyguard, in a belated show of firepower, led the way. It was not Marion Barry's finest hour.

3

DAMAGE CONTROL

R Kenneth Mundy, the lawyer Marion Barry had retained
after the Ramada Inn incident, was playing tennis when
he got word that his most famous client had been arrested. The veteran black criminal defense attorney and
admitted tennis fanatic finished the set—which he won—before
reporting to the mayor's uptown command center at 14th and
U Streets, NW, around 11:30 P.M. Still wearing his sweatsuit,
Mundy made his way past police guards, who were screening
out the press and public, to the elevator of the Frank D. Reeves
Center of Municipal Affairs, an ungainly steel, glass, and pink
concrete structure that Barry had built along the riot-torn 14th
Street corridor four years earlier. Grilled by reporters as he
waited for the lift, the normally loquacious lawyer—known
for his mischievous, gap-toothed grin and the many stylish
hats with which he adorned his balding pate—at first said only
that he was "not at liberty" to discuss the case. But then he
quickly returned to character and added, nonchalantly, "It's
a misdemeanor kind of thing."

To a man who had won acquittals in criminal cases with far
more damaging evidence and made his reputation, and a fair
living, defending criminally accused black men, rich and poor,
Marion Barry's case, though clearly a challenge, was not the
toughest Mundy ever had had to handle. The moment had
come more than a decade earlier when the 57-year-old Akron,
Ohio, native, who once had been a Golden Gloves lightweight
boxer and pursued lawyering with the same verve, style and
competitiveness he had shown in the manly art, represented
Terrence Johnson. The 15-year-old black Prince George's
County youth was charged with shooting to death two white
policemen at a police station. In that highly publicized, racially
charged murder case, Mundy had saved Johnson from the gas

chamber by winning acquittal for his client on one charge by reason of "temporary insanity;" he obtained a reduced sentence on the second charge, for which Johnson was convicted of manslaughter.

Mundy also had won acquittals for more high-profile black clients, including University of the District of Columbia president Robert Green, charged in 1987 with stealing an expensive stereo system and television from the university, and D.C. Council member Sterling Tucker, accused in 1977 of being on the Howard University payroll at the same time he was on the council.

"He really knows how to connect with a black jury," Mundy's former law partner, Joseph Gibson, told the *Washington Post* in February 1989. Gibson added, "With a black jury, he may do more preaching. With a white jury, he'll just lay the facts out."

On the night of January 18, however, Mundy had come primarily to listen. Emerging from the elevator on the penthouse floor, the mayor's attorney found several grim-looking senior officials. These included Barry's staff chief, Maudine Cooper, a former director of the D.C. Office of Human Rights and a National Urban League executive. She had unwittingly spoken to her boss at the Vista by phone during the sting. Also present were city administrator Carol Thompson, at 38 already a 10-year veteran of the Barry administration and one of the few bright stars on its clouded horizon; Joseph Yeldell, an aging bureaucrat whose sinecure was to direct the city's Office of Emergency Preparedness; and Isaac Fulwood, Jr., who had replaced Maurice Turner, Jr., as D.C. police chief six months earlier.

Fulwood seemed to speak for them all when he said about Barry's sudden arrest, "When I figure it out, I'll tell you."

While Barry's advisors conferred on how to rescue him from his latest self-sprung trap, the man who had helped Barry spring it, U.S. Attorney Jay Stephens, issued a characteristically terse and sober official statement.

"Tonight's undercover operation was part of an on-going public corruption probe under the supervision of the U.S.

Attorney for the District of Columbia," said Stephens in a press release issued jointly with Thomas DuHadway, chief of the FBI's D.C. field office. The statement said the mayor had been arrested at the Vista Hotel on "narcotics charges" but gave no details of the drug charges, nor how they related to the "on-going public corruption probe" of the D.C. government.

The following day Barry was arraigned before federal magistrate Deborah A. Robinson in United States District Court at 3rd and Constitution Avenue, NW. When he arrived, nearly an hour late for his scheduled noontime arraignment, so many people converged on his official limousine that a dozen policemen were needed to push them back. The somber-looking mayor, dressed in a dark double-breasted suit, blue shirt, and red tie, squeezed out of the Lincoln Town Car followed by Effi, mayoral press secretary Lurma Rackley, and Herbert Reid. Managing a wan smile but sweating heavily despite the cold winter day, Barry moved silently through the crush of humanity, ignoring questions shouted by reporters, until he reached the hulking limestone rectangle, built in 1952, where he had been tried and acquitted 20 years earlier on charges of assaulting two D.C. policemen in a scuffle over a parking ticket. Inside, the mayor was detained in a fourth-floor holding room for more than half an hour before being summond to courtroom eight, packed since early in the morning with reporters and spectators anxious to see the mayor of the nation's capitol stand before a judge.

While Kenneth Mundy conferred with federal prosecutors Judith Retchin and Richard Roberts, Barry, who had swaggered into the courtroom, smiling defiantly at reporters, sat in a black leather swivel chair at the defense table and rocked nervously. But when a courtroom artist looked at him through tiny binoculars, the mayor broke the tension by circling his own eyes with his fingers and staring back. At one point he left his seat to confer with Effi, who sat in a bench near the front of the courtroom. As they talked, the capital's First Lady touched Barry's knee and he smiled back at her. He lost his smile when the magistrate entered the courtroom and read the allegations against him.

"You are presently charged with the unlawful possession of cocaine base," said Robinson, "also known as crack."

As U.S. Attorney Jay Stephens looked on, Assistant U.S. Attorney Judith Retchin, a businesslike woman with short hair, briefly described the sting operation that formed the basis of the charges. If Barry's legal arch-nemesis, who had tried Watergate cases in the same courtroom, felt any elation at having bagged a quarry that had eluded his predecessor, Joseph diGenova, for five years and eluded him for nearly two, his face did not show it.

Mundy spoke for Barry, telling the magistrate his client would exercise his constitutional right to a jury trial.

Then Robinson asked the mayor to stand and raise his right hand and swear like any other common criminal suspect to accept the terms of his release on bond.

"You are to return to court on February 5 [for a status hearing]," Robinson ordered. "You are to submit to weekly drug tests, starting Monday, January 22." She told Barry he also must surrender his passport and phone the federal Pretrial Services Office in the District once a week. Then she warned, "Failure to return to court will constitute a separate offense," after which she told the defendant sternly, "You may have a seat while your release order is being prepared."

When Robinson announced the penalty upon conviction for drug possessin of one year in jail and a $100,000 fine, "Barry's facial muscles suddenly betrayed him," wrote the *Post*'s Courtland Milloy, who attended the arraignment. "For one agonizing moment he grimaced—with clenched teeth and furrowed brow. The cool smirk fell off his lips."

The legal formalities were completed in less than 15 minutes, but the greater ordeal for both Barry and the city he was elected to run would continue for months. As the mayor left the federal courthouse, Jay Stephens was holding a press conference on the front steps.

"I view this not as the end of an event but as part of an on-going investigation," said Stephens, who favored the patriotic red tie, white shirt, blue suit combination affected by many of Washington's power elite. He explained that the Barry sting

was only a part of a much wider federal probe of city government corruption that had begun under his predecessor and
picked up momentum after the Ramada Inn incident in
December 1988. Stephens added a human note to the occasion
by saying, "I think the events of last night are a personal
tragedy for the defendant in this case." Then Stephens
revealed why he had pursued Barry so fervently: "Narcotics
abuse and violence that has followed ... is also a tragedy for
many of the people of this city, for kids of this community,
for their families. I have said many times that narcotics abuse
is not a victimless crime. I think, as last night's events demonstrated, even a city can be a victim."

When asked if he was concerned Barry might claim an
entrapment defense because of the highly unusual way in
which he was arrested, Stephens replied: "When there is
predisposition [to commit a crime], there is no entrapment.
As a general matter, when we review undercover operations,
we look at it very carefully to make a determination where
there is a predicate, whether there's been some activity, some
basis, to believe that the subject of that undercover investigation may engage in additional criminal conduct.

"And I think it is fair to say that the operation conducted
last night was an operation that complies with the law, that
there is no entrapment there, that it was too scrupulously fair
to the subject of that investigation, Mr. Barry, and it was carried
out in an evenhanded and fair manner."

Finally, Washington's chief federal prosecutor emphasized
where the government saw the bottom line resting in this case:
"He [Barry] went to the hotel on his own volition. He went
to the seventh floor on his own free will."

A few minutes later the mayor, accompanied by his wife and
lawyer, stood before the same cluster of microphones and faced
the same unruly crowd of reporters and onlookers—some of
whom shouted encouragement or insults at him.

"Quit, Barry, quit!" yelled a well-dressed businessman.

"You still got my vote!" screamed a female supporter, as
if in response.

"I know that there will be a number of you who will be
interested and curious about these events and activities," said

the visibly subdued mayor, "but I cannot comment, react, or give any information about this particular charge." Then he turned to the horde of reporters and news camera operators jostling with each other for a better camera shot or microphone placement and added: "I urge you not to ask me any detailed questions about that because it is in the judicial system and I can't answer them. But on the other hand, I am going to leave here and go about the business of running the government." Beneath Barry's stoic public demeanor, and the defiance he had shown in court, was the privately held belief that, at least in one sense, his arrest had delivered him from a potentially greater disaster. If he had been allowed to continue his wanton lifestyle unchecked, Barry told WUSA-TV's Bruce Johnson shortly after the Vista bust, "I probably would have died out there drinking and drugging."

Mundy told reporters his client would plead "not guilty" to the drug-possession charge and that the defense team he led was in the "process of trying to find out as much information as possible about the charges."

As Barry left the courthouse, a black man yelled after him: "You all right Barry! You ain't done more damage than the white man do every day!"

The supporter's views were reflected in a poll taken the same day by the *Post*, a poll that graphically illustrated the deep racial schism in the capital. Four out of 10 black respondents in a random sampling of 661 black and white D.C. residents agreed that the Barry investigation was racially motivated. Only one out of 15 whites shared this view. One out of five black D.C. residents interviewed believed law enforcement officials were out to get Marion Barry any way they could, a belief held by only a third as many whites. While more than 70 percent of respondents of both races said they believed Barry was using drugs at the Vista Hotel, one out of five blacks—as opposed to only one in 14 whites—still felt Barry should run for reelection in the fall. In sum, concluded the *Post* in what could only be termed an understatement of the problem, "The repercussions of Barry's arrest have spread far beyond city politics, and may have further polarized the city's black and white communities, already deeply divided along social, economic and geographic lines.''

The responses to Barry's arrest—expressed in the *Post* poll and in numerous other media stories—did not always break down along racial lines. Some whites, for example, supported Barry while some blacks thought the mayor should resign immediately and get out of town. By and large, however, the residents of black neighborhoods defended the mayor—some claiming he had been unfairly entrapped by the city's white federal prosecutor—while white residents were generally quicker to conclude that Barry had invited the trouble and also disgraced the city. This split along racial lines, reported in great detail by both the local and national media, was not lost on Barry, his lawyer, or his political advisors. Such information would allow the mayor to predict that no jury in the predominantly black capital would convict him of a crime.

Meanwhile, on the day after the sting, some of Barry's oldest black political allies were starting to turn against him. D.C. Council member Nadine Winter, who for years had stood by Barry in good times and bad, expressed disappointment and outrage. She called the mayor's drug arrest ''a disaster,'' adding, ''I hope he has got more intelligence than that [to walk into a sting].''

Others, like D.C. Council member John Ray, the frontrunner in the 1990 mayoral race, put a political spin on the Barry crisis. ''I just think this is going to be a terrible shock to the young people of our city,'' said the Georgia-born lawyer and veteran city legislator who had won his first at-large council seat in 1978 with Barry's help. Ray was packaging himself in his campaign as a positive role model for the city's youth.

D.C. Council member Charlene Drew Jarvis, who also was set to challenge Barry in the Democratic mayoral primary nine months away and who still hoped to win his endorsement, said what nearly everyone was beginning to realize—that Barry's arrest would produce ''a dramatic change in the political landscape.''

Jarvis also said the sting had highlighted ''the larger issue facing the community,'' noting that ''this is the second elected official who has been involved with drugs recently.''

She was referring to James Herl, the white chairman of the county council of neighboring Prince George's County, who, a week before the Barry sting, had been caught in a similar undercover operation involving cocaine and a pretty undercover policewoman acting as a sexual lure. Unlike Barry, Herl eventually confessed his drug use, resigned from the council, and apologized to the people who had elected him, saying: "I think I am to be held, as a public official, to a higher standard. And I think part of being held to a higher standard is to forfeit my office at an appropriate time."

Mayoral candidate Sharon Pratt Dixon, a lawyer and former utility company executive, said bluntly that it was time for the mayor to leave Washington's political scene.

"All along I've said he ought not seek reelection because he wasn't up to the job," said Dixon, who had called on Barry to step down more than a year earlier, following the Ramada Inn incident. "It's clear he doesn't want to go on."

Perhaps the most charitable comment by a local politician came from the white D.C. Council chairman, David Clarke, another 1990 mayoral candidate. He called the Barry bust a "tragic moment in our history." But Clarke also insisted that "the city will continue to operate—the dignity of the city is more than just one person."

On Capitol Hill, where perceptions of the city translate into dollars—Congress provides about one-sixth of the city's annual operating budget and also retains veto power over the budget and all city council legislation—some key congressmen differed sharply with Clarke over how much one person can affect the city's dignity. "He [Barry] was so arrogant; he was an impediment," said Rep. Robert Dornan (R-Ca.), a member of the House District Committee. "This can only help the city. The city's leadership has become an irrelevancy, as far as the D.C. committee was concerned. We acted like the city government wasn't even there."

Dornan also gave Barry an unusual, if slightly premature, political epitaph: "What's the old expression, 'dance with the devil?' He's been dancing with danger so long the trap door finally fell open on him."

The House District Committee's ranking minority member, Rep. Stan Parris (R-Va.), said the mayor's arrest on drug charges would surely set back the District's controversial statehood drive, which already was crippled by a "never-ending series of catastrophic events—from the prison [over-crowding] situation to [poor] snow removal to an enormous operating deficit to simple administrative problems." As a result, said Parris, "Some [members of Congress] are talking openly about revoking home rule, although I don't think we've come to that."

Parris added: "I don't think the people of the United States want another situation like Mayor [James Michael] Curley of Boston, and I don't think the people of the District of Columbia do," said Parris, referring to the late, immensely popular Irish Catholic mayor of Boston. In the mid-1940s, Curley had been convicted on federal mail fraud charges and served part of his fourth mayoral term in a federal prison, before President Harry Truman pardoned him in 1946.

The pain and shock caused by the mayor's arrest were felt perhaps most deeply by the city's schoolchildren, many of whom had looked up to a man who had visited their schools to deliver an anti-drug message personally and who now appeared to be a total hypocrite. In the days following the arrest, Washington newspapers brimmed with stories of the betrayal and disillusionment felt by children and senior citizens, the two groups Barry had prided himself on helping the most.

The political fallout from the sting was not limited to the capital. Stories on Barry ran in every major U.S. newsweekly. *Newsweek* put the story on its cover. Ted Koppel ran a "Nightline" on the sting, and several other television news specials followed. In an editorial, the *Chicago Tribune* found it "inexpressibly saddening to see our capital city bloodied and its mayor arrested on narcotic charges. If he is convicted, this country should be infuriated. And perhaps finally understand that to conduct a serious war on drugs, we must cut the demand. We—or at least too many of us—are our own worst enemies."

A notable silence emanated from both the White House and the office of national drug czar William Bennett, who had targeted the District as the focus of his failed war on drugs and whose personal distaste for Washington's mayor was no secret.

Major black public figures, including the Reverend Jesse Jackson, generally offered support. "I'm too stunned to talk right now," said the normally garrulous and alliterative Baptist minister and Democratic presidential candidate, who was widely reputed to have his eye on the 1990 mayoral race in the District. When Jackson finally found his voice, it was the voice of a clergyman: "In this time of great private and public pain, my prayers and those of my family go out to Mayor Barry, his wife Effi and son Christopher."

Rep. Charles Rangel (D-N.Y.), chairman of the House Select Committee on Narcotics Abuse and Control, said, less sympathetically, "When mayors of great cities are indicted for drug abuse, it should show the depth of the problem."

NAACP executive director Benjamin Hooks, to the delight of the Barry camp, injected a racial element into the mayor's personal and political crisis by saying that the Barry case might fit into a national pattern of "selective enforcement of the law" against black elected officials by federal agents. He said the NAACP "felt that there has been undue emphasis on harassing black elected officials."

Hooks's charge brought an immediate response from U.S. attorney general Dick Thornburgh, who said any suggestion that the Justice Department based its investigative decisions on race "is sadly misinformed." Thornburgh added, "I think it would do at least an equal amount, if not a greater amount, of harm to forego prosecution on the basis of some characteristic of a prospective defendant than to target that person. Neither of those are admissible in a system that truly operates under the rule of law."

Overseas, reporters and editors of major news organizations were far less sympathetic and far less subject to the pressures of U.S. racial politics. In a summary of foreign coverage of the Barry bust, the *Washington Times* said it "was the lead story on French television's main evening newscast Friday [January 19]. It pushed the turmoil of Azerbaijan's civil strife in the Soviet Union to a secondary position for several hours in radio broadcasts in such diverse languages as Polish, Italian and Croatian." The *Times* said that "Barry's face stared at the readers from the front pages of hundreds of newspapers, including such prominent dailies as Milan's *Corriere Della Sera* and Madrid's *El Pais*.

"In Italian ('Il sindaco ha fatto crack'), German ('Washington's Burgermeister mit Kokain Entrapt'), or French ('Le maire de Washington pris au piege')," said the *Times*, "readers learned all about the crime scene in Washington and Mr. Barry's exploits. West European commentators reminded their audiences of the Chicago gang wars in the 1920s, pointing out that Washington was not only 'the capital of the free world' but 'the world's crime capital.'

"To many Europeans," the *Times* said, "the story had all the ingredients of a gangster film, and the press plunged into it with glee. The racial problem, the alleged sexual prowess of the capital's mayor and the activities of the FBI to trap him consumed a solid chunk of newsprint."

In Colombia, however, where hundreds of people are slain each year in a bloody drug war many Colombians feel is fueled primarily by U.S. demand, members of the media found little to be gleeful about. Instead, they were very angry. Bogota's newspaper *El Espectador* ran Barry's picture and story on its front page under the headline, "Drug-Addict Mayor." Bogota's other major daily, *El Tiempo*, also ran a front-page story by its Washington correspondent, Marino Perez Murcia, who told his readers, " Barry is considered a symbol of the hypocrisy in the fight against drugs, because he promotes anti-drug programs in the schools and black neighborhoods."

The tabloid *La Prensa* led its special extra late edition with a story and a photo of Barry wiping his brow. A radio talk show host in Bogota referred to Barry as the "narcomayor" of D.C.

The man who had helped set all this coverage in motion, Charles Lewis, was sentenced on drug charges in U.S. District

Court later on the same day that Barry was arraigned there. Pudgy, baby-faced, dressed in a three-piece buiness suit, Lewis asked Judge Stanley Sporkin for leniency, in part because he had provided the government with information that helped snare the mayor.

"For me, the bottom [line] was to believe that because I used drugs with other professionals, with others in government, with the mayor of the city, that I should lie to protect them and myself," said Lewis, explaining that he'd had a change of heart after realizing the unwisdom of his ways. In November 1989 Lewis had pleaded guilty to two counts of conspiracy to possess crack cocaine at the Ramada Inn Central in December 1988. He agreed to testify before the grand jury and at Barry's trial, should there be one. In return, prosecutors had agreed to drop 15 other charges against him. "Drugs have ruined my life," said Lewis, 49, a member of a prominent Virgin Islands family, who had met Barry nearly a decade earlier when he worked for the city's employment services department. "I have lost everything I had. I have lost a career. I have lost any material things I had. I have lost the respect of my family and friends. Most important, for a while, I lost my self-respect."

Lewis's attorney, Mark Shaffer, told the judge his client's testimony "has brought to a head the issue of whether this city can survive as a civilized place, if the city's chief law enforcement official, and its chief drug spokesperson, is a cocaine user."

Citing Lewis's cooperation with federal authorities, Sporkin sentenced him to 15 months in prison—six months less than the 21-month term prescribed under federal guidelines for a drug conspiracy conviction.

While his old friend Chuck Lewis took his lumps from Sporkin at the federal courthouse, the mayor was at the Reeves Center, closeted with a small group of old friends and advisors who reportedly told him that he finally had gone too far. They advised him to step down.

"This was not a pussycat conversation," one advisor later told the *Post*, adding that the politically beleaguered mayor "listened. He understood. He was not fighting us, he was not argumentative."

The group included Barry's black political campaign manager, Anita Bonds, who would play a key advisory role at his trial; campaign co-chairman and black television executive Robert Johnson; white developer and investment partner Jeffrey Cohen; and white restaurateurs Stuart Long and Jeffrey Gildenhorn, who had helped bankroll Barry's campaigns. According to the *Post*, "the group also told Barry that his remaining in office could exacerbate racial tensions in Washington, whereas with resignation, the scars caused by his arrest might begin healing."

One floor above the mayor, his cabinet, comprising about 40 top D.C. officials, was engaged in an emotional debate over the fate of both the mayor and the city government. Participants in that meeting told the *Post* that the officials divided into two camps—those willing to stick by the mayor no matter what and those who felt betrayed and deceived by a man who repeatedly had assured them he was not using drugs.

According to the officials quoted by the *Post*, Veronica Pace, executive director of the D.C. Office of Aging, "stood up and angrily accused officials present of leaking information against Barry and undermining his administration." They told the paper that Arlene Gillespie, executive director of the city's Office of Latino Affairs, had also assailed her fellow city officials for engaging in what she called a "conspiracy of silence" over the years while watching the mayor fall deeper and deeper into a deadly spiral of drug abuse.

The less sympathetic faction, the officials said, was led by parole board chairwoman Gladys Mack, who insisted that the mayor, at the very least, "owed us an explanation for his behavior."

Meanwhile the mayor himself held yet another emergency meeting on what was rapidly becoming the longest day of his political life. Barry told city administrator Carol Thompson and D.C. corporation counsel Herbert Reid that he would not resign, but at their request he agreed to put his political campaign on hold until he straightened out his legal affairs. Reluctantly, he also agreed to turn over temporarily to Thompson all executive powers allowed by the D. C. Charter. The document authorized her to run cabinet meetings, negotiate with the D.C. Council, execute contracts over $1 million, even declare a city emergency. Only the mayor, however, could sign or veto city council legislation or enter into contracts with the federal government. According to one cabinet member interviewed by the *Post*, the move really didn't alter the political landscape much, since Thompson and the cabinet already had been "running the government without the mayor's full attention for two years."

It was late afternoon when Barry finally entered the conference room where his cabinet had been waiting for more than two-and-a-half hours. He quietly announced his decision to delegate power to Thompson and told them he could not discuss any details of the arrest. Then the District's macho mayor, who earlier in the day had strutted into a federal courtroom for his arraignment as if he had not a care in the world, did something he never had done during nearly 20 years in public office: he broke down and cried.

Composing himself, Barry next turned his attention to the D.C. Council members who had come to the Reeves Center to meet with him. In a briefing that veteran council member John Wilson later described as "extremely depressing," the mayor told them of his arrest. Then, said Wilson, the mayor's grief momentarily turned to anger as he lashed out at unnamed council members whom he accused of finding "glee" in his predicament.

Barry remained at the Reeves Center until 9:30 P.M., receiving a steady stream of friends and advisors, as if presiding over his own political wake. At the end of the day he issued an official statement assuring the city's 574,844 residents they would continue to "receive the kind of professional service they deserve" and pledging not to "lose touch with the operations of government" during the crisis he had caused.

On Saturday, January 20, Barry summoned dozens of close friends and advisors to his Southeast Washington home to help him decide his next move. They included two old friends whose advice he sought on the critical question of drug abuse treatment: WRC–TV news anchor Jim Vance, who had been treated at the Betty Ford Center for cocaine and prescription drug addiction; and former comedian and civil rights activist Dick Gregory, inventor of the Bahamian Diet and health plan, which had been used succesfully to treat addiction. According to some who visited Barry's home that day, the mayor agreed that he needed to seek medical treatment and was prepared to accept a holistic regimen prescribed by Gregory. But, the visitors reportedly said, Barry was talked out of this plan late in the evening by other friends who warned him he would be committing political suicide by seeking treatment outside a traditional medical setting.

On the same day, a normally cautious Jay Stephens uncharacteristically tipped his strategic hand by telling reporters he would be "sensitive" to a Barry resignation in deciding how to proceed with his probe of the mayor's alleged illegal activities. The probe had reached the grand jury stage, and Stephens apparently was becoming increasingly confident that he would be able to convict Barry if the case went to trial.

"I believe there are issues here that go well beyond simply the punishment of Marion Barry," said Stephens, implying he might go easy on the mayor if he stepped down. "I'm sensitive to the needs of this community, in having the moral and political leadership that can deal with a drug and homicide crisis" as well as the need to hold "people accountable for their conduct."

After learning of Stephens's comments, the mayor reportedly authorized Kenneth Mundy to explore a possible plea bargain agreement with the U.S. attorney. Apparently, Mundy didn't get very far with Stephens, who clearly wanted as a minimum Barry's resignation—something the mayor was not willing to offer. Nor did Barry have much incentive to step down voluntarily. For one thing, Stephens had yet to bring an indictment against him, and Barry had no reason to believe the current grand jury would behave any differently than previous ones that had failed to indict him. Secondly, even if he were to be indicted, tried and convicted of drug possession—a misdemeanor in the District—he still could hold on to power legally. Under the D.C. Code, no sitting mayor can be removed from office unless convicted of a felony and jailed. Moreover, if Barry resigned, white D.C. Council chairman David Clarke would under the D.C. Charter be named acting mayor—an eventuality Barry and his followers wanted to avoid at all costs.

Early on Sunday morning, January 21, the day on which Barry had planned to announce his fourth-term run, the mayor instead "wept openly" in the living room of his Southeast Washington home while eight black ministers prayed for his recovery from drug and alcohol addiction. Around 9:30 A.M., Barry, Effi, and the ministers hiked 100 yards down Suitland Road to St. Timothy's Episcopal Church, where Barry faced a battery of television cameras and reporters.

Bolstered by his wife, who held his hand, and the ministers, the mayor delivered a sermonlike statement in which he dramatically pledged to "find a way to heal my body, mind, and soul" but failed to acknowledge his drug use, disclose any specifics about his personal or political plans, or apologize to the city.

"The events of the past few days," said Barry, "have been the most difficult of my life, more difficult than fighting my way out of poverty as a black youth born in the segregated Deep South, more difficult than the fear and hatred I faced as a civil rights leader in the 1960s, more difficult than I could have imagined, because this time I have come face to face with my human frailties. I have had to look my human weaknesses straight in the eye, had to realize I have spent so much time caring about and worrying about and doing for others, I have not worried about or cared enough for myself."

Without further explaining his statement about helping others—a claim Barry's political opponents would later characterize as self-serving, hypocritical, even ludicrous, considering the sad state of affairs in the District—Barry shook his head for emphasis and added, "How I wish I could trade this hour." No one could challenge the sincerity of that statement. "I've had to realize that God made Marion Barry the same as he made other people, a flesh-and-blood creation who will rise and fall just like any other human being.

"I felt for some time that I could do any and everything. But they [the ministers] have helped me to realize that God put each of us on this earth for a purpose and we may not always understand what the purpose is, but when we put ourselves in God's hands our way is made clearer.

"To all the people who love me and worry about me," continued Barry, carefully limiting the focus of his speech to his own problems, rather than those he had created for his constituents, "the best way to show your appreciation for me and our city and my family is to join together as a united community. We must at this hour be willing to forgive, to love, to reach out to each other and to serve our city."

The mayor concluded his personal message by calling up imagery from the Twenty-third Psalm: "I realize I'm going to have to walk this journey by myself. But I say to others who are pained and hurt as I am, join me, brothers and sisters, we can make it. We can make it. We will make it. It will be a lonely journey. But God stands with us."

A few days later he resurfaced at the Hanley-Hazelden Clinic in West Palm Beach, Florida, where Lurma Rackley said, the mayor would be treated for "a health concern" that included alcohol abuse. Like Barry, his press secretary was silent on the question of Barry's alleged cocaine use. A planned absence of a month would stretch into seven weeks when Barry transferred from Hanley-Hazelden to Fenwick Hall, a drug-treatment facility in South Carolina.

While undergoing drug treatment in Florida, Barry kept up the public relations campaign that he had started almost immediately after his arrest. The moves, made in concert with defense attorney Mundy and campaign manager Anita Bonds, seemed calculated to demonstrate his humility and sincerity in the wake of the sleazy Vista revelations, and later, when that didn't seem enough to fend off Jay Stephens, his willingness to relinquish, if the judicial price was right, his destructive grip on power.

Barry made his first important move while still in Florida. In mid-February during a Sunday visit to the New Macedonia Missionary Church in Riviera Beach, the mayor let it be known that he had rediscovered God. Barry told the southern black parishoners that he had "a friend bigger than the U.S. attorney, and that friend is Jesus Christ."

Barry continued to play the religion card on his return to the capital a month later by attending services at numerous black churches, where he presented himself as a poor lost sheep who had strayed and wanted to be readmitted to the fold. And he moved away from the multiracial and ecumenical All Soul's Unitarian Church, where he had worshipped for more than a decade, to attend services at the more fire-and-brimstone, sin-and-forgiveness-oriented Metropolitan Baptist Church, whose congregants were mainly black ex-Southerners like himself.

On February 15, only a few days after his purported religious reconversion in Florida, Barry was indicted in Washington on three felony counts of lying to a grand jury about his drug use with Charles Lewis and on five misdemeanor counts of cocaine possession at the Ramada Inn in 1988 and the Vista Hotel in 1990. Through a press release issued by his office, the mayor lashed out at Jay Stephens, saying the "indictment does not surprise me at all because it represents a continuation of the political lynching and excesses of the Justice Department."

Barry's by now familiar attempt to paint his accusers as white racists bent on bringing him down because he was black found resonance among local black opinion-makers. Radio station owner and talk show host Cathy Hughes had featured Barry's predicament on frequent broadcasts in which she propogated the dubious "fact" that the government had spent $42 million over the past decade to bring Barry down. She claimed that an official at the U.S. Justice Department, whose name she couldn't remember, had confirmed the figure, which she said she had gotten originally from the mayor's office—hardly a disinterested party. According to federal law enforcement officials, the actual cost of investigating and prosecuting not only Barry but at least 10 other city officials and contractors doing business with the city over an eight-year period starting in 1982 was actually somewhere between $2 and $3 million.

Barry got a strong partisan boost from virtually every local black publication as well. The *Washington Afro-American and*

Tribune, the *Metro Chronicle,* the *Washington Informer,* the *Capital Spotlight,* and the *Washington New Observer*—black weeklies largely ignored by the mayor in happier times—published stories under such headlines as "Bait Gate," portraying the mayor as the victim of a white federal conspiracy to dethrone him. Four days before the mayor's trial started, *Capital Spotlight* columnist James Strong had gone further than anyone by predicting that a conviction could bring about a racial Armageddon in the tension-filled capital. "To relieve racial tensions and restore racial calm," Strong had asserted, presumably tongue-in-cheek, "Washingtonians need to engage in a good old-fashioned, blood-soaking race war."

"You have to understand our perspective," *Afro-American and Tribune* publisher Frances Murphy had told a *Washington Times* reporter questioning her about the blatant pro-Barry slant taken by the city's black press. "It's not only Marion Barry that's on trial, it's the U.S. government that's on trial, not just in Washington but around the world."

Barry also had received a significant and unexpected boost from white journalist Robert Scheer, who had published an article in the July 1990 issue of *Playboy* magazine attacking the FBI's heavy-handed tactics—especially in "hounding an old [Barry] girlfriend [Rasheeda Moore] with troubles enough of her own."

"No matter what transpires in the trial," wrote Scheer in an article that was later quoted in the mayor's weekly campaign newsletter, "it's clear that the FBI should be found guilty. So maybe Barry is a pompous hypocrite—aren't they all? Politicians, that is. Who was he hurting other than himself if he did use drugs?

"Until the FBI and drug agents sandbagged the man, Barry was a popular mayor of one of the toughest cities you can run. Maybe he blew it and therefore deserves no pity. But what the FBI did smacks of goonsmanship of the kind J. Edgar Hoover used to encourage. And that is a far more troubling problem than Mayor Barry's libido."

Scheer's view was shared by black agents in the FBI's Washington Metropolitan Field Office. Said a black Washington

television reporter, who asked not to be named, "They were
furious over the heavy-handed tactics" the FBI used to recruit
Rasheeda Moore. "They [the white agents] told her, 'You'll
never see your children again.' "

He said that it was no accident that no black male FBI agent
had participated in the Vista sting.

National black leaders also had lined up behind Barry.
NAACP executive director Benjamin Hooks kept up his sharply
worded attacks on federal prosecutors, such as Jay Stephens,
who allegedly had "targeted" black officials for investigation.
The Reverend Jesse Jackson, not one to miss the chance to
weigh in on any black-related issue in the news, spoke
alliteratively of the government's "prosecution and persecu-
tion" of Barry. (Jackson's self-serving statement of support
came despite profound tensions that had developed between
the two men after Jackson moved to the District from Chicago
in 1989. In a tense meeting at D.C.'s Park Hyatt Hotel in
August of that year, Barry had reportedly told Jackson, who
was known to have his eye on Barry's job, "I feel like you've
just fucked my wife.")

And in early April, at the annual meeting of the National
Conference of Black Mayors in New Orleans, Barry, according
to the *Washington Post*, was surrounded by young people, who
"swarmed around him for his autograph and to have their
picture taken with him, while a number of mayors and other
officials showered him with hugs, kisses and words of encouragement." Savoring his hero's welcome, said the *Post*, Barry
told reporters in the City of Saints that his support back home
was even stronger, so strong, in fact, he said, that "it's been
frightening."

Later that same month Barry seemed to prove the point when
he showed up, nearly two hours late, at a debate among the
city's mayoral candidates held at a Lutheran church in Northwest Washington and stole the spotlight from the speaker.
Democratic candidate Walter Fauntroy was drowned out by
cheers and applause as the prodigal mayor strode down the
church aisle surrounded by television cameramen and well-
wishers, some of whom rhythmically chanted his name. By

mau-mauing the mayoral candidates and making numerous other campaign-style appearances around town during the leadup to his trial, Barry was flexing his political muscles at least enough to show Jay Stephens that, if he chose to run again, he might win. If he looked strong enough, the prosecutor might be forced to cut a deal.

While some prominent local and national blacks had been rallying around the mayor, Washington's white-controlled media had been bashing Barry in editorials and daily exposés of the criminal investigation, prompting Mundy to complain to the *Post*: "I think we have a very prejudiced press here. I don't say that racially, but I think we have a very biased press, editorially and in their commentary. There has not been one single, solitary, editorial commentary in print, electronic or otherwise from the general media here" favorable to Barry.

The split between black and white opinion makers in the capital reflected the larger schism between ordinary black and white citizens not only of Washington, but of New York, Detroit, Chicago, and other U.S. cities with large black populations. In all of these cities the schism had been widened by a decade of laissez-faire urban social policy under presidents Reagan and Bush, and by the country's growing but largely ignored economic recession, and the exodus of middle-class taxpayers from their troubled urban cores.

In Washington, as in New York—whose Howard Beach, Bensonhurst, and Central Park jogger trials had sparked an increasingly acrimonious racial debate—the tensions between the two major U.S. races would be addressed not in a healing dialogue, not even in government programs. Instead, they would be evoked angrily and without apparent catharsis by testimony in and publicity surrounding notorious trials. However, unlike the nondescript white youths in Howard Beach and Bensonhurst convicted of killing black youths, and the black youths in Central Park convicted of raping and assaulting a white female jogger, in Washington the defendant was a black middle-aged man who was well known, had acted alone, and committed crimes that hurt primarily himself.

Part Two: Marion Rises

4

ROOTS IN THE DELTA

What drove Marion Barry to transcend his start in wrenching poverty, becoming one of the nation's most powerful black leaders, only to self-destruct at the pinnacle? To find the key one must seek out his roots in the Mississippi Delta. By 1936, the year Barry was born on a cotton plantation near the crossroads hamlet of Itta Bena in north-western Mississippi, the stars and bars of the Confederacy had long since been furled. Slavery had been outlawed in this country for 71 years. The Magnolia State, like every other, bowed politically to Washington. But in the loam-rich Delta, cotton still was king and large planters still got rich riding the strong backs of slaves' descendants, who worked the land for rewards not much greater than those earned by their forebears.

Surrounding Itta Bena in Leflore County were half-a-dozen cotton plantations with fields that stretched up to 5,000 acres. The farms had quaint antebellum names such as Green Acres, Gold Dust, and Runnymeade. Some planters treated their sharecroppers like kin, toting their sick children to the doctor or otherwise helping out when a crisis arose. For the most part, though, life on the plantations, no matter how benign the planter, was anything but quaint. Sharecroppers lived in unheated shacks, hand pumped their water, answered the call of nature in outdoor privies. In the nation's poorest state— Mississippians earned an average of $215 a year compared to a national average of $515—they were the poorest of the poor.

During spring planting season Marion and Mattie Barry spent their days tilling and seeding the fertile brown "gumbo" soil of the Delta with a mule-drawn plow. Both animals and implements were furnished by the plantation owner for a fee. In the fall, when the cotton bolls ripened, before the weevils could get at them, they donned wide-brimmed straw hats and slung long burlap sacks over their shoulders to handpick the cotton they had grown. When Marion Barry was an infant, there were no day-care centers in the Delta, so Mattie carried him with her into the fields. He would later tell a *Washington Post* reporter that one of his earliest memories was "a lingering image of riding the tail of a cotton sack down a dark furrow at picking time."

At sundown each day Mattie prepared the evening meal on a potbellied, wood-burning stove. She could buy the fatback pork, peas, and beans many sharecroppers subsisted on at the planter's credit store. The Barrys also could purchase clothes and other essentials from the planter, who would deduct their bill from the proceeds of the crop sale. In a good year the crop might bring in $1,000. But after the planter took his half, then subtracted the credit store tab and the mule team rental fee, he might hand Marion Barry, Sr., only about $250.

The Barrys, like other sharecroppers, could find solace in churches or juke joints, where God at least could be counted on to lend a friendly ear, and music—Negro spirituals and Delta blues—became the medium of their deliverance. Many plantations had their own one-room churches, which often doubled as schools for the sharecroppers' children. At Love's Café in Itta Bena or the Hole-in-the-Wall on the grounds of the nearby D.T. White Plantation, a tired farmer could down a few beers or bolt white lightening while listening to ballads belted out, as often as not, on a broom, mouth organ, or one-string guitar.

On those rare occasions when the Barrys went into town, they could eat at Missy Burnette's Café or shop at Coffey's Grocery Store, black-owned businesses located in a neighborhood called Balance Due, so named because of the difficulty its poor residents often had paying their bills. But the Barrys also were welcome in many of Itta Bena's white-owned establishments, such as the Gibbs Movie Theatre, Shankle's Drug Store, or the Southern Café on Front Street, which had two identical lunch counters, separated by a wall. Black and white customers had their own entrances.

In town a polite civility prevailed between the races, so long as blacks—most of whom lived in Balance Due, east of the railroad tracks—maintained their designated roles. While no serious incidents of racial violence were recorded in Itta Bena, the potential for such outbreaks hung like a deadly specter over the entire Delta. Only a dozen miles away, in Money, Mississippi, a 14-year-old black boy named Emmett Till was lynched in 1955 after flirting with the white patroness of a country store.

Before Marion Barry grew old enough to inherit such problems, however, his mother took him away. He was just five years old when Mattie Barry, seeking a fresh start in life, moved north with her son and two older daughters to Memphis, Tennessee, joining what famed southern writer Willie Morris has described as "the largest and most dramatic migration of a people in the history of the human race." Her husband had been killed a year earlier in Itta Bena. Neither Marion Barry, Jr., nor his mother, who now lives in Memphis, will talk about the father or his untimely death, which, half a century later, still hangs like a dark, mysterious cloud over the family's past.

Built on a bluff overlooking the Mississippi River, Memphis back in the early forties was a bustling port city of nearly 300,000 people on the western edge of Tennessee. Although four out of 10 Memphians were black, Jim Crow laws barred them from mixing with white Memphians in schools, restaurants, hospitals, and all other public facilities, including the Memphis Zoo, which had a separate visiting day for blacks. Even the blues and jazz clubs on world-famous Beale Street, which featured primarily black musicians, were segregated.

Although blacks were legally entitled to vote, many were effectively barred from doing so by the dollar-a-head poll tax, which few blacks could afford. Even if they paid their dollar and voted, there were no black candidates. Whites controlled the city's political machinery and apparently felt no obligation to nominate a black person for office. In black neighborhoods churches picked up the leadership slack, shepherding not just long-time residents but newcomers such as Mattie Barry, who joined the Martin Temple Christian Methodist Episcopal church.

Mattie Barry found work as a maid, and she soon remarried, a butcher from rural Tennessee named Dave Cummings, who had two daughters from a previous marriage. Together, they had two more daughters. The combined family, which eventually comprised nine members, was crammed into a narrow, wooden "shotgun" house in South Memphis, one of four black enclaves in the city. According to local legend, if you stood in front of such a one-story house and fired a shotgun through the front door, the load would travel through every room in the house before exiting.

Life for young Barry—a tall, skinny child one former classmate at the Florida Avenue Elementary School described as an "ugly duckling"—was anything but easy. At home he slept on a couch and rose early each morning to chop wood for the stove. He stuffed cardboard in his shoes to fill the holes and sold his sandwiches to other kids at school, preferring hunger to being without pocket money. Though he couldn't carry a tune, he joined a church choir because the pastor had offered to pay the carfare of anyone who came to weekly practice. He walked to the church and kept the quarter. When all else failed and he needed money, he would put his younger sisters on the street where they would sing a cappella while he collected coins from appreciative passersby. Yet, says former schoolmate Aretha King, now a funeral home manager in Memphis, Marion Barry, Jr., like herself and so many other poor black children who grew up in South Memphis, was not "deprived." Rather, she insists, he had "a stout upbringing," meaning that he was taught Christian values by his parents, teachers, and scoutmasters, attended church every Sunday, and even belonged to a church youth group. One former member of Barry's church group, Zora Lee Davis, remembers that Barry, on talent nights, liked to recite poetry. His favorite, she says, was "The House by the Side of the Road," a poem by Sam Walter Foss that lauds those who maintain an open and friendly attitude toward others.

According to another old friend of the mayor's, one of his favorite childhood games was playing preacher—hardly a surprise for a boy who would use his charisma and verbal skills to become a leader at an early age. In fact, says Aretha King, even in elementary school Washington's future mayor was already showing the incipient skills of a "politician."

"I said some bad words in the [school] cafeteria and someone told my teacher," she recalls. "I said, 'Marion, please, go tell that woman I didn't say that, 'cause she's gonna believe you.' And he went to this schoolteacher and said, 'Miss Stephens, she didn't do that.' And she believed it because he was in good with her. He could always bridge between different groups of people."

But by the time Barry got to Booker T. Washington—one of only two black high schools in the city—it seems the boy whom his classmates later named Punching Bag had forgotten how to talk, at least to pretty girls. Years later the mayor would admit: "Actually, I was a very shy person during most of my life. I had trouble talking to girls, especially the pretty ones with big legs. A lot of my insecurities go back to those days."

Instead of spending his time hustling pretty girls, Barry kept his nose in the books. Although he was not an exceptional student, he was, according to former classmates and teachers, methodical and determined. At Booker T. Washington, he earned above-average grades and a berth in the National Honor Society. He stayed out of trouble, because troublemakers at the school sometimes earned a rap on the head with a big brass bell that the principal Blair T. Hunt carried with him as he patrolled the hallways.

The fact is, young Marion Barry had little time for mischief. When he wasn't studying or earning merit badges (he eventually became one of the first black Eagle Scouts in Memphis), playing basketball or boxing in club bouts after school, he worked at a variety of jobs. He delivered newspapers, bagged groceries, collected empty soda pop bottles, worked as a carhop at a drive-in restaurant. In the summers he traveled with his mother and sisters to Arkansas and Mississippi to pick cotton for 30 cents an hour.

In a 1976 interview with the *Washington Star*'s Robert Pear, Mattie Cummings said that, besides being exceptionally industrious, her only son also was somewhat of a mystery in his youth. "You could never tell what he was thinking," she said. "If he was worried, you'd never know it. He was independent, very proud and never was a quitter."

If Barry seemed to his mother to take life's hits and shrug them off, inside something very different was happening. Something dark. Former *Washington Post* staff writer Arthur Brisbane wrote in 1987 of this "dark side" of Marion Barry: "In later years, when he had power, it would take the form of an arrogance that waxed and waned according to how secure he felt. As a youth, it was rage, fluttering erratically inside. Barry controlled it, mostly, venting it secretly and with great satisfaction.

"He had a job waiting tables at the American Legion post, a place that gave little consideration to the innermost feelings of a sensitive black teenager. The men would look at Marion in his little white coat and say, 'Hey boy, come here, bring me my dinner.'

"Marion fought a private war with these men. He taught them, all right. While they weren't looking, he spat in their food.

" 'Here's your dinner, sir.' "

Barry would never lose that anger, no matter how successful and powerful he became. He'd suffered too many hits, starting with the death of Marion Barry, Sr. A just world doesn't take a little boy's father away. As Barry grew up, everywhere he looked, too many other things reminded him of the injustices black people suffered. Perhaps as a way of fighting back against his own sense of rage and helplessness, he made his people's struggle his own. If he could slay a dragon in the outside world, the little boy inside would feel protected, or perhaps revenged.

As a young civil rights leader and community activist, Barry would use the dynamo that churned inside him like Prometheus used the fire he stole from heaven: to benefit mankind. He seemed to have the energy and drive of a dozen men. Moreover, says author David Halberstam, who as a young newspaper reporter covered sit-ins Barry led in Nashville, during his civil rights days at least Barry was "this abidingly gentle and sweet youth with great personal courage.'' There seemed no limit to what a young man such as this could accomplish—both for himself and for his people—back then.

But in later years, when Barry transformed from outside agitator to political insider, the dark side gradually took over: he fell deeper and deeper into the grip of his admitted addictions—to Valium, Xanax [an anti-depressant], cocaine, and alcohol—and he lost control over the once-cleansing and inspirational fire inside. When that happened, Barry burned himself and everyone around him.

5

THE SHARECROPPERS' SON
GOES TO COLLEGE

In 1954, the same year the Supreme Court handed down
its landmark school desegregation decision, *Brown* v. *Board
of Education of Topeka, Kansas,* Marion Barry graduated from
his all-black high school, which, despite *Brown,* would not be
fully integrated, by court-ordered busing, until 1972. In the
Booker T. Washington yearbook, *The Warrior,* Barry was named
the "Smartest Boy" in his twelfth-grade section, an appellation
he'd worked hard for. That fall the sharecroppers' son became
the first in his family to attend college.

Barry chose small, predominantly black, LeMoyne College,
a co-ed school founded by the American Missionary Society
in 1862 for the education of Negroes. Its campus of modest,
red brick buildings was in the same run-down South Memphis
neighborhood where Barry had been raised. He lived at home,
since the college had no dormitories for its 450 students.
LeMoyne had a racially mixed faculty, student body, and board
of trustees—all rarities in the mid-1950s, South or North—and
a strong tradition of liberal learning. More important, the
school gave Barry a partial scholarship.

At LeMoyne Barry majored in chemistry, explaining years
later why he made such an unusual choice for a young black
man at that time: "I looked around me, and I saw everybody
was going to be a teacher in a black school or a social worker,
and I didn't want to be either of them."

Marion Barry, in fact had always made a point of being
different. Different from the kids he'd left behind in South
Memphis, some of whom would end up dead or in jail.
Different in the degree to which he, unlike so many of his
boyhood friends, was driven by ambition. In a 1962 interview

with graduate student Thomas Rose, Barry said, "I'm part of the same environment as my friends, and yet their values differ greatly from mine. I see them at home now, driving around in a big car, and this is their main existence. It puzzles me why I have the values that I have. And yet I know that I do."

Sometimes it seemed that Barry did things *just* to be different. One of the first things he did at LeMoyne, for instance, was to adopt the middle name "Shepilov." A fraternity brother of Barry's, George Cox, said the name was playfully given to Barry during a "fraternity program." But Barry later told a *Washington Star* reporter that he "was reading the newspaper one day and picked this name out of a story." Barry's story is more credible. Dmitri Shepilov was a high-ranking member of the Soviet Communist Party in 1956–57, years in which Barry attended LeMoyne.

Beneath the surface of this would-be nonconformist beat the heart of a young man who had always shown an almost desperate desire to be accepted, rewarded, and praised for his accomplishments. A young man who had used every waking second to earn something—whether it was an A in school, a merit badge, or a buck. Barry's college career was merely a more sophisticated extension of that early striving.

At LeMoyne Barry carried a B-plus average while involving himself in a host of campus activities. He pledged a national black fraternity, Alpha Phi Alpha, eventually becoming vice president of the campus chapter. He also was elected to the student council and joined the campus chapter of the National Association for the Advancement of Colored People. He played on the school basketball team, the Mad Magicians. Still, like most other LeMoyne students, he found time to hang out at the Fourway Grill, where he plumbed life's philosophical depths with classmates over beers and soul food. Those discussions sometimes exploded into arguments, epecially when the subject turned to race.

"He was very vocal and very hotheaded," former LeMoyne student Ulysses Campbell told the *Washington Post* in 1978. "He didn't care if we said that segregation was the way it is. He'd say it wasn't right and we ought to do something" to change it.

Barry indicated where some of that indignation came from when he told interviewer Thomas Rose of an incident at the Memphis fairgrounds during his junior year at LeMoyne: "They have two fairs in Memphis, one for the whites and one for colored. Four or five of us went to the fair when white people were supposed to be going, and we told all the people there that we wanted to see the science exhibit. We approached the lady and she said we could go in—but once we got halfway in the door a policeman stopped us and said, 'Where you going?' He said we had to have a ticket. He called the lieutenant.

"At that point, we didn't know what to do, because all of this was rather new to us. We went on home, but this sort of left each of us with an empty feeling. We felt inside that we should have done something, but we didn't know what. We had no power and no previous cases to look at. In the segregated Negro libraries there were no books or anything about race or Negroes. Still, I felt I should be doing something about the race problem."

Barry wasn't the only serious one among his close circle of friends. His Alpha Phi Alpha fraternity brothers included future utility executives, educators, college deans. Even back then, wrote Milton Coleman in a 1978 *Washington Post* profile of Barry, they "carried their books in briefcases, smoked pipes, wore wide-legged trousered suits, and drank Schenley's whiskey instead of two-bit wine."

But, he continued, they also knew how to let their hair down: "They gave their parties on Porter Street near the campus of little LeMoyne College, dancing the 'slow drag' and the 'nikey-hokey.'"

A former member of that inner circle, Allen Hammond, now director of financial aid at Memphis State University, says Barry liked to party as well as the next guy, but he never forgot what he'd come to LeMoyne to accomplish. "Whereas most of us would go out to parties and call it quits for the night," recalls Hammond, "Marion would go home and study."

Despite the high grades Barry earned, his new middle name, his participation in sports, and his campus leadership posts,

Hammond says that Barry still was considered "pretty average" by those who knew him at LeMoyne.

"If you started predictions on where you think people would be," Hammond adds, "I don't think anybody would have said that he would have been where he is today."

During the spring of his senior year, however, Barry finally broke out of the pack. By that time the "ugly duckling" had turned into a sleek black swan with a pencil-thin mustache. He dressed the part, often sporting a navy blazer with the gold crest of Alpha Phi Alpha emblazoned on the breast pocket. His shoes no longer had holes. And he apparently had lost his fear of pretty girls. The *Post's* Milton Coleman quotes a former college classmate as saying that Barry had become "so aggressive that he seldom waited for an introduction to any young lady who caught his fancy." He was becoming a man of action in other arenas as well.

In March 1958, as president of the LeMoyne College chapter of the NAACP, Barry challenged the white chairman of the school's board of trustees, who had made patronizing remarks about blacks in federal court while helping represent the city of Memphis during a bus desegregation suit brought against it by the NAACP. Walter Chandler, a former mayor of Memphis and U.S. congressman, had said: "The problems of the Negro will not be eliminated by permitting him to be seated alongside of white passengers on the busses in the city. If the NAACP would expend more of its efforts in trying to elevate the Negro morally, mentally, educationally and health-wise, it would be of far more benefit to the race.

"I have heard it said that the Negro is a second-class citizen. If he is a second-class citizen, it is just because he wants to be, and has applied the label to himself.

"We must think not in terms of the Negro only, but be considerate of our white citizens, whose health and public safety would be endangered by integration.

"The Negro is our brother, but he should be treated as a younger brother, and not as an adult."

When Barry learned of Chandler's remarks, he drafted an angry letter to LeMoyne College president Dr. Hollis Price, calling for Chandler's resignation from the board of trustees. The letter, published first in the college's mimeographed newspaper, and later reprinted in both the main Memphis dailies, said in part: "His [Chandler's] shocking statements not only had little bearing on the case, but were some of the biggest monuments to demagoguery that we have yet seen constructed. His conduct showed a complete lack of good will, and probably has had a devastating effect on race relations in this city.

"We feel that it is humiliating and embarrassing that such an obvious demagogue should have direct connection with our college, especially when this institution stresses to its students the importance of fighting for equal rights.

"Mr. Chandler's resignation should be requested immediately. Either that or the LeMoyne faculty should begin teaching the importance of second-class citizenship."

When NAACP executive director Roy Wilkins arrived in Memphis a week after Barry's controversial letter was published, he too attacked Walter Chandler.

"Nobody is complaining about Chandler's right to present a case for his client in a court as he sees fit," Wilkins told more than 3,000 people who had gathered at the Mason Temple in South Memphis. "But he should not sit on the trustee board of LeMoyne. He does not represent what we want our students taught in 1958. That man is looking into the 1920's. How can a college or any institution teach people to live in mutual respect and harmony when there is a member on the board who thinks Negroes are immoral and diseased adolescents?"

Wilkins then called to the podium the 22-year-old firebrand who had tried to unseat Chandler.

"The young man who asked for [Chandler's] resignation is one of the most righteous young men in Memphis!" he announced.

Barry, savoring his first major moment upon the stage, soaked up the applause. Then the tall, lanky college senior gave a forceful, if somewhat stilted, two-minute speech that evoked the activist path he would take in his future civil rights work.

"The major objective of the youth council of the NAACP,"
he said "is to serve as a training area where young persons
may obtain training and experience in the various techniques
for waging effective social action programs.

"Who can deny such leadership is badly needed in the
Negro's fight against the forces of bigotry and reaction, which
seek to keep segregation and discrimination status quo?"

Young Marion Barry was starting to define himself as a
person not afraid to speak out against racial injustice, to make
a stand, to take a hit, if need be, for doing so. More important,
by joining the struggle for black civil rights, Marion Barry finally
had found a way to use his anger constructively and at the
same time win serious attention and praise.

"He became a local hero for having spoken out," says Dr.
Vasco Smith, a Memphis dentist and veteran civil rights activist
who attended the March 21, 1958, NAACP rally at the Mason
Temple. "I think he was unusual in that most college students—
and in particular black college students—during that particular
time didn't care much about things one way or the other. I
think that he had a [strong] sense of right and wrong, and
what ought to be done."

LeMoyne president Price was less impressed by Barry's
move. In a 1978 interview with the *Washington Post*'s Leon
Dash, he said he considered expelling Barry because he feared
that "the college would have to suffer the consequences" of
his activism. Price, at least, was not convinced that Barry knew
what he was doing: "Marion was a bright young man and
he thought he was sort of a messiah. At the time, I did not
have much faith in his judgment. I did not understand [what
Marion Barry was about]."

The board of trustees thought they understood. In their next
meeting they declared that Barry's letter had been "imper-
tinent, ill-advised and did not provide facts on which the
conclusion it reached was based." They discussed asking Dr.
Price to expel Barry from LeMoyne but stopped short of
recommending such an action.

Despite the trustees' rebuke and Dr. Price's displeasure at
Barry's affront to a man who, in addition to being a trustee,

was a major financial contributor to the college, Barry was never officially punished for his remarks. He graduated with his classmates later that spring. In the meantime he savored his new-found notoriety. His unprecedented challenge of a powerful white city father had made him an overnight celebrity —not only at LeMoyne but in Memphis's larger black community, which was stirring to the drumbeat of the civil rights movement spreading throughout the South.

6

DAYS OF BOOKS AND PROTEST

When Marion Barry arrived in Nashville in the fall of 1958 to continue his chemistry studies at Fisk University, he merely transferred from one inner-city black school to another. But outside Fisk's eclectic 46-acre campus of Gothic white stone and modern red brick buildings was Tennessee's capital city, which gave the poor boy from South Memphis his first real window on the larger world.

In the late 1950s Nashville was not yet America's country music mecca; it was, basically, an overgrown farm town and trading center with a relatively large black population (43 percent) that also happened to be the state capital. Unlike Memphis, however, which was still bogged down in anti-segregation lawuits, Nashville was starting to integrate. Two black men—Alexander Looby and Robert Lillard—had won seats on the city council in 1951. The action had come largely because the city's white mayor, Ben West, while a state senator, had successfully sponsored a bill amending Nashville's city charter to give black residents the power to elect representatives from their districts. (The move had helped West win, and keep, the mayoralty by attracting black electoral support.) Selected elementary schools in Nashville had begun admitting black children, a grade at a time, the year before Barry arrived. Still, the city was ripe for reform, since all other public facilities except the airport restaurant were still segregated.

In Nashville Barry kept up his civil rights activism by first helping to organize an NAACP chapter at Fisk. Then he joined a small group of students from area colleges and universities who had fallen under the spell of a Vanderbilt University divinity student named James Lawson.

A tall, bespectacled, light-skinned black man in his early thirties, Lawson was a pacificist who had chosen jail rather than serve in the U.S. Army during the Korean conflict. After his release he had traveled to India as a Methodist missionary and came back reinspired by Mahatma Gandhi's teachings on nonviolent civil disobedience (he had long been a disciple), teachings that had spurred India's successful drive for independence from Britain. In his gently convincing manner Lawson spoke to the Nashville students of creating a multiracial "Beloved Community" based on the Christian ideals of love, sacrifice, tolerance, and forgiveness.

Barry and other future protest leaders attended weekly workshops in which Lawson—who later was expelled from Vanderbilt because of his protest activities—not only taught them the ethics and philosophy of nonviolence, but schooled them as well in such practical matters as how to keep from getting their skulls kicked in while passively resisting beatings and other abuse that might be inflicted on them by police or white bigots. Sometimes the training sessions resembled Marine boot camp drills, with instructors shouting in students' faces, hitting or kicking them, and otherwise testing their limits of self-control.

At the start of his second year of graduate school, Barry joined his fellow Lawson protégés in putting their newly acquired knowledge to a series of "test" sit-ins challenging Jim Crow laws at Nashville restaurants and lunch counters. Among this group was a future U.S. congressman, John Lewis (D-Ga.), a short, plain-spoken youth from the Alabama backwoods who, as a child, had been gripped with such religious fervor he had preached to the family's chickens and wept whenever a member of his baptized flock was slaughtered for a meal.

"Marion Barry emerged during those early days as a leader, as one of the spokespersons" of the student sit-ins, recalls Lewis, who back in the fall of 1959 was a divinity student at the American Baptist Theological Seminary.

Because the student protestors would leave calmly after being refused service, however, the test sit-ins had little impact on segregation practices in Nashville. But in February 1960, after the students organized a city-wide black boycott of the stores and began spending entire days sitting at the lunch counters quietly doing their homework and refusing to move, despite being refused service, the merchants grew concerned. Their profits were shrinking because of the boycott and sit-ins. Even white customers, fearing possible violence, were beginning to stay away.

At Woolworth's lunch counter on February 27, a group of young white toughs set upon about a hundred student protestors, including Marion Barry and John Lewis, while police stood outside.

"They put lighted cigarette butts in people's hair, down people's backs," recalls Lewis. "They were pulling people off their stools and dropping people, just pushing people" onto the floor.

The white assailants also poured condiments on students and cursed and spit on them before police finally entered the store and ended the attacks. According to Lewis, Barry, like everybody else, took the abuse stoically that day. The students had learned their lessons well from James Lawson. But their disciplined refusal to fight back did not save them from being hurt or arrested. Barry, Lewis, and 79 other students, black and white, were charged by police with disorderly conduct, while their attackers walked free.

Most of the detainees, including Barry and Lewis, chose to serve time rather than pay a $100 fine. The "jail, no bail" tactic later would become a crucial part of the protestors' strategy. Their aim was to clog the jails with protestors, while at the same time winning public sympathy for their plight as "Christian martyrs."

Later that year Barry was interviewed about his role in the sit-ins by protest singer Guy Carawan, who was cutting a disc on the Nashville sit-in movement for Folkways Records.

"I took a chance on losing a scholarship or not receiving my master's degree," said Barry about his first sit-in arrest in February 1960. "But to me, if I had received my scholarship and master's degree, and still was not a free man, I was not a man at all."

Barry was exaggerating the risks he faced in academia. In fact, the president of Fisk University, Stephen J. Wright, strongly backed the young rebels.

"I approve the ends our students are seeking by these demonstrations," said Wright, shortly after the incident at Woolworth's. "The point is not how to stop their efforts, but rather to find better alternative ways to end segregation."

But in his statement to Carawan, Barry, perhaps unwittingly, had revealed the degree to which his own quest for manhood was tied up with his people's crusade for dignity and equal rights.

Barry later explained to Thomas Rose his motivation for joining the sit-in movement: "This was the opportunity for me to express my convictions in terms of overt action, and be effective. I don't know why it [the civil rights movement] had to happen at this time, but it did. To me, the more I participated, the better I felt about doing it; it provided me with an outlet for many years of frustration.

"I feel too many people in the past have been too afraid to stand up for what they believe is right, and this is true now. The moral fiber of many communities has deteriorated. My participation was just a matter of expressing my convictions. I didn't mind sacrificing because I had waited so long to do it. It was a matter of conscience to me. It made me feel better inside. I felt bad when I didn't participate, which was only on one or two occasions."

Less than two months after the mass arrests in Nashville, which had drawn national media attention to the civil rights movement, Marion Barry and more than 250 other student activists and observers, black and white, from a dozen southern states, Maryland, and the District of Columbia, descended on Shaw University in Raleigh, North Carolina. They came to attend a conference organized by Ella Baker, a maverick senior leader of an activist ministers' group called the Southern Christian Leadership Conference. Baker felt it was time for the students to sit down with civil rights leaders to focus and coordinate the burgeoning student protests.

Foremost among those leaders was the SCLC's chairman, the Reverend Dr. Martin Luther King, Jr. Marion Barry admired the intense, erudite young preacher who, with fiery eloquence, had climbed quickly to the top of the civil rights movement after helping organize a successful bus boycott in Montgomery, Alabama, only five years earlier. In Barry's words, the 31-year-old King was bringing "a new kind of leadership" to black America, one that did not derive its power solely by cutting backroom deals with white power brokers.

In a speech midway through the April 15-to-17 parley, King paid tribute to the students from Nashville and nearby Greensboro, North Carolina, who had begun the spontaneous wave of sit-ins across the South in early February.

"These students are not struggling to save themselves," he told a racially mixed crowd of 1,600 people at Raleigh's Memorial City Auditorium. "They are struggling to save the soul of America. In less than two months more colored freedom fighters have revealed to the nation and the world their determination and courage than has occurred in many years."

King said the sit-ins showed that a new generation of Negroes, impatient with lengthy court battles and efforts to get action from an unresponsive Congress, were "moving away from tactics which are suitable merely for gradual and long-term change." He said the sit-in movement "has transformed jails from places of dishonor to badges of honor," as more and more students chose to serve time in jail rather than pay bail or fines for violating Jim Crow laws. "Through sacrifice," he insisted, we will be able to arouse the dozing conscience of the South."

In closed-door meetings later that weekend at the Shaw student center, the students, spurred by James Lawson of Nashville, hammered out a credo based on "nonviolence as it grows from Judaic-Christian traditions" and established a Temporary Student Nonviolent Coordinating Committee." After a struggle between the two dominant contingents from Nashville and Atlanta, the students named as their temporary chairman the tall, soft-spoken, 24-year-old graduate student who had led sit-ins in Nashville, Marion Barry, Jr.

Barry's election surprised some observers, who thought that the head of the Nashville Student Movement, Diane Nash, a petite, fiery Fisk University student from Chicago, would get the post.

"It might have been sexism actually at that stage [in the civil rights movement], " says Clayborne Carson, author of *In Struggle: SNCC and the Black Awakening of the 1960's.* "Also, she wasn't Southern. That might have been an even stronger reason."

John Lewis, on the other hand, says Barry's behind-the-scenes political skills won the day.

"Marion got out and worked [the meeting]," recalls Lewis, "and he had a relationship with the students in Nashville. It was a big delegation. And he was a tall, handsome guy, a serious student and he was out there leading the sit-ins. And I guess that's the image that people wanted [their new organization to project]."

At his first press conference on the Shaw campus, the newly anointed chairman of what Carson later would call "the first significant reform organization in this country run [exclusively] by young people," quickly set an assertive black nationalist tone for the new group. After identifying "the African struggle as the concern of all mankind," Barry took a gratuitous shot at the man in the White House.

"We understand there is a possibility President Eisenhower will make a visit to Africa this fall and agree that this is a desirable step," he asserted. "We feel that before going to Africa, the president should lend the prestige of his office to the solution of racial problems in this country, and thus he shall be even better prepared for his visit to Africa."

In taking the president to task, young Barry conveniently overlooked the fact that the moderately progressive Civil Rights Act of 1957 had been passed during Eisenhower's tenure, and that, three years earlier, the president had sent the 101st Army Airborne into Little Rock, Arkansas, to crush Gov. Orval Faubus's attempt to use state National Guard troops to delay school integration there—a politically risky, even courageous, move for a conservative Republican president. But, as King had noted in his keynote address, Barry was part of a restless new generation of blacks who felt no special reverence for

America's Great White Fathers, a generation that wanted to create real and immediate change on the civil rights front. Thus Barry was willing to risk provoking America's chief executive if it made him pay attention.

The day after the Shaw colloquium ended, on April 18, 1960, the Nashville student leaders suddenly were presented with a dramatic opportunity to put their nonviolent protest methods to work: the home of Alexander Looby, the black city councilman and attorney who had helped get some of them out of jail following sit-in arrests, was destroyed by a powerful bomb. Looby and his wife escaped serious injury but were badly shaken.

As soon as they heard the news, 3,000 outraged students, led by Diane Nash and the Reverend C. Tindell Vivian, marched silently to Nashville's Capitol Hill and confronted Mayor Ben West on the steps of the state courthouse. Nash demanded whether the city leader would use the prestige of his office to appeal to all citizens to end racial discrimination in Nashville.

"I appeal to all citizens to end discrimination, to have no bigotry, no bias, no hatred," replied West.

"Do you mean that to include lunch counters?" asked Nash.

"Little lady,"replied the mayor, "I stopped segregation seven years ago at the airport when I first took office and there has been no trouble there since."

"Then, mayor, do you recommend that the lunch counters be desegregated?" Nash retorted.

The mayor, confronted by the horde of angry marchers and the logic of this small, persistent woman, gave in.

"Yes, young lady," he finally admitted, "I favor the integration of the lunch counters and restaurants."

Three weeks later, on May 10, six stores in downtown Nashville, including Woolworth's, opened their lunch counters to black customers. It was a heady time to be involved in the civil rights movement, especially if you happened to be the leader and spokesman for a part of the movement that just had scored a victory for integration important enough to bring Martin Luther King, Jr., to town.

"I came to Nashville not to bring inspiration, but to gain inspiration from the great movement that has taken place in this community," King told 4,000 people gathered in the Fisk University gymnasium on April 29, 1960, two days after Mayor West had capitulated. He said the leaders and students of the Nashville sit-ins "have gained a better understanding of the [nonviolent] philosophy of the movement than any other group" and, with their actions, sent a message to others.

"We have been told for years that Negroes are happy with segregation and would be all right if it weren't for 'outside agitators,'" said King. "This sit-in movement is an eternal refutation of that lie. It has made it absolutely clear that the Negro is not satisfied with segregation."

Fired by King's words, Barry threw himself into his new organizational duties. He sent out a flurry of letters to such luminaries as the AFL-CIO's George Meany and the United Auto Workers' Walter Reuther (asking the labor leaders for both moral and financial support); Democratic senators John F. Kennedy, Hubert Humphrey, Stuart Symington, and Lyndon Johnson (asking for a chance to address the platform committee at that summer's Democratic National Convention in Los Angeles); Republican Rep. Charles H. Percy (making an identical request for the Republican Convention in Chicago); Vice President Richard Nixon (whom Barry scolded for "pleasing the power structure of the South" by refusing unequivocally to support the sit-ins); and scores of other prominent U.S. religious, political, labor, and civil rights leaders, asking them to attend the students' fall conference in Atlanta. Even former first lady Eleanor Roosevelt received a bid. She mistakenly addressed her reply "Miss Barry" when she sent her regrets.

The neophyte chairman of the Temporary Student Non-violent Coordinating Committee also found time to write to the not-so-famous. He advised students who had been expelled from college for participating in sit-ins that scholarships for continuing their studies were available from the National Scholarship Service and Fund for Negro Students.

The summer of 1960 was a busy one for Barry. When he wasn't drafting letters, engaged in further protests—or seducing some of the attractive women, such as Diane Nash, who were part of the movement ("He was hitting on everybody during those days," said a veteran civil rights leader close to Barry)—Barry was traveling to other cities to try to raise funds for his fledgling organization or attending meetings with civil rights leaders such as Dr. King, Roy Wilkins, and the Reverend Ralph D. Abernathy, King's chief lieutenant.

In July Barry led a SNCC delegation to the Democratic National Convention in Los Angeles, where John F. Kennedy and Lyndon Johnson were about to be nominated.

"For 350 years," he told the party's platform committee, "the American Negro has been sent to the back door in education, housing, employment, and the rights of citizenship at the polls. We have come to urge that this convention not only *speak* to these issues but *pledge* itself to see that the full weight of the federal government is used to eradicate our national shame, Jim Crow, and second-class citizenship.

"We are here today to urge the leaders and candidates of the Democratic Party to stop playing political football with the civil rights of 18 million Negro Americans and to take forthright and definitive action to make American citizenship a vital and living reality to all, regardless of race or creed."

In the 10 minutes allotted to him, Barry managed to cover a wide range of issues, from desegregation of public schools to greater protection for blacks seeking to vote—especially in the Deep South. And in a statement that presaged his rise to political power in the District of Columbia in part on the issue of home rule, young Barry urged the Democrats to "provide self-government to the voteless residents of our nation's capital."

Then in a pointed reference to former president Harry Truman's verbal attacks on student protestors, made during the recent sit-ins, Barry said: "To label our goals, methods, and presuppositions 'communistic' is to credit communism with an attempt to remove tyranny and to create an atmosphere where genuine communication can occur. Communism seeks power, ignores people, and thrives on social conflict. We seek a community in which man can realize the full meaning of the self which demands open relationship with others.''

Truman was not the first, nor would he be the last prominent American to accuse civil rights leaders of being communist-controlled or inspired. The most notorious was FBI chief J. Edgar Hoover. The aging G-man kept voluminous files on many U.S. civil rights leaders, including Martin Luther King, Marion Barry, and other members of the Student Nonviolent Coodinating Committee.

Apparently the party elders on the Democratic Platform Committee paid attention to Barry and other civil rights leaders. In what the *Congressional Quarterly* later described as the ''strongest civil rights plank in the history of the [Democratic] party,'' the Democrats called for federal aid to the desegregated school districts, strong federal backing for civil rights lawsuits, and the creation of a federal Fair Employment Practices Commission. In practically a paraphrase of the statement Barry had submitted, the platform committee stated: ''The peaceful demonstrations for first-class citizenship which have recently taken place in many parts of this country are a signal to all of us to make good at long last the guarantees of our constitution.''

A month later, in August 1960, Barry addressed the platform committee at the Republican convention in Chicago, making a similar appeal for urgent action on behalf of the nation's blacks. Then he turned to the more mundane task of finishing his education.

In September Barry traveled west to the University of Kansas at Lawrence, where he had accepted a teaching assistantship in chemistry. The move to the sprawling, 1,000-acre campus in the middle of America's wheat country took him far away from his beloved Southland—but not far enough away to escape racial prejudice. When white female students at the school were assigned to chemistry classes taught by Barry, some of their parents complained to university administrators. A man who had been hailed as a civil rights hero in Memphis was apparently seen by a few whites in Kansas as a sexual threat. It was not the kind of reception that makes a man, whatever his race, feel welcome in a strange town.

Only a month after moving to Lawrence Barry returned to Atlanta to attend a meeting of the Temporary Student Non-violent Coordinating Committee at its Atlanta headquarters. In a symbolic gesture of commitment to the four-month-old organization, Barry and other delegates voted to drop the word "Temporary" from the group's name. From then on it would be known simply as the Student Nonviolent Coordinating Committee, or SNCC (pronounced "Snick"). The delegates also reaffirmed the "jail, no bail" policy for arrested protestors and vowed to hold rallies during the November presidential election demanding immediate action on civil rights.

When the committee met again in November 1960, Barry resigned the chairmanship he had held for only seven months. Chuck McDew, a tall former athlete from South Carolina State College, was unanimously elected to serve as chairman "until the next meeting." (McDew actually served until John Lewis replaced him in June 1963.) Barry, however, remained on the executive Coordinating Committee and the Finance Committee.

After less than a year in Kansas Barry ended his unsuccessful foray into conservative, white-dominated mid-America and returned to Tennessee. He enrolled in the state university in Knoxville, where for the next three years he would be the only black student in his chemistry classes. He also took a teaching job at all-black Knoxville College and resumed his protest activities, which came to demand more and more of his time.

The following year, 1962, according to court records, Barry was arrested for allegedly passing bad checks. The charges were later dropped and the incident apparently was never reported. But, wrote Edward D. Sargent in the April 1990 issue of *Regardie's* magazine, "It seems unlikely it [the arrest] was connected to any legitimate civil rights activity. Did it represent the by-product of a racist system that was trying to discredit a young social activist? Or did it represent the misstep of a basically arrogant man whose penchant for challenging authority, breaking the rules, and tempting his fate started years ago? We may never know."

Nineteen hundred sixty-two was also the year Barry first married. The 26-year-old Memphian chose Nashvillean Blantie

C. Evans as his bride. Their marriage, however, was strained from the outset by Barry's efforts to lead civil rights protests while working on his chemistry doctorate. The couple stayed together barely two years; the marriage ended formally in 1969 when a Tennessee judge found that Barry had "abandoned . . . and neglected to provide" for his wife and granted her a divorce.

In the early 1960s Marion Barry's true bride was the movement. She was jealous and demanded all his time, energy, and love. But she also was sweet and seductive and whispered occasionally in Barry's ear that if he stayed with her, he'd become not only a part of America's civil rights history—he'd already done that by winning at age 24 the first SNCC chairmanship—but a major player in the continuing drama of his race. It was a siren song for a man with Barry's towering ego and seemingly bottomless hunger for approval and respect.

7

MARRIED TO THE MOVEMENT

In the summer of 1961 Marion Barry donned a T-shirt and overalls to blend in with the locals and joined more than a dozen other SNCC workers who had converged on McComb, the seat of Pike County, Mississippi, and a major railroad hub near the state's southern border with Louisiana. McComb and the state capital of Jackson, 80 miles north, had become the focal points of SNCC's Operation MOM, an acronym for Move on Mississippi.

Violence seemed to follow Barry into the town.

On August 22, only days after Barry arrived, Robert Moses, a black, Harvard-educated schoolteacher from New York City who had set up SNCC voter registration workshops in McComb and in neighboring Amite County, was attacked and savagely beaten outside the Amite County courthouse in Liberty, Mississippi.

The assault went unpunished after a six-man, all-white jury acquitted Billy Jack Caston, a cousin of the local sheriff, following a trial before a justice of the peace. The verdict was meant to serve as a warning to "agitators from elsewhere," as McComb's Mayor C. H. Douglas had branded the SNCC workers, to cease and desist their efforts to organize the local blacks to stage sit-ins and register to vote.

Some of the older black townspeople and farmers in the area also viewed Moses, Barry, and the other SNCC workers as troublemakers. Long before Robert Moses was attacked, they had learned what happens when a black man steps over the white man's line.

Many of McComb's younger blacks, however, saw the SNCC workers as heroes, identifying them with the Freedom Riders they had read about or seen on television. Those brave men and women, including John Lewis and other SNCC workers, had endured beatings and bombings as they rode buses into Deep South states to try to force desegregation of public transportation facilities.

Moses himself ignored the continued threats and the beatings he had received and, with fresh stitches in his scalp, continued his mostly unsuccessful efforts to register black voters at the Pike County courthouse.

Barry, meanwhile, set up a workshop on nonviolence for local teenagers. Although too young to vote, at Moses' behest they had been going door-to-door in McComb to try to persuade others to register. Two of the youths, Curtis Hayes and Hollis Watkins, grew tired of waiting for the adults to act and, spurred by Barry's workshop, on August 26 staged an unprecedented sit-in at the whites-only lunch counter in McComb's F. W. Woolworth store. They were immediately arrested for alleged "breach of the peace."

Marion Barry, albeit not a lawyer, respresented Hayes and Watkins at their summary trial. The youths were fined $400 each and sentenced to four months in jail.

Six high school students held another sit-in in McComb a few weeks later and received even stiffer sentences of up to a year in reform school. By that time Barry had left McComb for Jackson, where some other SNCC workers had been arrested and jailed. (Two years later, Jackson achieved national notoriety when Mississippi NAACP leader Medgar Evers was slain there by a sniper. White supremacist Byron De La Beckwith was charged with the slaying, but two 1964 murder trials ended in hung juries. In December 1990 Beckwith was arrested by authorities in Signal Mountain, Tennessee, and charged with Evers's murder a third time, based on new evidence. In March 1991, he was still fighting extradition to Mississippi.)

Barry left the far southern reaches of the Magnolia State at a propitious time. Within a week of his departure two more SNCC workers, John Hardy and Travis Britt, were attacked and beaten by local whites. Two weeks after that, on September 25, Herbert Lee, a farmer in rural Amite County who had been helping Robert Moses to register voters, was shot dead by a white man.

Lee's alleged assailant, state representative E. H. Hurst, was cleared at a coroner's inquest after claiming he had shot Lee in self-defense. Louis Allen, a black witness to the slaying, later told Robert Moses he had lied at the inquest out of fear and that Lee had been unarmed and slain in cold blood. Allen offered to testify for the prosecution if the federal government would guarantee his protection. However, Justice Department officials in Washington, who had been contacted by Moses, said they could not guarantee Allen's safety. Three years later Allen was shot dead outside his home by an unknown assailant as he prepared to move north.

After E. H. Hurst's exoneration, Moses, Chuck McDew, and Robert Zellner—SNCC's only white field secretary—led more than 100 high school students in a protest march to McComb's city hall. They were all arrested; everyone over 18 was charged with "contributing to the deliquency of minors." The three SNCC workers spent the next four months in jail.

The carnage and legal harassment were by now so great that Dr. King asked Attorney General Robert Kennedy to investigate what he termed the "apparent reign of terror" unleashed against blacks trying to register to vote in southern Mississippi. Except for a token FBI investigation, however, King's plea went unheeded.

Neither Robert nor John Kennedy was insensitive to the plight of the civil rights workers. But there were practical limits to Washington's ability to control the affairs of individual states. And there was political reality: in the next presidential election John Kennedy, who had beaten Richard Nixon by the slimmest of margins in 1960, would need the support of powerful southern politicians, including Mississippi senator John Eastland, if he hoped to stay in the Oval Office. Kennedy felt he could do more good by getting the southerners on Capitol Hill to back new civil rights legislation he was planning, than by putting the enormous prestige and power of his office on the line in one southern state. He let it be known through his brother in the Justice Department that money would be made available to help with voter registration. Then he called for a "cooling-off" period for "direct action" civil rights workers such as Marion Barry who were engaged in sit-ins or Freedom Rides in the Deep South.

The bitter irony of southern justice, coupled with the near-total failure of SNCC's Operation MOM and the Kennedy administration's failure to respond effectively to the attacks on civil rights workers in southern Mississippi were not lost on Marion Barry. He returned to Knoxville, somewhat chastened, to resume his studies and civil rights activities in an atmosphere far safer than Mississippi, and far more hospitable than Kansas.

While finishing his course work for a doctorate in chemistry, Barry led protests against segregation in restaurants and theaters in downtown Knoxville that resulted in more than 150 arrests yet failed to force any more changes in the city's century-old segregation laws.

Barry spent the summer of 1962 in Philadelphia, Pennsylvania, raising money for SNCC and learning about the perils of trying to organize angry urban blacks.

"Man, this is a jungle," he wrote in a letter to SNCC executive field secretary James Forman that summer, "but like the song says,'we shall overcome.'"

The following summer, in August 1963, while continuing his civil rights work in the South, Barry saw from afar the historic wave cresting when more than 250,000 Americans—a quarter of them white—massed on the Washington Mall near the Lincoln Memorial. From every state in the Union the marchers had come to the capital to demand that President John Kennedy and Congress end racial discrimination, speed up school integration, and provide jobs and decent housing to every American. Some carried placards and others sleeping bags. Some wore suits or dresses, some dirty overalls. All joined hands to sing protest songs and listen to an impressive array of speakers that included civil rights leaders, actors, and liberal lawmakers.

In confronting Kennedy, the protestors knew they would be heard. Unlike Congress, effectively in the grip of southern conservatives opposed to any new civil rights legislation, America's charismatic young president had actively supported the cause of America's minorities from the start. In his inaugural address, Kennedy had pledged to defend "human rights, to which this nation has always been committed, and to which we are committed today at home and around the world." In May 1963, just three months before the march on Washington, the president had met with civil rights leaders at the White House. A month later, after Alabama governor Wallace had stood in the administration building doorway and tried physically to bar black students from entering the University of Alabama, Kennedy had pledged in a nationally televised address to present federal lawmakers with a sweeping new civil rights bill that would make such constitutional insults impossible in the future.

According to John Lewis, who had recently been elected SNCC's third chairman, Marion Barry did not participate in the August 28, 1963, march, the largest civil rights protest in the country's history. But he no doubt was watching, along with tens of millions of other Americans, when the future congressman from Georgia, standing in the shadow of the Great Emancipator, gave a fiery speech in which he excoriated "politicians who build their careers on immoral compromises and ally themselves with open forms of political, economic and social exploitation." Lewis urged his fellow blacks to join the "great social revolution sweeping our nation" and to "stay in the streets of every city, every village and evey hamlet of this nation ... until the unfinished revolution of 1776 is complete."

But the day would be remembered most for another speech, delivered extemporaneously by Dr. King. He had just finished reading his prepared remarks and was about to sit down when his fellow speakers on the podium urged him to continue.

"I have a dream today!" declared King in the stentorian tone that had made his voice, and his message of nonviolence, familiar to millions around the globe. "I have a dream that one day 'every valley shall be exalted and every hill be made plain and the crooked place will be made straight, and the glory of the Lord shall be revealed, and all flesh shall see it together.'

"This is our hope. This is the faith that I go back to the South with. With this faith we shall be able to transform the jangling

discords of our nation into a beautiful symphony of brotherhood. With this faith we will be able to work together, to pray
together, to struggle together, to go to jail together, to stand
up for freedom together, knowing that we will be free one
day.''

King's impassioned eloquence was inspiring. Yet no matter
how noble the rhetoric, Marion Barry knew from much bitter
experience that words are only as powerful as the actions that
back them up. During his three years in the movement he had
seen fellow civil rights workers savagely beaten, even mur-
dered. He had seen the homes and churches of friends in
Mississippi bombed or burned to the ground. He had seen
how the Kennedy administration, genuinely concerned but
circumscribed by political reality, could do little to help. True,
Robert Kennedy had sent aides south to confer with resistant
white officials; and he had dispatched U.S. marshals to
Montgomery, Alabama, and Oxford, Mississippi, to rescue
protestors set upon by white mobs. John Kennedy was about
to submit a sweeping civil rights bill to Congress. But the
26-year-old activist was impatient. He wanted to stop the racial
violence, the bombings and the burnings, the discrimination
against his people *now*. So for the time being he would leave
the speech making and politicking to others. He would
continue to work directly with the people to bring about
change.

President Kennedy's assassination in Dallas only three
months later jolted Marion Barry, as it did the rest of SNCC's
leadership. But while the sudden and untimely death of a man
who truly had been a friend to America's blacks caused sadness
and concern, it brought no substantial change in the group's
basic strategy: to challenge the racial status quo in the South,
while trying to enlist Washington's help in the struggle.

At a meeting in late December 1963 the coordinating
committee, by then composed almost entirely of veterans like
Barry, who had dropped out of school, decided to turn up the
heat in the Magnolia State. In particular the committee was
considering a controversial plan proposed by Robert Moses
to bring up to 1,000 northern college students—most of them
white—to Mississippi in June 1964 to help register black voters.

The heavy participation of whites in the so-called Summer Project was hotly debated by the committee, some of whose members, including Barry, were already uneasy about the increasing number of whites taking leadership roles in SNCC.

"We were concerned about that, and how it is that you deal with the whole white-black thing," Barry later told SNCC historian Clayborne Carson. "It caused some very serious problems."

But while Barry shared the other black committee members' concerns, he also was a pragmatist. Arguing that the massive influx of white volunteers would grab the attention of the white-controlled national media and thereby increase pressure on the Johnson administration to pass the civil rights bill still foundering in Congress, Barry submitted a motion committing SNCC "to obtain the right for all citizens of Mississippi to vote, using as many people as necessary to obtain that end." The motion was adopted. The same man who had used his innate political skills to become SNCC's first chairman had once again brought those skills to bear on a controversial committee vote.

In June 1964, at the start of what historians later would call Freedom Summer, Barry was working as a SNCC fund-raiser out of Chicago when three Summer Project volunteers—two whites from the North and a black youth from Mississippi—disappeared near the town of Philadelphia, Mississippi. The search for the missing volunteers—which coincidentally turned up the bodies of several missing blacks without causing much of a stir—and the almost daily occurrences of violence against Summer Project workers all but eclipsed the signing into law by President Lyndon Johnson on July 2 of the groundbreaking Civil Rights Act of 1964: by August, four people were dead, 80 beaten, 1,000 arrested, 67 churches, homes, and businesses burned or bombed.

In *Freedom Bound*, civil rights historian Robert Weisbrot describes the act as "the most sweeping civil rights measure since Reconstruction." Summarizing the law, he says it "strengthened voting rights, banned discrimination in public facilities and in employment, empowered the attorney general to begin suits against school segregation, and authorized the withholding of federal funds from noncomplying schools."

Although Barry and other SNCC workers greeted the news with obvious pleasure and some justified pride for their role in forcing the President's hand, they knew their struggle for equality in the Deep South was far from over. But now at least they had the feds officially on their side in challenging Jim Crow laws.

On August 4, 1964, only a month after the new law was enacted, FBI agents, using a bulldozer, unearthed the bullet-riddled bodies of Michael Schwerner, James Chaney, and Andrew Goodman in Mississippi. The Freedom Summer volunteers had been shot and bludgeoned to death, and buried beneath an earthen dam on a farm near Philadelphia, the town where they last were seen.

The murders outraged the nation, which had avidly followed in the media the search for the missing workers. The killers remained at large, however, until the FBI reportedly paid $30,000 for information leading to the arrest of 20 local men, including Neshoba County deputy sheriff Cecil Price, who had allegedly used his official vehicle during the crime. Six of the accused, including Price, would be convicted three years later by a federal jury of violating the dead men's civil rights. They would serve brief jail terms. No state court would bring any charges against any of them.

Meanwhile, civil rights worker Barry and other SNCC leaders realized that these three young martyrs could significantly help the cause. Their deaths had triggered a national outpouring of anger and sympathy and focused unprecedented attention on the civil rights movement.

"After the killings in Mississippi," Barry told Howell Raines, author of *My Soul Is Rested*, an oral history of the civil rights movement, "we got James Baldwin to write a letter. We did a massive mail appeal. We had Harry Belafonte send out letters. During the summer and fall of '64, we must have raised out of New York alone at least $600,000."

Some of those funds were earmarked for the so-called Mississippi Challenge, in which delegates from the Mississippi Freedom Democratic Party, organized with SNCC's help, were going to try to unseat the all-white contingent from the

Magnolia State at the Democratic National Convention in Atlantic City.

In the two months leading up to the August 22 start of the convention Barry had made a hurried round of stops in Los Angeles, Sacramento, Salem (Oregon), and Seattle seeking money and votes for the challenge. He reached Atlantic City just in time for the showdown. Mississippi's all-white Democratic party had resolved at its July state convention to defy the Civil Rights Act of 1964. A Mississippi court had just outlawed the new Freedom Party. As a final insult the state government in Jackson had officially labeled the fledgling political party a "Communist organization."

Among the Freedom Party delegates who had preceded Barry to Atlantic City was SNCC worker Fannie Lou Hamer, a Mississippi sharecropper who, after registering to vote, had been evicted from the farm on which she had lived for 18 years. During a nationally televised hearing of the Credentials Committee, Hamer broke down in tears as she described the beating she had received from local whites after attending a civil rights meeting. After her moving testimony telephone calls and telegrams poured into Atlantic City from angry viewers around the nation. Many of them demanded that the Freedom Party delegates be seated instead of the official Mississippi contingent.

In an attempt to defuse the political crisis stirred up by a handful of backwoods but by no means unsophisticated Mississippi blacks, President Johnson offered a compromise in which two "at large" and 66 nonvoting Freedom Party delegates would be seated, in addition to the regular Mississippi contingent. He also promised to introduce a resolution calling for Dixiecrats to integrate their future convention delegations.

But the Freedom Party delegates rejected LBJ's offer. Using passes provided by Michigan and Massachusetts delegates, they occupied the seats of the Mississippi delegation, which by then had been reduced to three members. (The rest had stormed out in protest when LBJ offered his compromise deal to the Freedom Party delegation.)

The sit-in attempt failed. The Freedom Party delegates were unceremoniously ejected by convention guards, and to make sure the spectacle was not repeated, Johnson ordered all but three seats removed from the Mississippi seating area.

The Freedom Party delegates returned to the convention floor one last time, stood together, and led official delegates in the singing of "We Shall Overcome" and other Negro spirituals that over the past few years had been adopted into the protest hymnal. Such unscripted moments created by the Freedom Party delegates enlivened an otherwise dull convention.

In November 1964, the same month Lyndon Johnson crushed his conservative Republican opponent, Barry Goldwater (who won only six states—Alabama, Arizona, Georgia, Louisiana, Mississippi, and South Carolina), Marion Barry joined other SNCC leaders for a retreat in Waveland, Mississippi. They came to assess the extraordinary events in which they recently had participated and to shore up faltering morale. While acknowledging the pyrrhic victories they had won in Mississippi and Atlantic City, the members of the coordinating committee conceded that serious internal problems had surfaced during the Freedom Summer, problems that, ironically, threatened to turn the integrated "Beloved Community" envisioned by SNCC's founders only four years earlier into a viper's nest of racial conflict.

According to SNCC historian Clayborne Carson, arguments between white and black volunteers had begun to disrupt SNCC field meetings. He says the black volunteers resented the white volunteers coming down from the North and trying to take over key leadership positions in what was essentially an indigenous organization.

"Most of the work and most of the real decisions and most of the push [during the Freedom Summer] was with white people, with white students, and white people who had come down [to Mississippi]," Barry told Carson. "So a number of us were very disturbed and concerned about that."

Sexual tensions also arose between the races, said Barry, and were exacerbated when a surprising number of volunteers elected to stay in Mississippi at the end of the Freedom Summer.

"About one-third to 50 percent of those who had been there wanted to stay," Barry told Carson. "I think the majority of the people that wanted to stay were white women. And that was upsetting some of the blacks in the town because most of the white women were relating to black men [who] for the first time, I guess, had an opportunity to relate to a white woman."

According to Barry, the interracial intimacy also angered white Mississippians in whose towns the Summer Project volunteers were stationed. But, he said, "as long as it was in the black community nobody did anything about it."

Discipline had also become a problem, Barry told Carson. Barry was among those SNCC leaders who advocated a strong chain of command. Others, especially northerners, wanted more autonomy for field workers, prompting leaders such as Barry, who favored greater discipline and structure, to disparagingly label the autonomy seekers the "freedom high" workers.

"People were wandering in and out of the organization," said Barry. "Some worked, some didn't." And, he told Carson, "drugs started to be introduced at that point, particularly a lot of marijuana." (Many SNCC workers, according to Carson, would continue to use marijuana regularly until the organization died out in the late 1960s.)

At the end of the Freedom Summer Marion Barry took a personal inventory. Since joining the NAACP chapter at LeMoyne nine years earlier, he had straddled the fence between seeking the perquisites of the white Establishment in the academic arena and winning the endorsement of his fellow blacks, who were engaged in a historic struggle. He finally and unequivocally chose the latter by dropping out of school to work full time for SNCC.

"It was impossible to teach and work in civil rights at the same time," he later said of his 1964 decision.

In a way Barry's life-altering choice was an easy one to make. The civil rights movement, had, after all, provided the shy and angry young man from Itta Bena with an unprecedented opportunity. In what other arena was he likely to receive so much attention and adulation? Where else could he exercise his personal freedom and political power together, virtually unchecked? He finally had found where he belonged. Not in a classroom, nor on a basketball court, or in a boxing ring. Not even in the chairman's seat of SNCC, where he had gotten bogged down in paperwork and meetings. He had found his place instead on the front lines of his people's fight to dismantle, brick by invisible brick if necessary, the wall of racial separation dividing America.

8

GO NORTH, YOUNG MAN!

Following the Freedom Summer SNCC executive field secretary James Forman sent Marion Barry to New York, where he turned a challenging assignment into fun. While SNCC workers in the South staged sit-ins and mobilized rural blacks to get involved in the political process, Barry helped arrange star-studded parties at the homes of rich Manhattanites, to raise money for the organization.

"We had these fund-raising parties where we would get movie actors," Barry later told Howard Raines. "Sidney Poitier, Diahann Carroll, or Robert Ryan or Shelley Winters or Theo Bikel and others would come to somebody's house, and we would get somebody to have a party, and we would raise $13,000 or $14,000."

At the parties, held mostly, Barry said, at the homes of Jewish SNCC supporters, he would don his glad rags, paint on a smile, and hobnob with the rich and famous, who seemed insatiably curious about life on the front lines of the civil rights movement. Barry had plenty of good war stories. Still, he found it necessary to bring in fresh troops from time to time to keep the cash spigots flowing.

"We'd bring somebody up from the South," he told Raines, "and we'd say, 'Here is a living example of how tough it is down there,' and the person would speak. Some of them were very dramatic. Mrs. [Fannie Lou] Hamer [who had stolen the spotlight from more seasoned pols in Atlantic City] came one time [from rural Mississippi], and when she finished describing her situation, people were crying and all upset. That was easy to do then because the whole question of racism and segregation had not reached the North."

Barry, who had worked with hundreds of northern volunteers in Mississippi and had been a SNCC field secretary in

Philadelphia, Chicago, and New York, clearly was exaggerating. He knew better than most that many northern cities, though nominally integrated by the mid-1960s, still had sprawling black ghettoes whose residents worked at low-paying jobs, received little or no health care or insurance, sent their children to inferior schools, and held scant hope of sharing with their generally more affluent white brethren in the Great American Dream. But soon the once-poor boy from the Deep South would get a chance to change that reality for hundreds of thousands of his fellow blacks in a city that was, at least nominally, in the North.

In June 1965 Forman sent Barry to Washington, D.C., a city where blacks had lived alongside whites in relative peace for 175 years, while taking a back seat to them in virtually every aspect of their lives. SNCC chose the District as its first major experiment in urban—as opposed to rural—social reform, which it had been practicing in the South since 1960, says Forman, because it is "the capital of the United States" and, ironically, the only city whose residents "still don't have the right to vote" for fully enfranchised members of the U.S. House of Representatives and the U.S. Senate (the District has had a nonvoting representative to the House since 1974).

The city's most serious problem, Barry agreed, was its lack of representation in Congress, a problem he had first noted publicly while addressing the platform committees of the two major political party conventions in 1960.

"We had to shift locally to be relevant," he told the *Washington Post*'s Richard Prince in 1971. "To be in Washington talking about voting in Mississippi was irrelevant when we weren't able to vote here."

In 1965 Washington was, for all intents and purposes, a southern city in terms of its sultry climate, its slow-moving pace of life, its conservatism, and its large black population, which in fact, if not by law, was segregated. The federal enclave, for a variety of reasons, had been a mecca to blacks, both freedmen and runaway slaves, since Congress had sited the capital on the banks of the Potomac River in 1790. Although slave markets had flourished in the District of Columbia until the mid-1850s, and the city had Black Codes restricting the movement of black residents similar to those in the Deep South, those laws were far less stringent. Moreover, Washington had a large number of black freedmen who worked in such trades as carpentry, shoemaking, and barbering, and a small professional class of businessmen, teachers, and ministers. Their success attracted others.

The capital also offered unparalleled educational opportunities for blacks. In 1867 Congress had chartered Howard University, the first institution south of the Mason-Dixon line set up to educate both black and white students. During the Reconstruction era black men in Washington obtained the right to vote. And in 1872 and 1873 the city's territorial legislature passed laws prohibiting restaurants, ice cream parlors, barber shops, and other public establishments from refusing to serve black customers. Not surprisingly, tens of thousands of southern blacks streamed into the nation's capital, both during and after the Civil War, looking for greater opportunities.

By 1900, according to Howard University librarian Thomas C. Battle, Washington had enough educated blacks to support several labor and professional organizations and cultural societies. The capital had 89 black churches, a black-run bank, a black building association, and several black periodicals.

By mid-century, wrote Battle in the January 1989 issue of *Wilson Quarterly*, in the Shaw neighborhood near downtown Washington—the neighborhood Marion Barry adopted as his political base when he first came to the capital—blacks owned "hundreds of businesses, including barber shops, hardware stores, and groceries. Black doctors, dentists, and lawyers had their offices there. At Griffith Stadium, black sports fans rooted for the city's black baseball team, the Homestead Grays. Nearby, Howard University boasted many noted black faculty members, such as sociologist E. Franklin Frazier and political scientist Ralph Bunche. The main streets of black Washington were lively on Saturday nights. There were large dance halls and glittery nightclubs, such as the Bali, the Bengasi, the Capitol City, the Caverns, and the Howard Theater, where blacks could see performances by Billie Holliday, Pearl Bailey, and Nat King Cole."

On the other hand, despite a growing black middle class that soon would become the largest of any U.S. city, a majority of black Washingtonians still lived in poverty. Many of those on the lower economic rungs were angry, blaming the whites who held power for their predicament.

The anger was not limited to adults. Near the same Griffith Stadium where the Homestead Grays played, for instance, small boys who could not afford to watch their heroes play would, on days when the Washington Redskins or Senators staged games, threaten to slash the tires of white patrons who parked in their neighborhood unless they were given a quarter. The sense of anger and alienation among the children was stoked by the de facto segregation of Washington's public schools. They would not even begin to integrate, through court-ordered bussing, until 10 years after the 1954 *Brown* decision.

The indignities suffered by the city's blacks transcended the ghettoes. Although there were no formal laws banning them from such places, blacks knew they would not be welcomed at city parks and recreation areas, including the National Zoo. Until 1953, when the Supreme Court ruled such practices illegal, even affluent black Washingtonians and African diplomats were barred from some public eating establishments. And although black residents became a majority in Washington in 1957, until a decade later, when President Johnson appointed former city housing official Walter Washington as the city's first mayor-commissioner and put several blacks on a nine-member city council, only a handful of blacks held high-level management positions in the city government, which had been run for more than a century by a presidentially appointed three-member board of commissioners, almost all of whom had been white.

Although many blacks held low-level city jobs, the mid- and upper-level ranks of D.C. government, as well as the city's police and fire departments, were dominated by whites. The U.S. Congress—specifically, the white southerner-dominated House District Committee—effectively ran the city's day-to-day affairs. As a result many D.C. residents, black and white, felt they were living in a "colony" whose overseers did not necessarily have their best interests at heart. (In 1961 District residents were granted the right, by way of a constitutional amendment, to vote in presidential elections, but other than a token, nonvoting House delegate, they are *still* not represented in either the House or Senate).

In short, by the time Marion Barry arrived in Washington in June 1965, the federal enclave was an easy target for this battle-hardened black social reformer.

Working out of a rundown, three-story red brick townhouse at 107 Rhode Island Avenue, NW, which he rented for $225 a month, Barry wasted little time in setting an activist agenda. In August 1965, the same month the Voting Rights Act was passed—bringing sweet victory to Barry and thousands of others in the movement, some of whom had paid a steep price for it—Barry joined a massive anti-Vietnam War protest on the grounds of the U.S. Capitol. He was arrested along with 300 other demonstrators while carrying out SNCC's anti-war policies.

Five months later, in January 1966, Barry led a one-day "mancott" of the city's privately owned bus company, D.C. Transit. Its owner, O. Roy Chalk, had announced a nickel increase from the quarter fare.

According to *The Washington Afro-American,* at least 75,000 people stayed off the busses at Barry's request. No one was more amazed than Marion Barry.

"Washington was always a difficult town to mobilize," he confessed to the *Post's* Richard Prince. "To organize—that was considered a radical move. It's basically a government town, and there was always the feeling that you shouldn't be active in the community."

In his foray into the capital Barry also encountered the same problems other SNCC workers were finding in other U.S. cities, problems so intractable they would contribute to SNCC's dissolution in the late 1960s; problems so enduring they would continue to dog Barry throughout his future years as an elected official in Washington; problems that would not only defy solution but worsen before he left office as mayor in January 1991.

In his history of SNCC, Clayborne Carson underlines the extent of the problem when he writes that community organizers such as Barry "found that the poorest urban blacks, who were the focus of their efforts, were more alienated, anti-social, and angrier than their counterparts in the rural South. Lacking the sharply defined target of southern racism, SNCC workers in urban areas began the formidable task of building a social movement among blacks filled with undirected hostility and generalized distrust. They soon realized that their previous victories in the Deep South had exaggerated their sense of power to confront the entrenched ... social problems of urban, industrial society."

Nevertheless, Barry had to at least try to confront these towering problems. After scoring his small but decisive bus boycott victory, he took on a much bigger foe—the white-dominated Washington Board of Trade, whose members had sponsored a national advertising campaign asserting, unilaterally and without proof, that "a great many Washingtonians—including the overwhelming majority of local civic, professional and business leaders—are opposed to pending Home Rule legislation."

The board of trade's move angered both black and white D.C. residents, including Marion Barry, who used it as a fulcrum to generate action in the community. After enlisting the help of prominent D.C. religious leaders, black and white, and the local chapter of the NAACP, Barry held a February 1966 press conference to announce the launch of the "Free D.C. Movement" to promote self-government for the District. In his remarks Barry accused "white segregationists" in Congress of colluding with the board of trade's "moneylord merchants" to hold D.C. residents in "political slavery" by blocking passage of pending home-rule legislation.

Barry decided to attack the board of trade from an economic angle, something it would be sure to understand. He announced the movement would issue "Free D.C." stickers to local merchants who supported it and boycott those who sided with the board. Supporters would place the movement's sticker in the window and, according to Barry's plan, the picketers and boycotters would pass these friendly merchants by.

In mapping his strategy, however, Barry miscalculated when he set arbitrary levels for financial contributions by merchants. The move so enraged the city's white establishment it rolled out its biggest guns to silence this radical black agitator who already had proven himself a major nuisance by staging the boycott against D.C. Transit.

House District Committee chairman John L. McMillan (D-S.C.) called a special committee session to consider whether Barry's attempt to pressure merchants into making contributions to the Free D.C. Movement violated a federal anti-racketeering law that carried a 20-year jail term and $10,000 fine for anyone convicted of "interfering with business by threat of violence."

Sen. Robert Byrd (D-W.Va.) attacked Barry publicly, saying the tactics of the movement reminded him of "Chicago in the days of Al Capone." He called the Free D.C. Movement a "campaign of extortion" by "self-styled leaders."

D.C. police chief John B. Layton warned that the boycott plan could constitute "blackmail, extortion and everything else."

When several key allies threatened to bolt unless he changed his tactics, Barry finally backed down. He announced that henceforth all contributions, of whatever amount, would be strictly "voluntary." But he also fired a shot across the bow of those who had attacked him. "We have not demanded that any merchants give one penny to this movement," Barry said in a *Washington Star* interview only four days after the Free D.C. Movement was launched. "Our enemies are distorting this to make it seem that we are trying to blackmail businessmen."

The Free D.C. Movement fell far short of its announced $100,000 goal, the funds of which were to counter the board of trade's anti-home rule advertising campaign. And it failed to force immediate passage of home rule legislation, which was delayed for another seven years. But it put Barry on the map as a community organizer and leader to be reckoned with.

Nationally syndicated columnists Rowland Evans and Robert Novak wrote in a March 6, 1966, column: "The most important militant group in the teeming Washington Negro ghetto is the Student Non-Violent Coordinating Committee headed by tough, intransigent Marion Barry, a radical who was arrested last August when far left demonstrators stormed the Capitol to protest the Vietnam War.''

Four days later *Post* columnist William Raspberry devoted an entire column to Barry, whom he described as ''the 29-year-old former chemistry teacher who is fast becoming the leading catalyst for change in Washington.''

In October 1966—only 16 months after Barry arrived in Washington—he ranked an amazing fifth behind four longtime black D.C. residents in a poll that asked a sampling of the city's nearly half-million black residents who had ''done the most for Negro people in the area.'' Barry was succeeding beyond even his own ambitious expectations in establishing himself as a force for social change in the capital. And his new-found confidence was reflected in his demeanor: gone, in public at least, was the shy high school student who was too self-conscious to talk to pretty girls. Gone was the college student waiter who secretly spit into the food of white customers who called him ''boy.'' In their place stood a 29-year-old activist tempered into a steely toughness by his five years in the movement; a man who seemed to relish confrontation and rhetoric, the chief weapons of the social revolution he was helping lead.

9

A CATALYST FOR CHANGE

B y his words and by his example Marin Luther King, Jr.,
had taught Marion Barry that nonviolent confrontations,
especially when covered by the media, are the surest and
quickest way to militate for change. During the year and a half
in which Barry ran SNCC's Washington operation, he showed
that he not only had learned the axiom well but could put his
own creative spin on it.

In April 1966, for example, the 30-year-old activist tried to
break into the lily-white Cherry Blossom Festival Parade by
riding with a black beauty queen in a convertible with the Free
D.C. Movement slogan emblazoned on the side. Police diverted
the car, but Barry made the papers with his provocative and
unorthodox move.

Two months later Barry organized what he termed "Lunch
Hour" protests in downtown D.C. for those who "want to
get involved in this [Free D.C.] effort but are on the job while
we're picketing." To kick off the first day of the unusual protest
drive Barry showed up in a seersucker suit and straw boater
hat to lead a group that had gathered outside the 17th and
K streets, NW, offices of F. Elwood Davis, president of the
Washington Board of Trade.

At a rally near the White House the same month Barry and
others attempted to pitch a tent in the middle of Pennsylvania
Avenue to protest President Johnson's failure to protect civil
rights marchers in Mississippi or to support District home rule.

In July Barry hosted the first of a series of ghetto block parties
to give black teenagers a constructive outlet for their energies
and to introduce them to the concept of home rule. Dressed
in jeans, a T-shirt, and shades, he served as the party's DJ,
rapping over a loudspeaker about the virtues of self-government
between the soul discs he spun.

127

Barry made a hit with the kids, but as summer wore on and he threw more parties, the police were less impressed. On several of these occasions Barry was arrested for failing to obtain a city permit to hold such a gathering. Sometimes when the police moved in they were met with a hail of bricks and bottles thrown by the largely black crowd.

The resulting publicity turned off most whites in the city and many middle- and upper-class blacks, who saw Barry as a rough-edged troublemaker from out of town. But it raised Barry's profile considerably in the inner city, where people were grateful that someone cared enough about them to risk getting arrested.

"To most of the residents [of neighborhoods where the block parties were held], Barry is a man sent to show poor black people that all hope is not lost and to deliver them from Pharaoh's Land," wrote Bernard Garnett of *The Washington Afro-American* in July 1966. "The vast majority are poor. Many are on relief. Most have only menial jobs. Their homes often are overcrowded. And their concept of the power structure is not a complimentary one. These are the people who can walk down the turnpike of opportunity and find dead ends at all exits. And these are the people whom Barry and his [SNCC] sidekick, Lester McKinnie, want to convince that they have power."

Even Barry had to admit the convincing part was not going to be easy.

"Most Negroes come here from North or South Carolina and psychologically they think they're in freedom land," he told *Washington Post* columnist Dan Morgan in July 1966. "They're making two or three times as much money as they did back there. What's more, they weren't used to participating in political activity in their home states, anyway, so lack of politics here is nothing new to them."

If he wasn't altogether clear on how he was to educate the city's vast disenfranchised electorate, Barry knew how to use its press corps to further his agenda. When the police broke up a number of block parties in July, he staged a press conference on the steps of the District Building, a 60-year-old, five-story, stone Beaux-Arts structure on the corner of 14th Street and Pennsylvania Avenue, NW.

After blasting alleged "racial prejudice" by the city's 65 percent white police force, which earlier he had termed "an occupation army," Barry proposed a partial solution to the problem—a series of softball games between teams composed of what one reporter described as "youths most likely to get in trouble and the policemen least likely to be loved by the [inner city] community."

The novel and unexpected suggestion was quickly adopted by the city commissioners. They had learned to pay attention to the goateed agitator from SNCC who once had called them "slave masters" of D.C.'s "plantation system" of government, but who nonetheless usually followed through on whatever he had promised, or threatened.

The softball tournament, held in September, was judged by cops and street dudes alike to be an unqualified success. Barry had made his point: there are ways out of the deadly gyre of crime, race, and class animosity if you are creative enough to think of them.

Barry's efforts in behalf of the "core of the hard core," as he later referred to the city's trouble-prone youth, also was noticed by Mayor Walter Washington, who began turning to Barry for advice whenever violence loomed on the mean streets of the inner city. It was not unusual in those early SNCC days for Barry to stage a raucous rally in the morning and, if he escaped arrest, slip quietly into the District Building in the afternoon to confer with Mayor Washington about heading off a youth-related crisis.

This Janus-like behavior also carried over into other areas of Barry's life. *Washington Star* reporter Barry Kalb wrote in 1969: "Barry is almost always cool and restrained, often arrogant, never charming. In public, he exudes a forceful self-confidence and in private, at least, a towering ego."

Washington restaurateur Stuart Long, who met Barry in the late 1960s and soon became a close friend—and one of the few white members of Barry's inner circle—would concur that there are at least two Barry personae; but Long describes the private Marion Barry quite differently.

"He's just a decent, warm guy when you get him one-on-one," says Long, who owns several Capitol Hill restuarants. "He's a completely different guy when he's not putting on that front, you know, that political thing."

Ron Johnson, a former black SNCC worker in Washington in the mid-1960s, also recalls a gentler side of Barry: "Marion Barry wasn't a guy who would come in and take over a meeting. He would listen a lot. He wasn't nearly the uptight, angry person I've seen him become. He was open to different points of view."

Johnson said that Barry was also tolerant of drug-sharing at SNCC meetings. "I was in those SNCC meetings when joints were passed around," said Johnson, adding that Barry "never did partake" of the drugs that were shared.

Johnson's recollection of Barry's abstinence from marijuana was reinforced by a woman who was Barry's lover during the mid-sixties and also helped him raise funds for SNCC.

"The Marion that I knew was always a Boy Scout," recalls Geraldine Storm, then a Capitol Hill aide and now director of the community development division of the Appalachian Regional Commission in Washington. "A lot of people were into marijuana, and he very studiously avoided it. He would say to people, 'Why are you messin' with that?'"

According to Storm, "in the sixties when I knew him, he was [even] alarmed by the language that kids used on the street. I remember when he had the [SNCC] office on Rhode Island Avenue, he actually washed a kid's mouth out with soap who said 'fuck.'"

While Barry was capable of focusing, as in that instance, on cleaning up some of the smaller problems in the nation's capital back then, he mostly tackled more daunting ones such as a proposed freeway that potentially would displace tens of thousands of poor blacks who lived in Northwest Washington's Shaw neighborhood. At a mid-September 1966 meeting of the National Capital Planning Commission the SNCC leader first assailed the racial imbalance of the panel's staff, which he said was made up of "white people, planning for white people [who] fail to recognize they are talking about Negroes."

Then Barry warned that any project that further reduced the District's dwindling stock of low-income housing units could unleash civil disturbances similar to those that had broken out in the Watts district of Los Angeles the previous year. (Six thousand families already were on the waiting list in D.C., including many displaced by the massive gentrification of the Potomac Waterfront in Southwest Washington during the 1950s and early 1960s.)

"At some point their frustrations are going to cut loose," Barry warned prophetically. Riots came to the nation's capital 17 months later. If there was one thing Barry knew about, it was the darkness gathering inside the people he worked so closely with, because their rage mirrored his own.

Barry's frenetic activities in behalf of D.C.'s poor black residents left him little time for attending to other SNCC duties, including fundraising for the national organization, a matter which had become critical. Donations from white backers had dried up after SNCC's newly elected chairman, black nationalist Stokely Carmichael, had begun purging whites from the organization's ranks. The previous May, the same month Carmichael was elected, Barry had angered the group's executive committee in Atlanta when he defied an order from Carmichael to boycott President Johnson's national civil rights conference in Washington. Barry simply told them that the chance to promote D.C. home rule at the White House meeting was too important to stay away.

The rift with Atlanta grew wider when Barry informed Carmichael that he would be using most of the funds he raised in Washington for the Free D.C. Movement, rather than sending them to Atlanta as he had been instructed to do. In August 1966 Carmichael relegated Barry to a support role in SNCC's D.C. office. Barry resigned from SNCC five months later.

"The civil rights direction of protest is dead," he declared. "Now we must concentrate on control—economic and political power."

He explained the move later to the *Star*'s Barry Kalb: "I was getting tired of sitting-in, praying, and all that. I didn't think it was working anymore. Besides, my ideas on nonviolence were changing. I wanted to get into something where I didn't have to make the choice to be nonviolent.

"Like I believe, as far as blacks are concerned, we should use all and every means we want to, and those persons who want to go out and shoot policemen, that's their thing. You know it's not mine.

"I think that everything that anybody does is good. I'm serious. For instance, I know for a fact that white people get scared of the [Black] Panthers, and they might look at somebody a little more moderate and say, 'Well, let's give them a little money.' So I don't see how we can be hurt by anything that happens. Couldn't be no worse off."

Money—more precisely, the lack of it—was something that greatly concerned Barry. He had no income, and if he was to continue his full-time agitation, he could not work full time too. So he hustled where and when he could. Sometimes his methods were a bit unusual. Until Barry won elective office, for example, he would sometimes ask to be paid for interviews he gave to white reporters. In soliciting such a donation from Barry Kalb, Barry said he felt White America *owed* Black America for the deprivation blacks had suffered over the years. In particular, he implied, it owed Marion Barry.

"You can't do enough for me, really," he told Kalb. "Some blacks are satisfied with crumbs. But you can't do enough for me."

In that sense much of Barry's life could be viewed as an attempted payback on White America. Occasionally, however, Barry's anger backfired and ended up hurting him instead. In March 1967, for instance, after being arrested for jaywalking on 13th Street, NW, and disorderly conduct, Barry was also charged with destroying government property after he allegedly kicked in the rear door of the police paddy wagon used to transport him to the 13th Precinct station house for booking.

The young black militant, it seemed, had finally gone too far. Or had he? At least he was in the news, and the incident could be milked for maximum sympathy by a man who was growing increasingly canny about exploiting the media, no matter how adverse or unseemly the situation he had created appeared at first glance. In fact, Barry's trial three months later in D.C. Superior Court drew extensive media coverage when some of the city's most prominent religious and civic leaders testified in his behalf.

"I have known Mr. Barry for more than two years," Paul Moore, Jr., the white Episcopal bishop of Washington, who had helped launch the Free D.C. Movement with Barry, told the jury panel. "He is known as a man of peace, a man of nonviolence."

Eight other prominent Washingtonians, black and white, took the stand during Barry's nine-day jury trial to make similar statements, including Clarence Clyde Ferguson, dean of Howard University Law School, and Sterling Tucker, director of the Washington Urban League. Even two reporters who had interviewed Barry after the incident—Jim Hoagland of the *Washington Post* and Nicholas Horrock of the *Washington Daily News*—were called to the witness stand to explain the slightly different versions of events Barry had described to them in interviews following his arrest.

The arresting officers testified that Barry, when confronted about his alleged jaywalking at 13th and U Streets, NW, around 12:30 A.M. on March, 30, 1967, and asked to show identification, had retorted: "I ain't showing a white ———— a goddamn thing. . . . My name is nobody."

When Barry persisted in his refusal to cooperate, the officers testified, they tried to "escort" him to a paddy wagon, but he shoved them away. By this time about 20 people had gathered at the scene, they said, and they radioed for help. When reinforcements arrived, the former high school boxer had leveled one policeman with a punch in the face. They then claimed they pushed their struggling detainee into the back of a paddy wagon. During the brief ride to the 13th Precinct station house the officers alleged that the 6' 1", 200-pound activist "took the stance of a mule" and kicked the police vehicle's back door so hard it buckled.

Barry's attorney gave a very different version of events, a version that put a racist spin on the encounter.

"Hey boy, you must have a pocketful of money," the lawyer said one of the policemen had called out to Barry as he stepped off the curb. "You must be one of those smart-ass niggers."

Barry also took the stand himself. The incident had gotten out of hand, he told the jury, when a policeman arriving on the scene pointed to him and said. "That's Barry, get him!"

In Barry's version of events—backed up by the testimony of another SNCC worker who had witnessed the arrest—he had fully cooperated with the officers after simply demanding to know what he was charged with. He accused the police of arbitrarily kicking and punching him on the street and later at the station house.

After less than two hours' deliberation, a jury of 10 blacks and two whites (the same exact racial ratio as the panelists in his 1990 drug and perjury trial) acquitted Barry of the charge of destruction of public property. The jaywalking and disorderly conduct charges were later dropped by the D.C. corporation counsel, who conceded that the earlier acquittal had weakened his case.

In a post-trial statement Barry told reporters the verdict was "a great victory for Negroes and poor people" that "should prove to police that they can't arrest people without justification and get away with it."

By painting himself as a vindicated black victim of white police brutality, rather than the loud-mouthed, violent provocateur the police had described at his trial, Barry had turned a potentially embarrassing situation into a minor triumph—at least in the eyes of his sympathizers. He knew that the bottom line in politics is grabbing people's attention, the more dramatically the better.

Marion Barry was becoming a master of confrontation.

10

MAU-MAUING
THE U.S. LABOR DEPARTMENT

Youth Pride, Incorporated, the black self-help group that eventually became the springboard for Marion Barry's leap into the D.C. political arena, was launched in August 1967 on a dare. The gauntlet was thrown down by President Johnson's labor secretary, Willard Wirtz, who had invited Barry and other black D.C. activists to his office to review job-training proposals for the District.

Barry listened impatiently to several presentations. Then he told Wirtz, bluntly, that he was not impressed by any of them.

The labor secretary glared at the controversial activist, who recently had begun to emphasize his blackness by wearing long, African-style dashiki shirts and a towering Afro haircut, sometimes topped with a comb.

"Do you think you can do any better?" Wirtz snapped.

Barry replied that he thought he could.

To the labor official's surprise, Barry returned to Wirtz's office three days later with a detailed plan for training and putting to work hundreds of 14-to-18-year-old "dudes," as Barry called the city's unemployed black youths and young parolees whom the Labor Department had targeted for action. Unbeknownst to Wirtz, Barry quietly had been developing the proposal along with a 26-year-old ex-convict named Rufus "Catfish" Mayfield, who had already set up a smaller-scale version of Pride in his Northeast Washington neighborhood, and with two former SNCC workers—D.C. government official Carroll Harvey and phone company manager Mary Treadwell.

Barry would marry Treadwell—a heavyset, light-skinned black woman from Lexington, Kentucky, whom he had first met at Fisk University in Nashville—five years later. According

135

to Geraldine Storm, Treadwell "could lead him almost any-where. I think he loved her because she was such a tough character and had a lot of strengths that he didn't. She was a scary person and I think he sort of admired a black woman who wasn't afraid of anything or anybody and seemed to have her own resources."

While Pride's immediate goal was to put street dudes to work, its founders told the *Washington Post* they wanted ultimately to establish "employee-owned, profit-making businesses in the inner city that will employ and develop the productive talents of the 'core of the hard core' as well as educated blacks—and thus give the black community genuine participation in a capitalist society."

Wirtz was impressed with the proposal for Youth Pride, Incorporated, he told the *Washington Star*, because, unlike others he had seen, it had "the element of real [youth] participation."

The Johnson administration official also liked what former chemist Barry had to say about economic self-sufficiency, a component few others who had submitted proposals were even thinking of building into their programs.

"We want to reach a point where we don't have to ask for federal money anymore," Barry told him. "We just want catalytic capital from the government."

Barry's capitalistic aspirations put Pride "way out in front of all the other programs" his department was considering, said Wirtz. No wonder. At that volatile point in the country's history, the labor secretary and his boss in the White House were looking for ways to divert the tough street kids who otherwise might spark in D.C. the same kind of racial violence that had just ripped through Detroit, leaving 43 people dead. Wirtz and Johnson realized that if the unrest, which eventually would erupt in 59 U.S. cities by the end of 1967, spread to the nation's capital, it would make a mockery of Johnson's vaunted Great Society program, aimed at eradicating poverty through an expensive array of government-funded initiatives. The rioters would send a clear and unmistakable message to America's heartland—and, more important, to the law-makers

on Capitol Hill who controlled the legislative purse strings—
that Johnson's ambitious scheme had failed.

So Wirtz quickly approved $300,000 in "catalytic capital"
to fund a five-week pilot Pride program starting in August
1967. Soon more than a thousand dudes fanned out across
D.C.'s slums in bright green jumpsuits to clean up blighted
neighborhoods and kill rats for $1.40 an hour ($2.50 an hour
for supervisors). They killed so many rats (25,000) during the
trial period and cleaned so many streets and alleys (2,600) that
the city's Housing Division chief asked the city commissioners
to grant Pride funds to operate on a year-round basis. The
commissioners, however, who could make no such move
without Capitol Hill's approval, refused.

Some Department of Labor officials also were starting to balk
at providing long-term funding for Pride, despite the secretary's enthusiasm for the program. According to one official,
Barry and other Pride leaders had shown an annoying "pro-
pensity to pick up the ball and run all the way to the Huntley-
Brinkley report with it."

Using the electronic media to plead their case publicly may
have annoyed federal officials, but, says civil rights historian
Taylor Branch, such tactics were effective, and during the 1960s
they were new to the American scene. Branch said that black
activists such as Barry were then "developing new languages
and approaches" for attacking social ills, and some of these
new tactics were unabashedly aggressive.

"They mau-maued the Office of Economic Opportunity and
other government agencies," Branch said, by demanding
economic assistance and taking economic actions, such as
strikes and boycotts, against employers who did not serve or
hire people equitably. Branch said that at the height of the
Great Society, militants such as Barry were, in effect, working
both sides of the street at once: "On the one hand, they viewed
government as the enemy, and on the other hand they asked
for its help."

At the end of Pride's successful five-week test the Department of Labor doled out $1.2 million to keep the program going
for 40 more weeks. For the first time since leaving college, Barry

had a steady income ($15,600, figured annually). More impor-
tant, he finally had control of his own organization. He didn't
have to take orders from SNCC headquarters in Atlanta or even
the Department of Labor in running Pride. But he would have
to show results.

The first order of business was finding a place to hang the
new organization's shingle. He chose as Pride's main office
a handsome, three-story, gray stone building with tall, arched
windows and sculpted cornices on the corner of 16th and U
streets, NW. It stood next to a red brick apartment building
at the end of a row of once-elegant townhouses, on the dividing
line between the crime-ridden Shaw neighborhood and a
mixed-race neighborhood called Adams Morgan, which, in
architecture, commerce, and ambiance, is not unlike New
York's Greenwich Village.

Next, Barry leased a tiny Nash Rambler sedan to get around
town and rented a modest, three-room apartment only a few
blocks from Pride's new headquarters.

Roles for Pride's founders were divided up according to
leverage. Rufus "Catfish" Mayfield served as the group's
nominal chairman and occasional spokesman, but he had no
real power. Mary Treadwell handled fund-raising and the
business end of things, while Carroll Harvey directed Pride's
day-to-day operations. Marion Barry avoided such mundane
matters, focusing instead, said Harvey, in a 1969 interview with
the *Washington Star* on "the politics of the street," because he
knew "the moods and demands of the people."

Harvey explained: "Marion is not attentive to details, so he
needs a detail man around him. He realizes he doesn't have
capabilities across the board."

While leaving the detail work to others, Barry was learning,
very quickly, the politics of federal grantsmanship. After
discussing the matter with Pride's two other senior co-
founders, he decided it was too risky to keep Mayfield, who
balked at structure and had a criminal record for stealing cars,
as even the token chairman of an organization whose annual
budget was by now being measured in millions. Too many
times, they thought, Catfish had shown himself immature or
rebellious.

When Pride officials were called to Capitol Hill to testify about the program, for example, everyone but Mayfield reportedly agreed to wear work clothes to demonstrate the dignity of the working man. The flamboyant Catfish, Mary Treadwell said in a 1972 *Post* interview, showed up in a suit and carried a fancy walking stick. She said Mayfield was charging Pride for his weekend rental of convertibles and his home phone.

"Finally," Treadwell added, "he got this idea from the movies that executives stayed at home. He wanted us to call him on the phone."

In November 1967, just three months after Pride was launched, Treadwell, Barry, and Harvey effectively forced Mayfield out by stripping him of all decision-making powers.

"I grant you, friends and foes," Mayfield announced cryptically at his exit news conference, "I'm hip. I understand. And I'll forgive you."

Later, however, Mayfield publicly charged Barry, Treadwell, and Harvey with using him as a front man to launch Pride by telling federal officials that he and other youths employed by Pride would help run the organization. Once the senior founders got their money and no longer needed him, Mayfield complained, they simply dumped him.

Barry denied the charge, explaining that, in his opinion, running such a large and complex operation was simply "too much, too fast" for his former friend to handle.

"The Labor Department just doesn't give somebody that kind of money and say, 'Do with it as you please,' " Barry told *Post* reporter Courtland Milloy.

The day after Mayfield's departure Barry said that Mayfield would be missed but the organization would get along fine without him.

"Pride is bigger than any one individual," Barry asserted. He added that Pride "was my idea," despite common knowledge in the city's black community that Mayfield had set up the orgainzation before he even met Barry.

"Rufus was just pushed out ahead," claimed Barry. "We let him take the lead. He was just a symbol."

Then, inexplicably, Barry blamed Mayfield's resignation on L. D. Pratt, a white former SNCC worker who had helped Barry organize the January 1966 boycott against D.C. Transit. He told the *Star* that Pratt had "poisoned Mayfield's mind" in belated retaliation for a falling out that Pratt had had with Barry several months earlier. The conflict had led to Pratt's resignation from SNCC's Washington office, then headed by Barry.

"Pratt planted seeds in Rufus' mind about how awful Mary [Treadwell] and I were and about how we were trying to run the whole show," Barry charged. He said Pratt had done this in the vain hope of regaining his lost power in the civil rights movement. Barry did not elaborate on this accusation, nor did he provide any evidence to support it.

Mayfield's controversial departure embarrassed the fledgling black self-help organization that still was struggling for both acceptance and financial survival. (In the next three years, Pride would receive nearly $9 million in additional federal grants for job training and the development of related minority businesses employing "dudes" trained by Pride; but at that early stage, nobody in the Pride hierarchy could count on such funds.)

Catfish, meanwhile, was cooking up revenge. Three months after resigning from Pride, in February 1968, Mayfield called a press conference along with two dissident Pride board members at a Southeast Washington bar. He planned to demand the resignations of Barry, Treadwell, and Carroll. But before Mayfield could start the parley at the Terrace Lounge in Washington's tough Anacostia neighborhood, Barry and Treadwell stormed into the bar's tiny downstairs conference room ahead of some 200 Pride workers, some of whom had guns. The dudes surrounded Mayfield's outnumbered troops and chased out several newsmen.

"There ain't gonna be any press conference!" shouted Treadwell and Barry, adopting the tough street language and rough manners of their protégés.

According to Woody West and Barry Kalb of the *Star*, who managed to stay inside the Southeast tavern, the confrontation "hovered on the brink of violence for some minutes as members of both factions hurled charges and countercharges across the crowded barroom. At least three partially concealed pistols could be seen in the crowd, and it is known that others had weapons."

Undaunted, the bespectacled Mayfield, dressed in red slacks and a multicolored dashiki, climbed onto a table and angrily harangued his former colleagues who now surrounded him. He accused them of letting Barry and Treadwell "brainwash" them for a few dollars.

A few minutes later, West and Kalb reported, "the young men began to file sheepishly out of the bar. He [Mayfield] followed them, confronting individuals and continuing to berate them."

The violent confrontation, though effective, may have seemed out of character for a man such as Marion Barry who, as a matter of principle, had eschewed such tactics during his civil rights days, to the point of occasionally sustaining unanswered beatings and abuse from southern bigots and police. But, as Barry had made clear in public statements after leaving SNCC, the world was changing, and one had to change along with it, even if one came to resemble one's former enemies in the process.

The new Marion Barry carried a .32 pistol and had shown he could put hundreds of angry young blacks on the street to do his bidding any time he wanted. He later would claim that the gun was to protect him against the very people he was trying to help.

"You never knew what to expect from those guys [the dudes]," he said. "They carried guns like other people carried cigarettes."

Barry has never been known to use his gun. And, despite occasional replays of the mob scene he helped orchestrate that February 1968 day at the bar, and a later public comment that "every black person in America should have a weapon in his home to protect himself," no one ever would accuse him of directly ordering anyone to do violence to anyone. But Barry clearly had learned how to use an effective new political weapon: physical intimidation.

The flap over the Mayfield resignation was only a minor ripple in a sea of scandals and crises that soon would cascade over Pride and its business arm, Youth Pride Economic Enterprises, Incorporated—created by Barry and Treadwell in March 1968 to give jobs to Pride graduates and generate capital for the job-training arm. During Pride's first five years the black self-help group and its commercial spinoffs were investigated by the General Accounting Office (twice), the FBI, the Department of Justice, the Department of Labor, a District grand jury, and several congressional committees.

In 1969, 17 Pride employees were indicted by a federal grand jury on charges of misappropriating $10,000 in federal funds. The charges included payroll padding by creating "ghost" employees and forging signatures on paychecks. Although only three of those charged were ultimately convicted, while one pleaded quilty, the adverse publicity delivered another devastating broadside to an already vulnerable organization.

Barry, however, seemed unshaken by all the negative publicity. After all, he had warned everyone from the start about the risks involved in trying to put hard-core dudes to work in a structured environment. These were the young men who were left over after everyone else had been picked for a useful role in society. They were the ones who had flunked or dropped out of school, the ones rejected by the Army because they had a problem passing tests and taking orders. Even black power groups such as the Black Panthers rejected them for the same reasons. They were the victims and victimizers of society who all too often ended up in jail or the morgue. Given this reality, Barry scoffed at the relatively minor ripoffs by Pride employees that had been uncovered after a flurry of high-powered government investigations.

"The total amount involved was less than one percent" of the total amount of federal funds that Pride had received, he said, as if that excused the financial wrongdoing. But Barry conceded: "We've had cases where guys have not lived up to their trust. We moved them to other positions of less temptation."

Pride had other serious problems, which included the near-bankruptcy of Youth Pride Economic Enterprises, Incorporated, after less than two years of operation. By December 1970 PEE owned and operated half-a-dozen gas stations, a landscaping and gardening company, a painting and maintenance company, and a 55-unit garden apartment complex in Southeast Washington. Unfortunately, all but the Buena Vista Apartments, which were breaking even because of the rental income, were dripping with red ink. Overall, PEE owed creditors, including the Internal Revenue Service, between $150,000 and $200,000, not counting long-term mortgages on the Buena Vista Apartments and a warehouse Pride had just bought that quickly turned into a white elephant.

Pride escaped financial collapse only after D.C. residents contributed more than $50,000 to the Pride Survival Fund following a public appeal for help by Barry and Treadwell.

Some observers felt Barry could have avoided the crisis by focusing more of his time and energy on running the organization he had helped found.

"Commercial enterprise is a jealous mistress," one black leader told the *Star*'s Ronald Sarro and Fred Barnes. "It takes all your time. Marion's not that big and bright. You can't be a businessman and a politician. He tries to be a spokesman for the world."

A prominent black attorney expressed a similar view to the *Star* reporters: "He has a hard time defending the charge that he's spread himself too thin."

Barry shrugged off such criticisms, telling Sarro and Barnes that PEE's financial problems were practically inevitable.

"We have concentrated on service type businesses that employ a large number of hard-core dudes," he said, "rather than businesses that employ just the elite." He said: "We tried to do good at the same time we tried to run a business. It's almost impossible. We were doomed to fail according to the traditional business trends from the day we opened up."

While Barry's money problems were serious, they were, at least, potentially solvable with enough federal grants and private contributions. Much more difficult to turn around were "the dudes" themselves, some of whom reportedly had been shooting dice, fighting, or goofing off while out on work crews. Some black youths who worked at Pride-owned gas stations told white customers to take their business elsewhere, even pulled guns on customers. According to a retired D.C. policeman who patrolled the Shaw neighborhood during the 1960s, a major fencing operation for stolen goods was run out of an automobile service station owned and operated by Pride. "There were people walkin' in with TV sets," recalls the ex-cop. "They'd go and put 'em in the service bay. When they came out, they weren't carryin' the TV's."

Although he and other officers knew what was going on, he said they never made any arrests because they knew no one would be prosecuted if they did. "We just couldn't get [the D.C. corporation counsel or the U.S. attorney] to do anything," he said because, "they didn't wanta make waves."

Rich Adams, the black veteran producer for Washington's WUSA-TV, was a reporter back then. He says Barry and other Pride leaders in effect condoned such illegal activities because they knew that local and even federal officials would look the other way. "It was called mau-mauing," says Adams. "If somebody caught them, or if there was some hint that somebody was on their trail—particularly, the feds—the response from people like Treadwell and Barry was, 'Don't ask, honky motherfucker, because if you do, we're going to go out on the street, and we're going to start a riot and say that the white man is trying to destroy black ecomonic progress.' And it scared the living shit out of these liberals who didn't want any trouble.

"It was the cost of doing business. It was the cost of racial harmony or reduced racial tension because there certainly was not total harmony....So what if Marion and Mary Treadwell got a couple of hundred thousand dollars? It was worth it to the federal government not to have them stirring shit in the community."

Sometimes the trouble at Pride got more serious than a mere fencing operation. One former Pride worker said that when he rejoined a downtown cleanup crew after a lunch break, he found his co-workers sitting in the cab of a Pride truck "splitting up the money" after robbing the nearby Greyhound bus terminal at gunpoint. "The cops are going every which way," he recalled, "and this fucking Pride truck's on the corner. And these bastards are the ones that robbed the joint."

In early 1973, two years after Barry had left Pride to pursue politics full time—he was still the group's nominal head—four Pride employees were shot to death in less than a month. According to former D.C. homicide detectives assigned to the investigations, all but one of the four men implicated in the slayings were also Pride employees. Both victims and perpetrators, they said, also belonged to a gang that had staged a rash of armed street robberies in the District. They said most gang members were parolees from Lorton Reformatory, the prison the District runs in suburban Virginia.

All four murders were carried out by fellow gang members to silence potential snitches, the former detectives said, and two of the shootings took place at Pride's 16th Street, NW, headquarters. (They said the body of the first victim, Yale Dewitt Harris, was found in an alley a few feet from Pride's back door on January 14, 1973.)

The former homicide detectives got a big break in the case when the body of the final victim, John Theodore Moore, was found on February 13 alongside a rural highway in The Plains, Virginia. Moore's bullet-riddled corpse had been wrapped in a drapery. The detectives also found a note: "This is for all the stickup boys," it said. "He's number six and we are going to kill again. Sign [sic], Executioner, Eliminator and Exterminator." (The note contained fingerprints that led the former detectives to one of the perpetrators, a young man with the unfortunate name of Jesse James Martin.)

About 10 days after discovering Moore's body, the former detectives said, they went to Pride headquarters armed with a search warrant and made an unusual discovery. "We go up on the second floor," one of them recalls, "and there's a drapery missing, and [hanging next to the empty curtain rod] there was one that matches the composition of the one that

Theodore Moore was wrapped in. So, of course, we took if for comparison, and in there is a damn bullet that matches another [one of the four Pride] murder [cases]."

Altogether, four District men were eventually convicted of murder or manslaughter in the scandals that further tainted the already controversial organization.

While Barry was still actively at Pride's helm, rumors also persisted about rampant drug use by Pride workers and staff. Jim Money, another former D.C. policeman assigned to the district where Pride was headquartered, said Pride employees "on their lunch breaks would go over to a vacant townhouse a block [from 16th and U streets, NS] and shoot up" heroin. According to a former Pride worker, the organization "had drugs coming all the way through it." He said it was easy to obtain marijuana, cocaine, heroin, and other narcotics from fellow workers, although he saw no evidence of any organized drug distribution by Pride workers or managers.

On more than one occasion, the former Pride worker said, he saw Marion Barry and Mary Treadwell smoking marijuana at parties he attended. (This was confirmed by a former D.C. musician who also attended the parties.) Of course, marijuana joints also were being passed around in thousands of Washington homes during the late 1960s and well into the 1970s. And marijuana was an integral part of the counterculture to which Marion Barry belonged. Not to use it would have been unusual, rather than vice versa. Barry, however, apparently never stopped using drugs, while most of his activist colleagues left them behind when they moved into the 1980s.

Many of the young dudes Barry was trying to help in the late 1960s, however, were into harder drugs. One former Pride worker said the former Lorton inmates he worked with on a cleanup crew kept heroin and Dilaudid (a synthetic narcotic) and syringes in their truck and shot up several times during the day.

"These guys [also] were carrying guns and knives," he said. "Some of them were just out of Lorton. This was the dumping spot for anybody who was going on parole. They could get a job at Pride."

When confronted with such allegations, Barry angrily defended Pride, which he reminded critics had tackled perhaps the most difficult job in American society—trying to turn around "the hustler, the dropout, the ex-junkie." In his words, "Criminals didn't slip into Pride. The program was set up in the first place to take in young criminals and try to straighten them out."

Three years into the experiment, Barry told the *Star*'s Sarro and Barnes: "What Hitler could have done in this situation with this population would have been to burn it up, because they are no asset to society, because they are not putting anything into society, because it's a drag on society.

"We're at the end of the failure syndrome. We get people 17 or 18 when they have gone through about 10 or so institutions which have failed them. We weren't talking beginning failures. We were talking end failures."

Barry admitted to the *Star* reporters that he had "really underestimated the severity of the problem. "We thought we could get a cat through Pride in a year and he's ready to go to work. This is one assumption I made and it was wrong. Pride cannot in one year undo the effects that society has left on a person over 17 or 18 years of his life."

Despite the towering odds against the youths served by Pride, however, some succeeded in the conventional sense. They went to college. Got and kept jobs. Kicked their drug habits. Put enough money in their pockets to pay their bills and taxes. And, through its economic arm, Pride eventually trained thousands of black youths in such marketable skills as house painting and renovation, auto mechanics, gardening and landscaping, and over-the-counter retail sales.

Pride's success also brought accolades to Barry, who was consulted frequently by city officials, including then-mayor Walter Washington, on youth problems.

Even Barry's rivals conceded that he had made a significant impact on the city's black community by creating Pride. "As Pride goes, so goes the community," Jeanus Parks, director of another black self-help group called United Planning Organization, told the *Star*'s Sarro and Barnes. "Pride has an absolute monopoly on the business it is in—its business is the dudes. Unless we support Pride, this city, this metropolitan area, will become a land of 'look behind' because there will be no one working with the dudes."

Another black community activist, Reginald H. Booker, was even more blunt in his assessment of Pride's importance to D.C.'s inner city residents. "If Pride fails," he told the *Star* reporters, "the whole community fails."

Barry himself was more philosophical. Two years into the experiment, he told the *Star's* Barry Kalb: "What Pride is doing is no panacea. I'm not so sure that what we're doing in the final analysis—if the country continues the way it's going—is going to make that much difference."

11

"A MAN FOR ALL STORMY SEASONS"

When the Kerner Commission, empaneled by President Johnson to study America's tense racial situation, released its findings on March 1, 1968, it warned that the country was "moving toward two societies, one black and one white—separate and unequal." But it also said, optimistically, that "the movement apart can be reversed. Choice is still possible. The alternative is not blind repression or capitulation to lawlessness. It is the realization of common opportunities for all within a single society."

A little over a month later, on April 4, 1968, in Marion Barry's boyhood home of Memphis, an assassin's bullet ended such hopes when it tore through the neck of Martin Luther King, Jr., fatally wounding him. While speculation continues even today over convicted white assassin James Earl Ray's role in a possible conspiracy, the immediate reaction to King's slaying was swift and furious. Blacks in Memphis and in 129 other cities across the nation took to the streets, throwing bricks and molotov cocktails at police and firemen, looting and burning in a self-destructive orgy of pain and rage.

In D.C., wrote Keith Harrison in a retrospective *Washington Post* article, the rioting began only two blocks from Pride headquarters. It started, said Harrison, just "minutes after King was pronounced dead at 7:05 P.M. Central time (8:05 P.M. in Washington), when the window of a drugstore was splintered at 14th and U streets, NW.

"Soon angry crowds had taken over the street, breaking windows, looting stores, setting fires. The destruction spread and continued for three days. . . . President Johnson called in federal troops. They set up machine guns around the Capitol and surrounded the White House. The nation's capital had the look of a teetering South American republic. Before the end, federal troops occupied the city, whole blocks were consumed by flames, thousands were arrested and 13 were dead.''

Near the riot's ignition point, former SNCC leader and black power advocate Stokely Carmichael, accompanied by a band of youths, had first asked the merchants along 14th Street to close their stores out of respect ''until Martin Luther King is laid to rest.'' When some white shop owners refused, the youths became enraged and began trashing the stores. Carmichael led the historic confrontation, he said in a 1988 interview with the *Post*, because ''our role would be to properly coordinate [the riot], to inflict as much damage as possible on the enemy and then to receive as much concessions [as possible] from the enemy on behalf of the people.''

Relatively speaking, Marion Barry's was a voice of calm back then. Although not necessarily motivated by altruism—he'd stated before that bricks and bottles in the hands of blacks are no match for a policeman's gun, and that if you're going to mount a revolution, you'd better have the firepower to back it up—he kept a low profile during the rioting. When it was over, he emerged as a leader of the effort to change the situation that in his view had caused it—white economic control of the black inner city.

''Everybody and his mother used to be able to come in black communities and operate,'' Barry told one of numerous forums held in Washington to study the effects of the riot, ''and whether they boycott or burn, people in black communities aren't going to stand for that any more.''

''White people should be allowed to come back [to riot-torn areas],'' he said, ''only if the majority of the ownership is in the hands of blacks. That is, they could come back and give their experience and their expertise—and then they should leave.''

Barry told the D.C. Council that rebuilding the city according to the old, white-engineered model would not solve the problem. ''There's a black culture, there's a black psychology, there's a black value and there's a white culture, there's a white psychology and there's a white value,'' he explained. ''You can't plan for black people like you can for white people because there is a difference." Then he warned: "If this city is rebuilt the same way it was, it is going to be burned down again."

Washington saw no more large-scale riots, and in neighborhoods savaged by rioters, some black merchants eventually moved in and started businesses. By April 1969, however, the first anniversary of King's assassination, the rebuilding process had barely begun, and Barry's dream of black economic power rising from the ashes of the inner city seemed further away than ever. In a brief speech marking the anniversary of a man who had been Black America's hope, and his civil rights mentor, Barry could no longer mask his bitterness at King's death and at other injustices he had witnessed, and at the numbingly slow pace of change.

"I've been in this thing for 10 years," he said hoarsely when his turn came to speak. "And I'm tired of going to memorial services for my friends. I don't care what your thing is, we've got to get together."

Barry, meanwhile, was doing what he could to carry on King's legacy by creating greater opportunities for blacks in Washington. And his work was not going unnoticed. By October 1970 the *Post*, which in 1966 had editorialized that then-SNCC leader Barry had "deliberately flouted the law," ran a complimentary article calling Barry "D.C.'s Man for All Stormy Seasons."

The article praised the young activist for defusing tensions a few months earlier when violence had nearly broken out between black youths and police a few blocks from Pride headquarters. It also cited Barry's role in mediating a 1970 teacher's strike by holding an all-night session between teachers and school board members at Pride headquarters. The *Post* also reminded its readers that four years earlier, in 1966, Barry had ranked fifth behind four longtime Washington residents in a poll asking black city residents who had "done the most for Negro people in the area."

At the same time other powerful white-dominated institutions in the city—most notably the U.S. Congress—continued to snipe publicly at Barry.

Rep. Joel Broyhill (R-Va.) led the charge, calling Barry a "street rioter" and "one of Washington's worst agitators." Broyhill described Barry's creation, Pride, as a multimillion dollar ripoff promoted by liberals "convinced that permissiveness and coddling of criminals and back alley creeps is the surefire shortcut to peace and safety on our streets."

Barry in turn charged that lawmakers who criticized Pride, such as Broyhill and Sen. Robert Byrd (D-W.Va.), were part of "a racist conspiracy" to destroy the antipoverty organization, which had been set up to help people to whom privileged whites could not easily relate.

"It's the same old stereotype of black folks with their hand always in the till," Barry complained. "Nothing but witch-hunting."

Barry's race-baiting effectively silenced Broyhill. In 1970 a spokesman for the former Virginia Republican congressman said Broyhill was so upset that his efforts against Pride had resulted in his being branded a racist, the Republican congressman had decided to hold his tongue.

"We are not going to pursue this [investigation and criticism of Pride] anymore," Broyhill's spokesman said. "It's not that we don't think we're right. It's just that it's self-defeating."

Says WUSA-TV's Rich Adams, "He [Barry] was crafty. He knew exactly which political buttons to push. He knew exactly how to manipulate the system. And, quite frankly, you and I might say, 'That's morally reprehensible.' [But] in the mind of somebody from Itta Bena, Mississippi, and all the racial bullshit and everything he put up with, this was the chance for the black guy to fuck over the white system. And he did it with style. It wasn't just rob a 7-11. It was rob the whole goddamn federal government and, you know, use it to his advantage. So it's the ultimate power trip for a guy with that kind of [deprived] upbringing."

Barry's political enemies were not limited to Capitol Hill. The People's Republican Committee of Washington charged that Barry had created "a junior black power movement" in Pride and called for a cutoff of federal funds. An attorney for Pride, Incorporated, John Rigby of the prestigious D.C. law firm of Arnold and Porter, said that at various times FBI agents had questioned Barry and other Pride officials about possible connections with the Mafia, Red China, SNCC chairman and black militant H. Rap Brown, and with local drug pushers.

Both Barry and Mary Treadwell appeared before a federal grand jury to answer charges of financial manipulations within Pride. Although Treadwell would be convicted of diverting Pride funds to her own use several years later, at that point both she and Barry escaped indictment. Once more Marion Barry had slipped out of a legal noose. Personally and politically the young black activist seemed to have as many lives as a cat.

Although many of Barry's personal and political battles during his early years in Washington seemed to involve whites, Barry denied any racial animosity—at least, not against those whites who shared his values or beliefs.

"I don't dislike white people," he told the *Washington Star* in a July 1969 interview. "I do dislike white institutions. There are a lot of white people in the country that philosophically are in tune with me."

During his early civil rights days Barry had held a far more tolerant view of whites, some of whom, he knew, had fought, even died, alongside blacks while striving for the same civil rights goals he embraced.

"I think it's good that whites are participating [in the civil rights movement]," Barry had told graduate student Thomas Rose in 1962, "because in the South you've had for so long this gulf between the white and Negro. When you find a white person who is participating actively you find they really get to know Negroes better because it takes a close bond in order to go downtown and sit in together, and go to jail together. As a result, Negroes get to know whites better and vice versa. I think contact is a good way to break down stereotypes."

Still, admitted Barry, even back then: "There is the tendency [among some black people] in the South not to trust white people. I think this is not good. It's putting white people in that category that they put us in; it's not taking people as individuals."

From his civil rights days onward Barry maintained close friendships with individual whites. He had an innate charisma that drew people to him, and he could be ingratiating and charming. But Barry also was capable of using those same skills to manipulate people—whites or blacks—to get what he wanted.

At a guest appearance at Howard University in November 1968, Barry reportedly told a group of black middle-class students: "I think a lot of my black talk frightens you. You've been brainwashed. Black has always been a very negative thing in this country. But no matter how much Nadinola [a skin lightener] you use, you're still going to be black."

"You know what those dudes call you?" asked the leopard-skin, dashiki-clad black activist, referring to the young Pride workers he had recruited from the city's slums and from Lorton Reformatory. "They call you 'shirt-and-tie niggers.'"

Then, satisfied that he'd made his point, Barry reversed himself and asked the same young men and women he had just insulted to tutor Pride workers by appealing to their sense of black pride. It was a classic Barry move: jab for shock effect, put people on the defensive, then stroke them by telling them how important their contribution to the common black cause can be. Several students volunteered as tutors that night. The Rogue Charmer had worked his magic again.

12

LOVE YOUR ENEMY

M arion Barry had barely launched Pride when an irresis- tible chance came along to take on his old nemesis, the Metropolitan Police Department. This time the confron- tation would be strictly legal: in May 1968 the U.S. Office of Economic Opportunity offered to fund an experiment in defusing tensions between police and residents of the crime- ridden 13th Precinct in Northwest Washington. The precinct includes the Shaw neighborhood where Pride was located, where Barry lived, and where he occasionally had been arrested—mostly for minor infractions such as "failure to move along."

Under the proposal for a "Pilot Police Precinct Project," which carried an OEO grant of $1.4 million, precinct residents would elect a citizens' board to work closely with the officers who patrolled their neighborhood. The proposal called for "sensitivity" training for beat officers and the creation of storefront police substations in high-crime areas and special police units to handle domestic disturbances. The idea was to build trust on both sides and to learn if greater civilian contact with police would bring fewer clashes between police and neighborhood residents and an overall reduction in crime.

On paper the project looked solid; everyone, it seemed, would benefit. D.C. Mayor Walter Washington appointed a director, Robert Shellow, and a support staff. The trouble began when Shellow invited community groups to provide their input. No single group of 13th Precinct residents could agree on the final structure for the project or on how to elect the proposed citizens' board.

Although some residents seemed content with the way Shellow was handling the project, others, including Marion Barry, who had become chairman of the so-called Ad-Hoc

Committee for a Real Pilot Precinct, wanted far greater control over the police and the project. Barry demanded, among other concessions, the resignation of Robert Shellow and his entire staff; board control of the project's budget; and co-equal power with 13th Precinct police commanders over the hiring, firing, promotions, merit increases, transfers, reprimands and demotions of all officers under their command.

Barry's extreme demands prompted D.C.'s acting public safety director, Charles Duncan, to remind him: "The pilot precinct is designed to maximize citizen participation. However, precinct control, in the final analysis, is vested in the chief of police," not in a hypothetical citizens' board. Duncan added, pointedly, that the project "is an experiment that's going to require good faith on both sides, or it's not going to work."

Duncan's statement reflected the frustration city officials felt with regard to Barry and other militant critics of the project who already had delayed its start for more than a year.

In October 1968 Mayor Washington, hoping to resolve the dispute, appointed a committee made up of 46 community leaders, including Marion Barry. A month later Barry joined four others in resigning from what they termed a "puppet committee," a "sham," and a "fraud."

They wanted it their way or no way at all.

Unlike the project's other critics, however, Barry was in a special category. For in the midst of his drive to gain greater community control of D.C.'s "occupation army"—as he called the Metropolitan Police Department—Barry was betrayed again by his dark side. In May 1969, in an alley beside Pride headquarters, Barry clashed with officers of the same police precinct he was trying to reform.

According to court records and published news accounts, the trouble began about 7 P.M. on May 13, when Barry rushed out of the building and began cursing two white police officers who were standing near a Pride employee's car that was parked illegally in the alley.

"If you write a ticket on that car, I will kill you," Barry reportedly threatened, after the officers failed to respond to his explanation that their precinct captain had agreed not to ticket cars there belonging to Pride employees. (Barry did not know that the officers were members of a roving patrol unit composed exclusively of Special Operations Division officers, who owed no allegiance to precinct commanders.)

SOD officer Randy Lehman wrote the ticket and placed it on the car's windshield, the reports said. Barry ripped up the ticket and threw it in Lehman's face. Lehman tried to arrest the Pride leader for depositing trash. Then, according to Captain Charles Monroe, deputy commander of the Special Operations Division, Barry "struck [Lehman] on the throat with his hand and grabbed the officer's shirt and ripped the front pocket out."

At that point, said Monroe, Barry was joined by three other Pride employees who "assaulted both officers." He said a dozen more policemen arrived. With about 50 other blacks looking on, some yelling, "Kill them! Kill them!" Monroe said, Barry and the others struggled with the officers before finally being subdued. He said Barry and his three co-workers were loaded into a police paddy wagon and hauled away.

At the 13th Precinct station house, Captain Monroe said, one of the prisoners tried to escape. He said Barry then "jumped" an officer who was trying to stop the fleeing prisoner. This started a free-for-all, the deputy commander said, and during the melée SOD officer Paul McConnell "struck Barry one time on the head with a blackjack to subdue him." The blow sent Barry to the hospital for treatment of scalp lacerations and a possible brain concussion.

After being treated for his injuries and released on $2,100 bail on charges of disorderly conduct, depositing trash, and two counts of assaulting an officer, Barry wasted no time in putting his own spin on these events. The very next morning, Edward A. Hailes, president of the D.C. branch of the NAACP, issued a statement implying the police were at fault.

"In addition to demanding an investigation," Hailes said, "we demand an immediate suspension of the officers involved pending an outcome of the investigation of this incident. We request a reply to those demands within 24 hours."

On the same morning Barry, wearing a bandage on his head, arrived in the D.C. council chamber at the District Building, where about 300 Pride workers and students from predominantly black Federal City College were waiting for him.

"We have just declared war on the police department and this city," Barry declared to cheers and clenched-fist Black Power salutes. "The police are like mad dogs. If it can happen to me, it can happen to any black man [in the city]. We must unite together, fight together and die together."

A short time later Mayor Walter Washington, who had been meeting in his District Building office with one of Barry's attorneys, Howard University professor Frank Reeves, announced he would conduct an official investigation into the incident. Reeves emphasized to reporters that the inquiry would be separate from any that might be conducted by the police department. Walter Washington never released his findings.

As Barry's supporters left the building, several reportedly became disruptive, breaking glass bottles against a stairwell and trying unsuccessfully to set an American flag ablaze. Outside they shouted obscenities, pushed and shoved white pedestrians, and punched a news vendor in the face. They stole bouquets from a flower vendor and a carton of beer from a station wagon parked outside a market. Once again Barry had shown what could happen when his followers got angry enough at the way he was being treated. He would have to wait nearly a year, however, for a chance to vindicate himself legally of the charges he faced.

By August 1969, 15 months after the OEO announced its plan for a pilot police precinct in Shaw, no such project had materialized. Meanwhile, the Metropolitan Police Department announced a plan to divide the city's old precincts into six larger administrative areas called "districts." Upon learning this, Barry demanded, and received, a meeting with acting public safety director Charles Duncan and Mayor Washington. He was concerned that the redistricting would, in a single stroke, wipe out the political base he had worked to build in the 13th Precinct, which had only half as many residents as the expanded district. However, while these top city officials apparently were willing to try to placate Barry, they refused to ask the police department to change its reorganization plan.

"Just say the war is on," Barry melodramatically told reporters as he left the meeting.

The first battle of that war was waged not against city authorities, however, but against fellow residents of Shaw. In September Barry and some followers raided the Garrison Elementary School at 12th and S streets, NW, where Shaw residents on the mayorally appointed planning committee had gathered to draft a plan for electing the board of directors of the Pilot Police Precinct Project. Only minutes after the forum began, Barry, backed by his cohorts, strode to the podium and seized the microphone.

"We've got to come together and fight this thing [the pilot project] until we can get control of it," he announced to the startled participants.

When the parley's moderator, Gladys Harris, attempted to regain control, she was shouted down by Barry's followers, who began chanting slogans. The meeting quickly degenerated into pandemonium—with some participants vocalizing their support for Barry while others hurled invectives at him. Police officers on the scene ordered the unruly crowd to disperse after a female Barry supporter slapped one officer in the face.

The same month that Barry took over the elementary school meeting, he staged a bizarre confrontation with project director Robert Shellow and an assistant at their offices in the basement of the Roosevelt Hotel on 16th Street, NW. After holding a press conference outside, Barry led about 20 supporters into the building, where they confronted Shellow and staff member Russ Morgan. Shellow tried to talk to them but left with Morgan after they began cursing and shouting him down. This time Barry added a new twist to his confrontation methods by staging a mock trial of Shellow, Morgan, and acting public safety director Charles Duncan by a "people's revolutionary court."

After a two-hour "trial," complete with a "judge," witnesses, "bailiff," "prosecutors," and a "defense counsel"

(Russ Morgan, who later returned to his office, was allowed to play this role), the officials were found "guilty" of "defrauding the black community" and misappropriating black people's money. Shellow, Duncan, and Morgan were all sentenced to "resign" their posts.

Barry's guerrilla theater was dramatic, but it did not please everyone in the newly reconstituted Third District, where more than 100,000 people were crowded into an area roughly one-and-a-half miles square. Some residents were openly hostile to Barry and his followers, whose tactics they found rude, even threatening.

"There are a lot of moderate and older Negroes who are boxed in on this issue by the militants," one community leader told *Star* reporter John Fialka. "They don't want to give orders to the police, but they're afraid to speak out."

"There should be some way to keep the militants out," Willis Jackson, district deputy of the Improved Benevolent and Protective Order of Elks of the World, told the same reporter three months after the takeover of the project's office. "They don't give the people a chance to be heard. They cuss and carry on so the older people get up and walk out."

"Most people are afraid of those folks," said Gladys Harris, the woman who earlier had been driven from the podium by Barry supporters at Garrison Elementary School. "They bring their people in and start this profanity and the mothers and the grandmothers leave. We have a lot of people who will never come back again."

"They complain about rights," said Jose Roig, a leader of the Third District's growing Hispanic community. "Yet when the time comes that they violate other people's rights, they don't see the distinction. If there ever is an election [for the pilot precinct's board], they will be defeated, make no mistake about that."

Mrs. Lee Aiken, white president of the Swann Street Block Club, echoed Roig's sentiments when she told Fialka, "Barry uses disruptive tactics. The people who are for this are rather timid souls and are not about to face down that sort of thing. But an election will be a different matter."

A former head of the District's NAACP chapter, Eugene Davidson, was equally adamant about excluding Barry. "If it comes to the city losing $1 million [in OEO funds earmarked for the project]," he told Fialka, "or giving control of it to Marion Barry, I think we should lose the money."

Despite such strong opposition to Barry, in February 1970 candidates of the People's Party, which he headed, won a majority of seats on the 27-member board. They were helped by voter apathy: only about 2,000 of the Third District's more than 100,000 residents bothered to cast ballots. Barry, who still received more votes than anyone else, was named chairman of the board, which quickly adopted his aggressive brand of politics.

According to Stephen Romansky, an OEO project director for the renamed Pilot Police District Project from 1969 to 1971, Barry quickly demonstrated that he was more than just an agitator.

"He would come to meetings incredibly well prepared," recalls Romansky, who later moved to Boston and became a psychiatrist. "He had all the information, he would bring notes, he really knew what was happening in the community, and he was very committed [to the lower-income residents]."

In May, when the OEO announced it would grant the board only half the project's allocated funds—making payment of the balance conditional on how the board performed during its first six months—the board called the move "incredible and unacceptable." Barry personally delivered a letter to OEO director Donald Rumsfeld, in which the board complained that the agency's decision in effect "relegates the board to everlasting proposal drafting." On the same day, Barry and some other board members staged a press conference in the project's 16th Street offices, saying the board was deeply concerned about the proposed budget cuts.

Rumsfeld quickly agreed to meet with the dissident board members, who also were backed by Mayor Washington. The mayor, who had worked with Barry on solving a number of youth crises, said he would not sign the project funding agreement with OEO unless its elected board, led by Barry, first endorsed it.

Faced with a potentially embarrassing situation in which the whole purpose of the grant would be vitiated by soured relations with the D.C. government, Rumsfeld backed down. The OEO released the funds for the full 12 months. Once again Barry had mau-maued a federal agency and won.

In April 1970, only two months after the confrontation with Rumsfeld, Barry faced another showdown—with a judge and jury in U.S. District Court for his alleged assault, 11 months earlier, on two D.C. policemen who were ticketing cars outside Pride headquarters.

Barry's attorney, Herbert O. Reid, Sr., 54, who would serve in future Barry mayoral cabinets and become over the years what one observer accurately described as "the closest thing to a mentor in Barry's life," argued in court that no one had tried to flee the police station house where a brawl had allegedly broken out on May 13, 1969, the day Barry and several other Pride workers were arrested. Reid contended that police had contrived the tale to cover up their unprovoked beating of his client. To buttress the defense case, he introduced photographs of the altercation taken at the station house by a Pride photographer.

After a day and a half of deliberations, the jury sent a note to the judge saying: "We, members of the jury for criminal case No. 1036–69, are not able to reach a unanimous decision on the two counts for Mr. Marion S. Barry, Jr."

Unofficial reports said the vote was nine to three to convict Barry for assaulting Officer Randy Lehman in the alley beside Pride headquarters and six to six on starting the station house brawl. A new trial date was set, but the U.S. Attorney's Office decided to drop the case.

The same month he stepped out of his latest legal noose, Barry almost stepped into another one—once more over the dubious issue of parking tickets. This time Barry confronted no less important a figure than America's first lady, Patricia Nixon.

President Richard Nixon's wife was attending a luncheon at the exclusive Congressional Club, just across the street from Pride headquarters, when Barry, Mary Treadwell, and about

75 Pride workers invaded the club to protest the special privileges congressional wives were given by police while double-parking outside the club.

"I want to talk to you!" shouted Barry as Mrs. Nixon was escorted downstairs by the club's president, Mrs. Winston Prouty, wife of the Republican senator from Vermont.

Mrs. Nixon, thinking Barry meant her, smiled and waved to the angry, mustachioed man in the club's lobby before being whisked away by Secret Service agents to a waiting limousine.

Barry quickly turned his attention to Mrs. Prouty. "If we double-park, we get tickets and are fined," he complained. "If you can do it, we want to do it, too," he said.

Then he lectured the senator's wife on larger issues. "We're interested in economics, not politics," Barry said. "It's difficult for the boys we work with to understand the laws when lawmakers' wives break the law."

Mrs. Prouty, a middle-aged woman with a mane of wavy white hair, was anything but intimidated. "Maybe the husbands of those here will think about that when they make appropriations," she snapped.

"You're not threatening us, are you?" Barry asked.

"I didn't say that," Mrs. Prouty retorted. "I thought you were talking about not having special privilege."

The confrontation ended when Mrs. Prouty promised to make an announcement asking the hundreds of luncheon guests to move their double-parked cars.

"Let's call a truce today," she suggested, then promised to look into the possibility of using a neighborhood parking lot in the future to handle the overflow of cars, instead of having people double-park in front of the club.

Barry, Treadwell, and the Pride workers retreated. No one had been arrested. No one had gotten hurt. They had made their point peacefully to the elite audience they had commandeered.

In July 1970 the pilot project faced its first real test when Third District police clashed with Black Panthers at their "community center" near the corner of 17th and U streets, NW. Two policemen and at least one Panther were injured after police broke up a loud singing session outside the three-story brick townhouse that was within shouting distance of Pride headquarters. The officers arrested 20 Panthers and seized five unregistered guns, including one deemed a machine gun under D.C. law. Several Panthers complained that the police had unnecessarily roughed them up, destroyed personal property, and beaten one Panther at the Third District station house.

As chairman of the citizens' advisory board, Barry pledged an investigation. His statement to reporters was markedly devoid of the inflammatory rhetoric he had used in the past to brand police as "mad dog" members of a racist "occupation army."

"Our purpose is to find out exactly what happened," he said. "We just want to make sure the police department is doing its job and that our people [the Panthers] are cooperating with them." Barry said the board would reserve its judgment as to possible wrongdoing by either side until it had completed its investigation.

The city's top prosecutor for misdemeanors, acting D.C. Corporation Counsel Francis Murphy, apparently feeling the heat of the board's investigation, dropped disorderly conduct charges against 19 Panthers. He told a reporter that "the facts didn't indicate enough evidence to avoid a reasonable doubt" of their guilt. Felony charges lodged against another Panther for possessing a machine gun also were dropped by the U.S. attorney.

By September 1970 Barry's relations with police had improved so dramatically he was asked to help in a police recruitment drive for minority officers. Barry recorded public service announcements inviting young blacks to apply for jobs on the force. They were played on several of D.C.'s black radio stations. Twenty-two minority recruits responded, of whom 12 passed the department's written exam.

The recruitment spots also brought a less positive reaction, when local black militants reportedly criticized Barry "for saying nice things about being a policeman."

Barry let the matter slide. He finally had learned when to keep silent in the interest of promoting his political future. There would be time enough to get into public showdowns—if the issue was important enough—once he had gained more power. He had proven he could win an election, however parochial and limited.

Almost immediately, he set his sights on the D.C. school board race coming up in the fall of 1971.

13

A NATURAL POLITICIAN

U ntil 1974, when the first mayor and council members were elected under the District's new home rule charter, a seat on the Board of Education of the District of Columbia was the *only* elective office for which a District resident could compete—and that had been true only since 1968, when Congress deigned to allow District residents to select their own school system overseers. In the off-year election of 1971 dozens of candidates—not all of them experienced or even interested in education (Keith Jones of the Socialist Workers Party said right out front if he won he would use his seat as a platform to "stop the war in Vietnam")—lined up for the school board race.

Although a relative newcomer, Marion Barry was still one of the best-known candidates for the at-large seat held by board president Anita Allen (the remaining 10 seats were held by members elected from each of the city's eight wards). His leadership of Youth Pride, Incorporated—often at the center of controversy, but seen by many blacks as a positive force in the city—and his chairmanship of the Pilot Police District Project had given Barry a distinctly high profile, especially among black residents.

To run for his first citywide elective office, Barry shed his dashiki and donned a coat and tie, telling a reporter: "Of course, I've changed. The whole nation has changed. I'm a situationist. I do what is necessary for the situation."

But while Barry's dress had transformed to reflect his desired role change, his ego and militant rhetoric had not. From the start the Pride leader displayed a bristling confidence that bordered on arrogance. First, he announced he would run a slate of candidates from across the city—a move designed to ensure being named president of the board by a majority of

167

seat holders. After failing to sign up enough allies, Barry approached Allen directly, offering to run as a ward candidate, rather than at-large (he obviously believed he could take the seat away from her), if she would promise to anoint him as the next board president.

"I told him no," said Allen, a career employee of the U.S. Office of Education. "I was not prepared to make that kind of deal."

Nor was Allen impressed by Barry's activist credentials. She said the man who wanted her position might know how to organize protests and give young people jobs, but he "doesn't know two cents' worth about the D.C. school system." Allen also charged that Barry and his supporters "are not interested in the public schools, but in control of the city and the local Democratic party." She said the men who had endorsed Barry—former appointed city council chairman and local hardware magnate John Hechinger, attorney and former head of the U.S. Equal Employment Opportunity Commission Clifford Alexander, and D.C. Democratic Central Committee chairman Bruce Terris—were would-be political kingmakers who "need someone whose name is known [to run against her], not someone who knows anything about education." She added, presciently—in 1971 there *was* no higher office in the District to which to aspire—that her challenger was only interested in the school board as "some sort of political office, a steppingstone to somewhere."

Barry brushed off Allen's criticisms, while castigating her for allegedly presiding over a divisive board known more for its "personality clashes" than its effectiveness in helping the city's 140,000 students, who were stuck in a system which was, and still is 20 years later, in shameful disarray. He accused Allen of being "rigid, doctrinaire, and dogmatic" in guiding the board, whose members were then fighting over whether or not to retain D.C. school superintendent Hugh Scott, who had held the job less than a year. But when asked about his own intentions, the Pride leader was vague, saying only that District schools "are not doing what public education is supposed to be doing—teaching students marketable skills with

which they can become valuable community members."
Ironically, Barry did specifically recommend the instruction
of both students and teachers about illegal drugs, which were
invading the schools. Some teachers, Barry quipped, couldn't
differentiate between the smell of marijuana and "an off-brand
cigarette."

According to a former girlfriend of Barry's who still lives in
Washington, Barry was using the drug himself at the time.
She recalled an evening together when they smoked marijuana
so strong that they both fell asleep in the front seat of Barry's
Volkswagen bug and didn't wake up until dawn. The former
girlfriend said that after their relationship ended, Barry still
kept calling her, asking, " 'Can you get me an ounce? Can
you get me an ounce?' " When her pot supply dried up, she
said, "he stopped calling."

Barry got a big boost for his school board candidacy when
D.C.'s nonvoting congressional delegate, the Reverend Walter
Fauntroy, formally endorsed him.

"I am convinced," said Fauntroy, a civil rights leader and
former neighborhood activist who, after winning a congressional seat earlier in the year, had become the city's most
powerful elected politician, "that our educational system needs
a man of [Barry's] strength and talent to bring order out of
chaos....Marion Barry represents hope for change and I urge
your support."

Although Fauntroy was a minister and enjoyed strong
church support in his successful delegate bid, he was unable
to persuade most black religious leaders to back Barry for the
school board. The committee of 100 ministers, which claimed
75,000 D.C. parishoners, and the Baptist Ministers Conference,
which boasted more than 100,000, both backed Allen, whose
husband, the Reverend Willie B. Allen, was a Baptist minister.
When Barry invited 400 ministers to hear his views at a candidate luncheon, only 20 showed up, including the Reverend
David Eaton, pastor of All Souls Unitarian Church, of which
Barry was a member.

"I've been hearing some mean things about Marion Barry,"
Eaton told the other clerics. "I hear people say that he knows

pimps and whores and dope addicts. Well, I know pimps and whores and dope addicts, too, and so should you. If we understand what the gospel is all about, that's who we ought to be talking with. And we ought to be telling people that if they understand what the gospel and humanism is all about, they should vote for Mr. Barry.''

Not everyone held such a lofty view of the Pride leader. Former school board member and community activist Julius Hobson denounced Barry for allegedly being ''tied up with a Daley-type machine.'' Hobson was referring to the late Chicago mayor, Richard Daley, who back then dominated the Windy City's politics. He also took a shot at Barry's comparatively large campaign war chest of $10,000—more than four times what Anita Allen had raised. ''I am sure that the education and welfare of D.C. school children will be affected adversely by politicians who purchase their elected offices,'' he grumbled.

His three opponents also accused Barry of plagiarizing their campaign speeches. ''He said just what I do,'' Anita Allen charged about Barry's embrace of an experimental reading plan being introduced to the schools—a plan Barry originally had opposed. '' 'All normal children can learn if they are properly taught.' How can he object to the plan?'' Allen said Barry had stolen so many ideas and phrases from her that ''I've had to throw away my standard speech because everything I call for he says too.''

D.C. schoolteacher Ira Mosley, another at-large candidate, said Barry had stolen his analogy of the 1969 firing of Redskins football team coach Otto Graham because of the team's poor record to the need to assemble a ''winning team'' on a reconstituted school board. Mosley also accused Barry of being a ''hoodlum'' with an extremist background, and of having used profanity in his speeches to public school students.

Barry, who admitted sending an assistant with a tape recorder to tape speeches by Allen, Mosley, and other candidates, defended his use of their phrasing, sometimes word for word. ''What's wrong with that?'' he jibed. ''That's sophistication.''

If he'd been a candidate for a national office and done the same thing, Barry would have been laughed off the stage. But he wasn't. During this time of nascent local politics in the District, marked more than occasionally by such permissiveness and absurdity, a candidate, if he was popular enough, could not only steal speeches and ideas but he could even have few ideas of his own—and still win big. On November 3 Barry coasted to victory against Allen and his two other opponents, winning 58 percent of the vote in an election that saw nearly twice as many voters go to the polls as in the previous one. The turnout only sharpened the perception that Barry and his backers were creating a political "machine."

D.C. Council member Joseph Yeldell, who had run second to Fauntroy in the D.C. delegate race, was not impressed. "Without trying to discount what Barry may do [in his new post]," Yeldell observed, "any reasonable candidate against [the unpopular] Mrs. Allen would have won."

Mayor Walter Washington, on the other hand, was convinced that Barry's victory presaged a sea change in District politics. "From now on, winning elections will take three ingredients," he predicted. "Organization, funds, and hard work. There's a very definite move from the civic organization pattern to the straight political pattern."

At a victory rally, Barry told his supporters to hold him "accountable for what I do or don't do. If I don't produce . . . I'll quit."

The *Washington Post* welcomed Barry's victory, saying the Pride leader and veteran activist "brings proven political savvy to this job—which could be just the plus that has been missing up to now." It called on Barry to help "end factionalism and arguments over plans, motives and personalities that—fairly or unfairly—have damaged the image of the school system."

Barry immediately went to work to increase his leverage on the board. He endorsed several candidates for ward run-off elections, knowing that if they won they would owe him their vote for board president. The strategy proved even more effective than Barry could have hoped. In January 1972 he was unanimously endorsed for president by his 11 board colleagues.

He pledged to "put [his own] ego last and put [the board's] political operations behind." Then he added, "The changes aren't going to be made without pain and effort, but I believe everyone on this board is committed to putting the children first."

The following month, during his first formal meeting with U.S. Congress members who oversaw the District's budget, Barry seemed more concerned about the perks of his new post than the students he pledged to help. He asked members of both the Senate and House appropriations committees to reassign two chauffeur-driven cars that had once been at the board's disposal. "This is basically a volunteer board," Barry contended. "Many members don't work, and can't afford to operate a car." The committees, citing budgetary reasons, turned down his request.

It was now time for Barry to get down to the business of running the school board and promoting his own political agenda. According to veteran D.C. school board member Calvin Lockridge, Barry was quickly becoming a master at both pursuits. "I remember [then-school board member] Hilda Mason talking about the fact that they were getting ready for a budget committee meeting," recalled Lockridge, "and he knew nothing about the budget. She said he learned the budget overnight."

Lockridge said that the 37-year-old Pride leader "came on the board because he was looking to be accepted. He was looking to increase his visibility and his power in the city, and he wanted to make some particular changes. He wanted to open up the system to the ones who had been left out, to put pressure on the business community to be more responsive to the residents. I think he saw the city being run as a political plum for southern congressmen, and he thought it should be in the control of local citizens. And he was trying to make some inroads [to change that]."

Six months after Barry took over leadership of the school board, the city's school children still were no better off, but Barry had found, among other things, a bully pulpit from which to launch fresh attacks against the city's white establishment—*and*, in a new and unexpected twist on racial politics, against the white-dominated national antiwar movement as well.

On June 16, 1972, former antiwar activist Barry led a group of 60 black community activists who condemned the anti-Vietnam War movement as "racist." In a press conference at All Souls Unitarian Church Barry charged that, among other things, the mass demonstrations in Washington, which had helped turn the country against the war, were led almost exclusively by whites, with only "token" blacks in leadership roles. He charged that the antiwar movement used blacks and other minorities "as a drawing card to legitimize the racist goals of the existing peace movement" and announced a "summit conference" on the alleged problem for June 22, the same day antiwar protestors planned to assemble tens of thousands of women and children to form a human chain around the U.S. Capitol.

One of the white organizers of the "Ring Around the Congress," Edith Villastrigo, called the black group's attack "deliberate sabotage." She said, "It is not realistic, it is not right for them to condemn the movement as racist," a charge that seemed particularly bizarre since antiwar activists long had charged that the U.S. government was "racist" in killing Vietnamese and sending young black American soldiers to their deaths in disproportionate numbers.

Villastrigo's sentiments were shared by several well-known black female leaders of the antiwar protest, including Coretta Scott King, Fanny Lou Hamer of Mississippi, and Willie J. Hardy of Washington. They went ahead with the demonstration.

The use of race to challenge the antiwar movement represented a dramatic shift for Barry who, a year earlier, along with community activist Julius Hobson, had used the occasion of the third anniversary of Martin Luther King's assassination to stage a series of antiwar protests. Echoing the late civil rights leader, Barry then had called for an end to the decade-long war "so we can spend the money [now used for the war] at home."

But by mid-1972, apparently, times had changed, or at least Barry concluded that a more militant racial stance was now called for. Meanwhile, he used his ascendancy to the school board to challenge the powerful, white-dominated *Washington Post*, which had been, for the most part, unusually supportive of him. Responding to a photo caption of black school children attending a concert at the Kennedy arts center that read, "Mozart, But Dreaming of the Jackson Five," Barry accused the paper of "bias" and "shallow thinking." He ended his letter to the editor—which the *Post* published—by saying, "Black people can dig both James Brown and Mozart or Beethoven."

Though relatively trivial, the incident nevertheless revealed Barry's willingness to take on anyone in town, no matter what the move might cost him in terms of white political support, if he felt a slight had been made to his race.

Racial politics came up again at the end of Barry's first year as board president. This time white school board member Bardyl Tirana, fed up with what he considered to be Barry's grandstanding, circulated memos urging his colleagues to replace Barry in January when they voted for a new president. All but one board member stuck by Barry, who responded that Tirana "wants to be a power broker, and when he finds that he cannot control us (Barry and superintendent Scott), he then attacks us. This is the typical pseudo-liberal reaction to strong black male leadership."

Barry need not have played the race card to trump Tirana—he was easily re-elected school board president in 1973 and was able to persuade the board to retain Scott as public school superintendent—but his move had once again shown how effectively he could use the race issue to mau-mau his political opponents, and how quickly he resorted to such an extreme when challenged by a white man.

By August 1973, however, even Barry was ready to replace Hugh Scott, who had not been able to solve the problems in the city's perennially troubled schools. But when it came time to pick Scott's successor, the board once again split into resolutely intransigent factions. Barry's faction backed the Bronx, New York, educator Andrew Donaldson, who was the uncle of Ivanhoe Donaldson, a tall, thin, extremely shrewd

New York policeman's son and former SNCC worker who had become Barry's chief political advisor. Barry's opponents, led by Charles Cassell, backed Barbara Sizemore, a strong-minded Chicagoan who shared Cassell's grass-roots approach to education.

When the two sides squared off, Cassell, surprisingly, won most of the skirmishes by outmaneuvering selection committee chairman Barry on such issues as whether or not to hold public interviews, public disclosure of the candidates' names, and the selection of finalists for the superintendent's job. Cassell used familiar Barry tools against him in the fight: he leaked information to the press about whom the board was considering for the job, and he and his supporters publicly criticized Barry for his alleged sexism in opposing Sizemore. But when the dust cleared at the end of the fight, Barry's candidate, Andrew Donaldson, was still among the three finalists.

At this point Barry, in one observer's words, had "sniffed the political winds" carefully enough to know that a majority of the board's constituents favored Sizemore. Claiming that he too had preferred the Chicago educator all along, he abandoned Donaldson and cast the decisive vote for Sizemore on an evenly divided board. Then he took credit for selecting her, cleverly co-opting Cassell. Like any astute politician Barry had discovered that no political stance, no matter how hard-earned or ostensibly sacred, was exempt from abandonment when greater power could be obtained from such a move.

As it turned out, Barry's last-second switch to Sizemore paid handsome dividends. When he ran in the September 1974 Democratic primary for an at-large seat on the newly minted, 13-seat District of Columbia Council, Barry gathered more votes than anyone except the Reverend Douglas Moore. One observer speculated that women voters, pleased with Barry's choice of a female public school superintendent, helped him beat out Delano Lewis, a utility executive who trailed Barry by less than 3,000 votes.

Barry had intended to run for council chairman—what other post would do for this go-for-broke politician who had resigned from the school board in July to seek a seat on the first elected

District legislature in a century? But, after "sniffing the political winds" again (Mayor Washington indicated he would back the appointed council chairman, Sterling Tucker, in that race), Barry settled for a shot at one of two at-large seats designated for Democrats (there were four in all).

The general election in November was a mere formality in a city dominated by the Democratic party. In that same election black attorney and Democratic candidate Walter Washington, who had served as the District's first appointed mayor-commissioner, became its first elected mayor; black community activist Sterling Tucker also traded his presidential appointment for an elective title as city council chairman.

Once on the council Barry seemed to turn away from the strictly social agenda he had emphasized throughout his activist and school board days to focus on fiscal matters. But after winning the chairmanship of the council's powerful Finance and Revenue Committee by the friendly arm-twisting that typifies successful politics, he almost immediately introduced a bill to require all D.C. employees to live in the District. The move failed—among other things such a law would violate the home rule charter—but it won points from the many disgruntled D.C. residents who felt "outsiders" from the suburbs were taking away their jobs. (Their fears were, in fact, justified: as recently as 1989, according to D.C. government figures, 60 percent of all income earned in the District is earned by workers who live outside the city. And, because of the congressionally drafted home rule charter, none of that income is taxable.)

Realizing he had found a fulcrum with enormous leverage in his committee post, Barry quickly proposed a series of fiscal measures, including cuts in the D.C. budget that supposedly would not reduce city services, and legalized gambling—tongue-in-cheek, he proposed holding chariot races along Pennsylvania Avenue between the White House and the Capitol, in addition to casinos and a lottery, to raise badly needed revenues.

In May, Barry proposed "far-ranging" hearings into local real estate speculation, charging, not without justification, that white developers were destroying low-income neighborhoods to make way for gentrified office buildings and apartment complexes. The same month he and fellow council member Douglas Moore proposed that the District government invest tens of millions of dollars it would soon have for deposit only in banks that pledged to aid minorities. The proposal was shot down by the city's white budget director, who said that "other tools should be used to stimulate the kinds of social goals you have in mind." But Barry again had managed to portray himself as a hero to the city's disadvantaged blacks.

He raised his pro-black profile even higher in a confrontation with the mayor over city hiring practices. On the eve of a council hearing to examine the issue, Barry wrote to Walter Washington accusing his administration of allowing "incredibly racist and sexist" hiring practices to exist in the city's police department. Washington got so angry at Barry he refused to permit Barry and other council members to question his aides in depth on the matter at a scheduled hearing, and he publicly accused Barry of seeking purposely and irresponsibly to "arouse racial passions" with his unsubstantiated charges.

In fact the Metropolitan Police Department had undertaken a vigorous minority recruitment effort that already had made it 50 percent black. According to a police official the force's 320 female officers probably also made the District the distaff police capital of the country. Barry may or may not have been aware of these facts when he launched his attack on the mayor. But the confrontation won him points with militant black residents who considered the incumbent mayor a tool of the white establishment.

During the next three years, Barry shifted tactics frequently, but whether confronting the mayor or some other entrenched D.C. power or schmoozing them, he kept churning out proposals for boosting the District's income—by among other means, imposing a commuter tax—and redistributing some of that additional revenue to the poor. The *Post*, which Barry had accused of "bias" and "shallow thinking" during his school board days, swallowed its pride and praised the Revenue and Finance Committee chairman in July 1975, as a "savvy street protestor of the 1960s, now considered by fellow council members to be one of that body's influential and knowledgeable mainstays.''

When the same newspaper revealed that the Metropolitan Police Department, aided by the Central Intelligence Agency, had surveiled Barry, fellow council members Sterling Tucker, Douglas Moore, and David Clarke, and other local civil rights and antiwar activists during the 1960s—reportedly compiling files on, among other things, their drug and sex habits (the department claimed it had destroyed the files), Barry said he was ''appalled that the police had nothing better to do with taxpayers' money than watch those of us in the civil rights movement who were pushing hard against the system,'' but hardly surprised. Nor, Barry indicated, was he worried that such police state tactics would be used against him in the future. (According to the *Washington Star*, Barry's name also appeared on a ''master computer list'' of some 5,500 black activists compiled by the federal government during the late 1960s and early 1970s).

''I guarantee you they won't keep any files on me now—at least not legally,'' Barry said. ''We've got budget control'' over the police department.

Barry's flip comment showed how far he had come from his activist days when his rhetoric was more militant but his real power limited. He remained wary of the police—using his future mayoral powers to virtually control the department—but, for at least the next decade, he no longer had to fear them. In fact, he and his wife, Mary Treadwell, already were able to thumb their noses at police with virtual impunity whenever they got parking tickets. The *Washington Star* reported in June 1975 that police in the neighborhood in which the Barrys lived had failed to impound Barry's Volvo, which had 26 outstanding tickets on which Barry owed $390. ''With 26 tickets, the car should have been towed away,'' Captain Joseph Mazur of the police department's special operations division said of Barry's Volvo. The *Star* said Treadwell had accumulated 11 tickets on her Mercedes for total unpaid fines of $215. It said the police cracked down on the pair only after Barry had successfully cut Mayor Walter Washington's proposed 1976 budget. For the time being, at least, the police answered to Washington, not Barry, although it was clear that rank-and-file officers were protective of the city council member and his wife, who was widely respected in the black community as the leader of Youth Pride, Incorporated.

In November 1976 two years after being elected, Barry and several other council members who had drawn short straws were forced to relinquish their seats and, if they wanted to stay on the council, compete in an off-year election. The move was made to stagger elections so every council member wouldn't come up for re-election every four years. Shortly before the race, which he won handily, Barry, then 40, told the *Post*'s Stephen Lynton he was anxious to win re-election to a council seat, but that his real ambitions lay elsewhere. Someday, he said, he would have Walter Washington's job. "The only question," he told Lynton, "is when."

14

IN THE POWER SEAT

Marion Barry had to wait two more years before he landed his dream job. In the meantime he almost got killed. On the afternoon of March 9, 1977, a small but well-armed band of Hanafi Muslims had just taken over the fifth floor of the District Building, where the mayor's office and D.C. Council chamber are located, when the unsuspecting D.C. Council member entered an elevator on the ground floor. He was on his way, he thought, to a scheduled meeting of the council's judiciary committee.

"There were two guards on the elevator," Barry recalled from his bed at the Washington Hospital Center the day after he was shot by an unidentified Hanafi. "One of them said, 'There's trouble on the fifth floor, so you better watch out.' When we got off the elevator they walked toward the council offices and started to pull their guns out of their holsters. I stopped in the hall to talk to someone about a bill that's coming up for a hearing. Then I heard two shots. I didn't know where the hell they were coming from. I dived to the right. And then I felt a hot, burning sensation in my chest. I knew I'd been shot."

Barry picked himself up and staggered, clutching his bloody sternum, into the D.C. Council chamber, where he collapsed again. Several people, crouching behind furniture, managed to reach him and tried to stop the bleeding. "The worst part was I didn't know my condition," Barry recalled. "I kept calling for a doctor. People grabbed me and took off my coat."

He had been hit an inch above his heart by a shotgun pellet, which apparently had richocheted from a distance, reducing its impact.

Two D.C. fire department paramedics, led by a young police lieutenant, Isaac Fulwood, Jr., braved the fusillade to drag the city council member to safety. Twelve years later Barry would appoint Fulwood chief of police. Altogether it took 23 minutes to evacuate Barry, who was strapped to a litter and carried down a stairwell to safety. The wounded politician told reporters before being rushed to the hospital by ambulance: "Nobody wants to die, but in this violence-torn society, with all our problems, you expect that sometimes in life somebody's gonna do some things, and so you just, uh, you just take it."

At the Washington Hospital Center, Dr. Howard Champion, who led the surgical team that operated on Barry, tersely summed up the city council member's prognosis: "He's a very lucky man. The bullet stopped in front of his heart without penetrating the bone, and there was no injury to the vital organ."

Other victims of the tripartite terrorist attack—Hanafis also seized the Islamic Center and B'Nai B'rith headquarters in Northwest Washington in a vaguely defined "revenge" mission—were not so lucky. Howard University radio reporter Maurice Williams was shot dead in the same hallway where Barry was wounded. Another man, taken hostage at B'Nai B'rith, was paralyzed. All 12 suspects were later convicted of multiple felonies related to the takeovers, but their reign of terror had left its bloody imprint on the city, and on Barry, who was left puzzling over the irony of nearly being killed by a fellow black. "I've been in all kinds of situations," he mused, shortly after being wounded. "I was in Mississippi in civil rights marches and everywhere else, but this kind of thing never happened before. I didn't know who did it, and I don't know why."

The incident may ultimately have helped Barry politically, according to one veteran observer of the District's political scene. "If he hadn't been shot," opined a former Capitol Hill reporter who first met Barry in the late 1960s, "he'd never have gotten elected mayor."

Indeed Barry barely won the Democratic mayoral primary race 18 months after being shot, squeezing by D.C. council chairman Sterling Tucker and Mayor Walter Washington by one and two percentage points, respectively. But his victory was due less to sympathy and more to good, old-fashioned politicking, voters' disenchantment with the incumbent mayor—whom Barry accused during his campaign of "bumbling and bungling in an inefficiently run city government"—and a strong endorsement by the *Washington Post*. Ironically, white middle-class voters, who saw in the former activist a hope for getting the moribund, debt-ridden city government moving again, put Barry over the top.

During his campaign Barry raised more than $100,000, much of it from wealthy white businessmen he once had tarred as "moneylord merchants." Why the sudden change of heart on both sides? Simple. With his eyes on the District's highest political prize, council member Barry had introduced a series of bills reducing the tax liability of developers and merchants operating in the District. The Metropolitan Board of Trade was so pleased with what Barry was doing it threw a $500-a-plate luncheon for him, raising $60,000 in an afternoon. Barry's Machiavellian moves won some former enemies to his side and filled up his campaign chest. But they brought harsh criticism from others, including fellow council member Douglas Moore, who scornfully proclaimed Barry a "tool of the landlords."

Tool or not, by mid-October, Barry was the runaway favorite to win the general election against Republican Arthur Fletcher, a conservative black attorney who had served in both the Nixon and Ford administrations. In addition to the white business community's financial support, Barry won key endorsements from the District's police, firefighter, and teachers unions and from the Gertrude Stein Club, representing the politically influential gay community. He also picked up support from women voters, who remembered his backing of Barbara Sizemore for public schools superintendent, and from young black and white activists. But he failed to garner much support from poor blacks, who, at that point, saw him as a friend of the white establishment, or from more conservative members of the black middle class, senior citizens, and churchmen, many of whom came from families that had been in the District for generations and felt they'd gotten along just fine without the help of a man whom they viewed as a militant outsider.

Nevertheless, on November 7, 1978, a 42-year-old black man who as a child in the Deep South had once picked cotton for 30 cents an hour, decisively beat his well-to-do Republican rival to become mayor-elect of what he would later proudly call "the international capital of the world."

Two months later, on a rainy winter morning, a triumphant Barry rode from the Washington Hilton Hotel to the District Building in an open car with his third wife, Effi. Barry had married the tall, elegant, former airline stewardess, teacher, and city health inspector 11 months earlier. He had divorced Mary Treadwell the previous year. As the inaugural parade wound through the Adams Morgan and Shaw neighborhoods in Northwest Washington, making its way toward the 14th Street riot corridor, which it would follow downtown, it passed the headquarters of Youth Pride, Incorporated. The three-story building at the corner of 16th and U streets was decked with a black, red, and green Afro banner that read "You've come a long way, Marion. You've a long way to go, Mr. Mayor."

In a day replete with such symbols of black power and pride, Barry was sworn in by Supreme Court Justice Thurgood Marshall on the steps of the District Building, becoming the first black activist mayor of a major American city.

"I have one immediate objective," Barry announced in his inaugural speech, "and that is to bring all of the people of this city into a full governing partnership with my administration."

Later that evening, the mayor, surrounded by hundreds of friends and supporters, rocked with Effi to the music of Peaches and Herb in the Grand Ballroom of the Washington Hilton hotel. Before the dancing began, the Reverend Jesse Jackson lent his inimitable verbal touch to the occasion. "Marion Barry deserves to be the mayor of this city," the future Democratic presidential candidate declared. "He is flesh of our flesh and blood of our blood. . . . We know Marion from the trenches."

Barry responded, "I will never forget where I came from, and I will never forget the people who made me what I am."

Whether Barry ever lived up to his lofty words of January 2, 1979—the promises he made on the steps of the District Building, the gratitude he professed at the Hilton ballroom—is debatable, but at least in his first mayoral term he tried.

From the start, however, the going was tough. He inherited from Walter Washington an unwieldy bureaucracy, a budget deficit topping $100 million, and a government beholden for part of its revenues to the U.S. Congress, which, despite granting limited home rule in 1973, still could veto any decision taken by the D.C. Council and held approval power over the District's budget. Five months after Barry took office the House Appropriations subcommittee "stunned" the new mayor when it cut the annual federal payment to the District by more than $25 million. Barry had no alternative but to roll up his sleeves and get to work—not only to solve these problems, but to win the hearts and minds of those who could keep him in power long enough to make a difference.

During his first term he wooed the city's black clergy by funding church-sponsored programs in housing, nutrition, drug and youth counseling, and aid to the elderly. The churchmen, most of whom had supported Washington or Tucker in 1978, would stand behind Barry in future elections. The District's second elected mayor in a century also set aside 35 percent of all city contracts for minority firms, rewarding upwardly mobile blacks with contracts worth hundreds of millions. And Barry sorted out the city's chaotic financial picture well enough to get the General Accounting Office, which had declared D.C.'s accounts "unauditable," to change its mind. "We balanced the budget," Barry's first city administrator, Elijah Rogers, proudly recalled to the *Post* on the eve of Barry's departure from the District Building in January, 1991. "We did the first audit in 100 years. And we achieved seven or eight years of reducing the accumulated deficit."

Rogers was only one of the highly respected members of Barry's first-term administration, a team on which Barry conspicuously placed talented women, such as human services director Audrey Rowe, and Hispanics, such as chief purchasing officer Jose Gutierrez. Long before Jesse Jackson coined the term "rainbow coalition," Barry's administration offered a successful working model of just such an approach to governing. Their primary goal? To jump-start the city's moribund bureaucratic machinery and make it more responsive to everyone—especially those most vulnerable residents—the very young, the very old, and the very poor.

Some longtime Barry observers believe that the mayor was motivated not so much by altruism as by a desire to expand his political base. "He was purely a political animal," Barry's former director of intergovernmental relations, Dwight Cropp, told the *Post* in December 1990. "The majority of programs and policies initiated during the Barry administration were geared to expanding his constituency and [winning] reelection. With Marion, I could not separate out what he was legitimately interested in for the public good and what he was interested in for his political gain."

A perfect example of this ambiguity of purpose was the Marion Barry Youth Leadership Institute, which Barry founded shortly after he took up the reins of power in the District. Over the next dozen years the institute provided positive role models, guidance, and training to thousands of low-income youths. But not coincidentally, it also created a cadre of young voters loyal to Barry.

According to D.C. government employee and former *Post* reporter Edward Sargent, Barry viewed many of these youths as his protégés. "For many years after he'd hung up his dashiki," wrote Sargent in the April 1990 *Regardie's* magazine, "he carried himself like a jovial, paternalistic African prince, surrounding himself with young people, imparting his wisdom, trying to mold and shape them in his own image. He wanted to point black youth in the right direction. He wanted to teach them how to use discipline and strong character to rise above the odds, even though ultimately he couldn't show them by example."

At first Barry could and did show by example. He had barely become mayor when he purchased a $125,000 red brick colonial in the Hillcrest Heights neighborhood of Southeast Washington, whose predominantly black, working-class residents had spurned him in 1978. (They would back him strongly in future elections.) The move typified this quintessential politician who during his long, methodical climb to power had learned the importance of wooing his political enemies.

But the capital city's new mayor alienated many other potential constituents when, in an effort to cut the budget deficit, he laid off municipal workers and reduced city services, moves that affected the residents of poor black neighborhoods disproportionately. To head off criticism, the mayor rode a garbage truck one day to show he understood the working man's plight, and, when challenged by black students during a visit to the campus of the recently founded, predominantly black University of the District of Columbia, responded: "Let us not use the fury and anger we feel toward [the white-controlled] society and injustices, and turn it against each other."

Such clever public relations moves and rhetoric seemed enough to carry Barry through most first-term challenges, although he took several resounding hits from the press over such things as a discounted home mortgage from a D.C. savings and loan to whose board of directors his wife had recently been named, a lengthy trip to Africa of questionable relevance to D.C. residents, the $50,000 his administration spent near the end of Barry's first year in office for an advertising insert in *Time* magazine filled with praise and pictures of Barry, and the 1982 indictment of Barry's ex-wife Mary Treadwell and four other Youth Pride, Incorporated, administrators for allegedly stealing or misappropriating hundreds of thousands of dollars from the federal government and from tenants of a low-income apartment complex owned by PI Properties, a business spinoff of Pride. Treadwell was later convicted and imprisoned for these crimes. Barry was called before the grand jury to testify about any knowledge he might have about the scandal, including why he never became suspicious after Treadwell bought him a new Volvo and herself a Mercedes convertible plus expensive art and jewelry, and traveled frequently to the Caribbean—all on her $23,000 annual salary—but he was never indicted.

Unbeknownst to most of his constituents, by the end of his first term Barry was secretly on the verge of an even greater disaster. According to a knowledgeable source, a federal grand jury in the District, convened in 1982 by then-U.S. Attorney Joseph diGenova, was investigating allegations of illegal drug use and contract corruption by Barry, some of his friends, and members of his administration. Despite sworn testimony that included friends of the mayor's saying they had used cocaine with Barry or supplied him with the drug, the source said, "nothing was ever done" because the grand jurors seemed "intimidated" by the high positions of Barry and others whom they were being asked to indict. "They were your real quiet, law-abiding, upstanding, church-going type of people," the source said, and "the vast majority were black." The source said the grand jurors apparently concluded that "none of it [the allegations] was gonna stick anyway, so there was no point in doing anything." The source claimed, "They had all the evidence they would've needed [to indict Barry]."

According to the *Post*'s Juan Williams, the known scandals and Barry's first-term policy of "calloused realpolitik" regarding whom he *had* to help, rather than whom he *should* help "combined to take a tremendous toll on the poor in Washington." Williams said that during the city's 1980 budget crisis, for example, Barry, "in cold political terms, listed the groups he would protect in the face of budget cuts. 'I'll tell you who supported me [in the 1978 election]—the labor unions, police, firefighters and teachers, the gays and 30 percent of the black voters. I lost Ward 8 where all the black people live. They didn't support me.'"

Williams noted that the mayor "created a special office to address gay concerns and increased the police department budget, but scrapped a scheduled, long overdue welfare increase and cut the education budget, the two parts of the budget most important to poor blacks."

During a mayoral walking tour of a Northwest housing project, an unemployed 27-year-old resident seemed to speak for many of the city's disaffected poor when he told a reporter, "We expect more from a black mayor. He's supposed to have been through everything we've been through. He was something in the old days . . . in his dungarees and tennis shoes. Now he's back in a three-piece suit, and he's too good for home.''

While Barry seemed willing to risk alienating inner-city residents who shared his humble southern roots by imposing cost-cutting measures that unfairly burdened them, he was careful not to alienate more affluent Washingtonians with whom he had little in common, other than a shared interest in developing the downtown area. Still, the mayor never believed that the white business and real estate moguls whom he had provoked during his activist days had suddenly fallen in love with him. ''They are supporting me because I'm a good politician,'' he said in 1982. ''I know how to win [elections]. It don't matter if they don't like me. If people who don't like me vote for me [in the November, 1982, election], I'll be mayor again.''

As his first term drew to a close in the fall of 1982 Barry told reporters he had ''a surging self-confidence'' about winning re-election. He also said, ''I have some qualities that are unique in the mayor's office. One, I really care about the people.'' Citing his 20 years in public service, he contended unabashedly, ''It has been one constant demonstration of caring.''

The incumbent mayor faced eight opponents in the September 1982 Democratic primary. None could match his fundraising abilities or his use of the incumbency to commandeer the media.

In an interview shortly before the primary, Barry admitted he had made mistakes during his first term but declared that some of the District's problems were out of his control, like Congress's reduction of the federal payment and President Reagan's penurious social policies, which affected all U.S. cities. He said he understood the workings of the District government better than any of his challengers and boasted about his first-term accomplishments. ''I don't think any potential candidate can attack my record,'' he asserted, ''in terms of our efforts to fight crime, our efforts to clean up [the] summer jobs [program], our efforts to help senior citizens, or my handling of the financial situation.''

Barry's Democratic challengers attacked him every way they could but lost anyway. In the November general election Barry trounced his Republican opponent, black attorney E. Brooke Lee, Jr., winning 80 percent of the vote. He now had the mandate he wanted and an unprecedented opportunity to show how much he really cared about "the people."

During his second term, however, Barry seemed more concerned about building up downtown and fattening his campaign coffers than in improving the quality of life for Washington's poor. By expediting the process for obtaining building permits and inspections and cutting red tape, his administration cleared the way for developers to build a new convention center in downtown Washington, as well as more upscale shops, hotels, and office buildings than the District could use for the next decade. Between 1980 and 1988 D.C. office space increased by 10.1 million square feet and the city gained 3,124 new hotel rooms. Still, there were some trickle-down economic benefits. The downtown construction boom generated tens of thousands of jobs and tens of millions in tax dollars for the city. It had been initially set in motion by Barry's predecessor, Walter Washington, but Barry, naturally, took credit for it. Unlike mayors in some other U.S. cities, however, Barry failed to oblige developers to build affordable housing elsewhere in the city in return for the right to develop the lucrative downtown area.

Had the mayor lost sight of the "left out, kicked out and just plain kicked" for whom he had always been a self-described champion? In a second-term interview with the *Post* Ivanhoe Donaldson, Barry's close friend, chief political strategist and, most recently, his deputy mayor for economic development, suggested to a *Post* reporter that the answer at that point may have been yes. "Government can't eliminate poverty," Donaldson admitted. But he added that the Barry administration *could* provide contracts to minority businesses, which in turn might create jobs for other blacks. "Patronage isn't evil," Donaldson insisted to the *Post*'s Juan Williams, "it's just good politics."

Aside from the construction boom, Barry had other second-term successes—most notably the hiring and training of thousands of disadvantaged city residents. His administration also significantly improved delivery of such basic services as trash collection and road repairs. By untangling the Gordian knot in the city's financial records, the District was finally able to enter the bond market for the first time. In September 1986 Barry dedicated a new $40 million municipal center on the corner of 14th and U streets, NW. The eight-story building, topped by a huge skylight, rose like a pink concrete phoenix from the ashes of the 1968 riots that had destroyed many of the stores in the neighborhood. To get the D.C. Council to approve the funds to build it, Barry had convinced council members it would spark a resurgence of black economic power in the neighborhood which, even before the riots, had been a major flesh-and-drugs market. Unfortunately it remained so after the new municipal center was built. No investors materialized to pour money into the neighborhood until years later, after a new subway line made it economically viable. But Barry got his name on the building and a fancy satellite office out of the deal. More important, he had shown that he could get just about anything he wanted from the pliable D.C. Council.

Even as the mayor publicly flexed his considerable political muscle, however, behind the scenes, he was secretly undoing himself. According to Barry intimate Stuart Long, around 1980 the mayor started drifting away from "daytime" friends like himself who were married, had kids, and "headed home at a certain time" each night, into the embrace of a faster crowd, which often assembled at a popular Potomac waterfront restaurant.

Barry began using cocaine, says Long, in order to hustle the attractive young women who frequent the pricey Channel Inn restaurant on Maine Avenue, SW. "They always used like to get high before they made love," said Long. "That's how he got into all that shit. He wanted to be hip, you know, and that's where it all came from."

As the drug use and womanizing increased, so did the scandals. The most politically damaging occurred in 1984, when media stories broke about Barry's alleged cocaine use three years earlier at the "This Is It?" nude dancing club and his alleged cocaine purchases that year from Karen Johnson. In both instances Barry was investigated but never indicted. Nevertheless, both allegations haunted Barry for years afterward.

In 1987 WUSA-TV's Mark Feldstein reported further details of Barry's visit to the club, based on a March 1982 D.C. police report that quoted a woman employed by the club as saying that club owner Herbert Cole had offered her and two other female employees $100 each to "engage the mayor in sexual activity." She said she didn't accept Cole's offer because of "a previous commitment," but the other two women approached by Cole did. The same witness told police she was wary of cooperating with them further because, "If the mayor of D.C. could come to 'This Is It?' and use coke in the open, it was obvious that there was no fear [by Barry] of police."

Two years later Feldstein reported that when Inspector Fred Raines, head of the D.C. police department's intelligence unit, had attempted to pursue the allegations in 1982–83, he had been discouraged by then-police chief Maurice Turner, Jr. Feldstein, now with Cable News Network, said that when Raines, in frustration, later took his information to the FBI and Justice Department—both reportedly declined to investigate— Turner castigated Raines for going outside the chain of command and assigned him to night duty as a disciplinary measure.

During this period scandals also hit top members of Barry's administration. In 1986 Ivanhoe Donaldson was jailed after being convicted of defrauding the city of $193,000. A year later, another deputy mayor, Alphonse Hill, was convicted of extortion, income tax evasion, and defrauding the District government in a kickback scheme involving city contractors. Barry aide Robert B. Robinson resigned after pleading guilty to misusing city funds to help buy Effi Barry a fur coat. And Dr. Robert L. Green, who had resigned under fire as president of the University of the District of Columbia, was tried, and acquitted, after being charged with diverting university funds to his own use. (Green was defended by R. Kenneth Mundy).

No scandal was more damaging to Barry, personally and politically, than the fall of "the Hoe," as administration insiders referred to Ivanhoe Donaldson. According to former D.C. school board member Calvin Lockridge, Donaldson actually ran the day-to-day operations of city government while the charismatic Barry greeted the public and politicked with the D.C. Council. Lockridge said Donaldson was the one cabinet member Barry deferred to and that in 1983, the year in which Donaldson—and another strong cabinet member and close advisor, city administrator Elijah Rogers—left city government, Barry's addictive behavior went out of control. "Once Donaldson left the scene," said Lockridge, "there was no one else left who could have any semblance of acting as a brake to say 'You ought not do this, Marion, this is wrong.' You had too many yes people around him. And so his personal life, his drug addiction, his drinking, everything just got out of focus, because there was no one else left there to stand up to his ass."

According to Lockridge, even Barry's long-time friend and minister, the Reverend David Eaton, could not convince Barry to curb his excessive behavior, once the Hoe was gone. "David would go and talk to him," said Lockridge, "and it got to the point that the mayor would tell Eaton, 'Go deal with your own habit. You drink too goddamn much. Don't come telling me about my [bad] habits.'"

During Barry's second term, two city officials, Jose Gutierrez and Alvin Frost, added to the litany of disgrace by publicly exposing alleged corruption in the Barry administration. Gutierrez, who held the cabinet-level post of chief purchasing officer for the city, accused city administrator Thomas Downs of steering a $20 million contract to the Chesapeake & Potomac Telephone Company for political reasons. C&P's executive vice president, C. Delano Lewis, was a longtime political supporter of the mayor's. Barry publicly flogged Gutierrez, the highest-ranking Hispanic in his administration, then demoted him. Frost, a black Harvard MBA and the city's senior cash-management analyst, asserted publicly that the city's finance department was "rife" with corruption, then changed the password to the finance computer and announced a "guess-the-password" contest for city schoolchildren. Frost was forced to resign, but before he left he sent a letter to Barry in which he offered an unsolicited but fascinating insight into Barry's character. The letter, quoted in the April 26, 1987, issue of the *Washington Post* magazine, reads, in part: "The press devotes considerable attention to what you've done since your activist days as a college student and your work with SNCC. I believe that the real story goes back to your very early days and holds important clues to psychological development. . . . The combination of poverty, race, loss of father, etc., created very conflicting drives of insecurity and vulnerability with your ambition and agressiveness. At bottom, you have always been an opportunist, willing and prepared to take advantage of anything and anyone to achieve your own personal need for power, control and acceptance. Isn't it frightening to be so powerful and yet so insecure?"

For the most part Barry kept his own counsel regarding the mounting scandals. When he spoke publicly, he said only that some "bad apples" in his administration "let me down."

Barry's second-term scandals reached beyond his administration. In 1982 Effi Barry was criticized for accepting $1,150 worth of clothes from a lawyer who lobbied the city government. In February 1985 news reports revealed that the city paid $11 million to Jeffrey Cohen, a real estate developer and godfather to Barry's son, for land it valued at $6.7 million. In 1986 Effi made the news again, this time when a Barry aide used $1,500 in city funds to help buy D.C.'s First Lady a new fur coat. Barry later repaid the funds.

This cascade of setbacks and scandals prompted a discouraged Barry to briefly consider stepping down at the end of his second term. Perhaps he changed his mind when he realized the paucity of his alternatives. For one thing, there was nowhere else for him to go politcially: the District of Columbia has no governor or senators, only one, nonvoting member of the House of Representatives, a "shadow" House representative and two "shadow" senators, elected in November 1990, to lobby for D.C. statehood. If he tried to move into the private sector, what company, even a black-owned one, would want to hire an ex-mayor who had left office under a cloud of suspicion? So the choice actually was easy.

Shortly before the November 1986 election Barry and his wife enrolled their son, Christopher, in a private school. Having once led the city's school board, the mayor knew that his bright and sensitive child wouldn't stand a chance in the rough-and-tumble environment of the city's public school system. This move should have telegraphed to the "left out, kicked out, and just plain kicked" Barry purported to be serving that he was no longer with them, but, surprisingly, it didn't. In November 1986 Barry was reelected for the second time, outpolling Republican council member Carol Schwartz by 61 to 39 percent. This time, however, most of Barry's votes came from blacks. The mayor had come full circle from 1978, when he won the closely contested Democratic primary largely on the strength of his white electoral support. And by the end of his third and final term fours years later, even most black D.C. voters would abandon him.

15

BIG TROUBLE FOR
D.C.'S "MAYOR-FOR-LIFE"

To launch his third term Marion Barry threw a four-day inaugural party that included a formal ball and parade. The $1 million celebration, along with Barry's expensive wardrobe, his increasingly aloof governing style, and the large security contingent that followed him everywhere, earned him the press moniker "imperial mayor." This unsolicited sobriquet galled a man who had been born to Mississippi sharecroppers and liked to say that he could "walk with kings and queens and not lose the common touch." But he was now in the power seat and didn't really have to worry about what the increasingly critical media were saying about him.

His third term had barely begun when the "barracudas" renewed their attacks. In January 1987 the city was paralyzed after sustaining a record snowfall while its mayor was in sunny Pasadena, watching the Washington Redskins, led by black quarterback Doug Williams, drub the hapless Denver Broncos 42–10 in the Super Bowl. The media had a field day reporting on the anger and frustration of District residents at the failure of road crews to clear the streets in a timely manner. Barry was doubly skewered when he alleged that his constituents were exaggerating the problem in describing it to newsmen, then delayed his return to the East to recover from yet another reported flareup of his alleged "hiatal hernia" (which, according to testimony at his drug and perjury trial, was in reality a near-fatal cocaine overdose).

Lesser embarrassments had followed, including two late-night car crashes involving the mayor's official limousine. Barry explained each time that he was on his way to a social gathering and admitted that he was something of a "night owl." Reports of Barry's alleged extracurricular romantic activities also continued to surface. In May 1987 the *Washington Post* reported that Barry had visited 23-year-old black model Grace Shell at her Capitol Hill apartment two months earlier. Dressed in a blue velour jogging suit and a cap with "Mayor" emblazoned on it, Barry was reportedly rebuffed by Shell and shooed off the premises by Shell's landlady. The unabashed mayor later said through his attorney that he had been invited to the apartment by Shell to meet her three-year-old son. Shell denied it. In the same month Barry's mother-in-law, Pollie Harris, made the news after allegedly torching her ex-boyfriend's house in a Maryland suburb. In December 1987 the *Post* reported that Barry had spent Thanksgiving weekend in the Bahamas with Bettye L. Smith, a former city official who then worked for W.R. Lazard & Company, which advised the District on bond issues. (Barry explained that Smith, who was reportedly fired by Lazard after the Bahamas incident was publicized, was a family friend, so familiar that his son, Christopher, called her "Aunt Bettye.")

Also in 1987 reports began to surface of a D.C. police internal affairs division probe into an alleged drug network run by and for city employees. The *Washington Times* reported that "drug use among District employees is epidemic and involves some of the city's highest-ranking officials as both users and dealers, according to law enforcement authorities and District sources." In a series of investigative articles the *Times* said that a syndicate, using a private jet, flew drugs from the Virgin Islands and the Bahamas via Atlanta and Miami to Washington National Airport. The paper said that it was not uncommon for D.C. government personnel to be snorting cocaine at their desks.

The drug probe coincided with an ongoing federal grand jury investigation of contract corruption, which eventually led to the indictment and trial of more Barry administration officials and minority contractors. Two close Barry associates—former Department of Human Services director David Rivers and minority contractor John Clyburn—were among those tried for bribery and conspiracy. Both men were acquitted.

Other Barry aides and friends were investigated but not indicted. They included bonding company owner Gwendolyn Joseph, who reportedly offered from a federal prison cell in California to testify before a federal grand jury that she had had sex with the mayor and used drugs with him. Joseph also reportedly offered to testify about her alleged knowledge of bribes paid to Barry by minority contractors, but federal officials apparently failed to meet her demands to be freed from prison first. Marcia Griffin, who sat on the board of two companies that were reportedly awarded nearly $5 million in city contracts, also admitted having an affair with the mayor and sharing what she believed was cocaine with him. Sallie Melendez, another woman linked amorously to Barry, was reportedly on the city payroll for two months (receiving an annual salary of $63,185, the sixth-highest salary of any city official) before obtaining a job description. As it turned out, however, it was the investigation of Barry's relationship with a man that finally began his downfall.

In late December 1988, the *Washington Post*, the same paper that 14 years earlier had helped topple Richard Nixon with its Watergate revelations, reported that Barry had repeatedly visited his old friend Charles Lewis in the latter's downtown Washington hotel room, where traces of cocaine were later found by police. Quoting an unnamed source, the paper said two D.C. vice squad detectives were on their way to room 902 of the Ramada Inn Central at 14th Street and Rhode Island Avenue, NW, to make an undercover drug buy from Lewis when they were called back—presumably, by their police commander. The paper said the detectives had aborted their December 22 mission after learning that Barry was in the room with Lewis. The *Post* said the detectives were answering a hotel maid's complaint that Lewis had offered her cocaine in exchange for sex.

The *Post* said Barry tried to head off the subsequent investigation, first by calling police brass repeatedly in the days following his last visit to Charles Lewis, then visiting a police communications center where such calls are taped, and finally by urging police chief Maurice Turner, Jr., to announce that the investigation had been completed. Instead, Turner turned the investigation over to the U.S. attorney's office. (Turner would later tell the *Post* that during his eight-year tenure as chief he was "well aware of the allegations and innuendos and rumors" regarding Barry's drug use. He said there were "four or five ambitious grand juries that were undertaken and there were some stings [planned against Barry] that didn't materialize.")

At a news conference shortly after the drug allegations were made public, a visibly shaken Barry, mopping his glistening brow under the heat of the television lights and the gaze of reporters, flatly denied any wrongdoing. "At no time did I see any drugs, use any drugs or have any knowledge of drugs," he said, echoing what he'd said on previous occasions when faced with similar accusations. "It would be inconsistent with my character, with my integrity, with my veracity to be involved in such activity or to be around such persons who would knowingly do this."

Yet the mayor ducked the challenge made almost immediately by D.C. Council member Nadine Winter—a long-time Barry supporter and friend-turned-critic—to take a drug test.

Barry also questioned what he called "rumors, innuendoes that started with one maid, one whose veracity no one even knows about" and said that he had visited "Chuck Lewis" only once, on December 22, the same day detectives had gone to the hotel, not "at least six times," as the *Post* had reported.

The mayor refused to take any questions and lashed out at the gagged reporters, complaining that he'd been "tried, convicted, and doing time [sic] by some members of the media."

Time, Newsweek, U.S. News & World Report, and *People* magazine all carried January 1989 stories on Barry's latest crisis. ABC's "Nightline," CBS's "48 Hours," PBS's "McNeill-Lehrer News Hour" and "The McLaughlin Group," and CNN's "Capital Gang," all aired shows on Barry and on the wave of drug violence sweeping what they were calling "Dodge City" and "Beirut on the Potomac." Some foreign newspapers got in their licks too. The *London Daily Telegraph* ran a story under the headline "The Capital of Sleaze." Even the Voice of America, which broadcasts from Washington to an estimated 190 million worldwide listeners each week, ran stories on Barry's troubles and on D.C.'s drug and murder epidemic.

The criticism from Capitol Hill, where D.C. gets part of its operating budget, was even more vitriolic. The national law-makers were angrier at the District government than they'd been in 115 years—when the District had been run by a crooked territorial governor named Alexander "Boss" Shepherd—and in an equally vengeful mood. "The state of affairs in our nation's capital is a national disgrace," said Rep. Douglas Bereuter (R.-Neb.). "It is an international embarrassment and dishonors the name of our first president, George Washington. Mr. Barry has sent a message to the young people of Washington that he tolerates corruption, abuse of power and the drug culture."

"Look at the management of the District's affairs," said Rep. William Dannemeyer (R-Ca.). "It's a tragic joke. Somebody is not watching the shop. That's cause for Congress to step in and take some action."

But what probably stung Barry most was the criticism leveled at him by other blacks. A few days after the new scandals hit, black *Post* writer William Raspberry asked in a column: "What do we do about our embarrassment of a mayor?"

Jay Stephens quickly answered that question when he summoned a grand jury to investigate possible drug use and obstruction of justice by Barry—the latter because of his calls to D.C. police brass and his visit to the police communications center. Soon the grand jury was also investigating the joint D.C. government/U.S. Virgin Islands personnel project. The man who co-managed the project? None other than Charles Lewis.

Lewis, however, would not cooperate with police—at least, not initially. Barry was thus able to elude the pursuing federal lawmen once again.

In December 1988 Barry took another major hit to his image when *Regardie's* magazine published titillating excerpts from

Barry paramour Karen Johnson's diary. The following month *The Washington Monthly* magazine published a cover story under the headline, "The Worst City Government in America." Citing hair-raising examples of incompetence and corruption during Barry's 10-year reign, the article ripped into the mayor's overpaid minions for running an operation that all too often ignored the crying needs of the very people the mayor purported to care most about—the poor and disadvantaged—while drawing five-figure salaries and doing a minimum of actual work.

Despite these stories and many others like them, and despite the public trials and jailings of former top aides, the mayor nevertheless remained popular with many of D.C.'s black voters, who seemed endlessly willing to forgive his administrative failures and reported indiscretions. "I don't know what it's going to take to convince the white media that the mayor's personal life—his sex life and whether or not he does drugs—is not of importance to the black community," radio personality Cathy Hughes told *Washingtonian* magazine. "You know, we have lived through centuries of white political leadership that drank or practiced deviant behavior. We had a congressman (Wilbur Mills, D-Ark.) jump in the Tidal Basin with a stripper. Others were chasing little boys in the bathroom. So why are we going to get upset if our mayor is chasing a go-go dancer?" She was referring to the 1984 "This Is It?" scandal.

Barry had exploited such attitudes, along with the fear of some less affluent black Washingtonians that if he were removed from office, the city's white minority would bring in one of their own, who would set back the progress blacks had made under Barry.

Thus it was understandable that when Barry showed up for the first day of grand jury testimony in the Ramada Inn incident on January 19, 1989, he could playfully shadowbox for reporters and boast: "I'm stronger than ever before."

According to the *Post*'s Juan Williams, because of the unspoken racial element blacks who were *not* enamored of the mayor felt compelled to maintain their silence. "What he creates is a Teflon coating," Williams told *Time* magazine's Michael Riley in June 1989. "If you're white, you can't say it. If you're black, you can't say it. In this town, who does that leave? The ultimate irony is that if this guy were white, black people would be on their hind legs screaming."

Within the political ruling circles, however, D.C.'s "Mayor-for-Life"—as the *Washington City Paper* had satirically dubbed Barry during less troubled times—was rapidly losing ground. In late January 1989 Nadine Winter called her old friend the mayor and four black colleagues on the city council to her Northeast Washington home. They asked Barry to step aside at the end of his term in January 1991 and give some other Democrat with an untainted record—one of them perhaps—a chance to hold D.C.'s highest political office. News of the meeting was leaked to the *Post*. Though Barry angrily denied he'd been asked to step aside—saying pointedly a few days later there was a "60-40" chance he'd run again and he expected his aides to back him to the hilt or resign—he had sustained another jarring political blow.

"It pains me that people have accused me of things that are not true, guilt by association," he complained in a television interview taped around the same time. "When I ran for mayor ... I didn't run to be pope, or to be bishop, or to be a Zion elder, or to be a preacher. I ran to be mayor. I figured my private life—as long as I didn't do anything illegal, didn't do anything outrageous—was my private life. The rules of the game [have] changed. I'm under scrutiny 24 hours a day. No other mayor in America has this much scrutiny. I guess I've sorta become bigger than life."

Barry had in a sense become bigger than life: millions around the globe were following his escapades in the media. In London, for instance, the *Daily Telegraph* told its readers in February 1989 that the nation's capital "is fast becoming the murder capital of the U.S., with more than one killing per day last year. It is infested with drugs ... and the streets are patrolled by an army of beggars who congregate outside the chic restaurants and shops. The city is corrupt, inefficient and extremely dangerous. Mr. Barry's recent behavior has become a national scandal.''

Here at home, said Sen. Arlen Specter (R-Pa.), who once chaired the Senate Appropriations Subcommittee on the District, Washington's controversial mayor, who had long crusaded for D.C. statehood, had, ironically, ''set back decades'' any such hopes for District residents by alienating the very congressmen who would have to vote on a constitutional amendment to grant it.

Juan Williams concurs. ''I think that much of the momentum in that movement has been drained by the sense that the District has not done a good job of governing itself,'' said Williams in a February 1990 interview with the author, ''and particularly that Marion Barry has brought a lot of shame to the nation's capital and not only to the nation's capital but to the federal government. For instance, in terms of this drug war that the president is now waging, suddenly we see international headlines that say: 'My gosh, the President has this crack-using narco-mayor under his own nose!' And that's embarrassing not only to residents of the District of Columbia, it's embarrassing to the people of the United States.''

The views of Specter and Williams were supported by a national poll the *Post* conducted in March 1989: half the respondents said they believed the D.C. government was more corrupt than other big city governments and a majority opposed statehood for the District.

While Barry hemorrhaged politically, the city was hemorrhaging literally. Shortly before the Ramada story broke in December 1988, Barry said he would soon announce a major anticrime initiative. Two months later there was no such plan. The non-move characterized the perhaps well-meaning but increasingly ineffectual and distracted mayor. Washington was drifting like a ghost ship, moving with purpose only when a puff of hot air from the District Building filled its sails briefly with rhetoric. Its decks were awash with the blood of the 372 people slain in 1988, mostly young black men involved in the city's runaway crack trade.

Because of the record number of murders—highest per capita in the country—the media had anointed Washington America's "murder capital," prompting leaders of the city's $2 billion-a-year tourism industry to worry that potential visitors would start avoiding Washington. One downtown hotel, the Capital Hilton, began giving guests who jogged specially marked street maps so they could avoid dangerous areas when they ran. And in the city's 57 public housing projects, home to 40,000 of D.C.'s poorest, many residents were afraid to leave their apartments, day or night, because they knew they might get caught in one of the turf battles sporadically being waged in 90 open air crack markets located near them.

Even D.C. police chief Maurice Turner, Jr., had publicly conceded that his 3,990 outgunned officers were losing the war on drugs. Forty-nine more murders had been recorded in January 1989, nearly doubling the record-setting pace of the previous year. "We arrest them but they don't go to jail, they don't fear jail," he complained, referring to the city's unprecedented 46,000 drug arrests during Operation Clean Sweep in 1988. Only 1,400 of those arrested had reportedly been locked up. But Turner also had said, defensively, "This city isn't different from any other major city. A lot of other cities are experiencing problems with drugs, homicides and violence."

Actually things were a lot worse in the District than in most other major U.S. cities. In a 1988 survey of 11 metropolitan areas besieged by drug-related murders, D.C. ranked last in number of cases solved. More than half the 372 slayings investigated by the city's overworked 46-member homicide squad that year had gone unsolved, partly because the police ballistics lab was hopelessly backlogged with more than 600 cases. Despite the rash of murders, the city had only one certified pathologist at the morgue and the office of chief medical examiner had been vacant since 1983.

Washington's most effective law enforcement was being provided gratis by the Nation of Islam, which sent unarmed patrols into the Mayfair Mansions project in Northeast Washington to confront, occasionally beat up, and eventually chase out drug dealers. And in the drug-ridden Shaw neighborhood in Northwest an arsonist was burning down crack houses.

By February 1989, when the mayor gave his annual "State of the District" address, he was calling for anyone who knew the identity of any at-large killers to "come forth, come forth! Tell us who did it!" But the likelihood of any such turn-ins was slim. Barry himself knew that values were different in the inner city, that cooperating with "the man" was seen by some residents as a copout. Besides, the tough-talking, gun-toting street dude in the dashiki and Afro haircut from the 1960s no longer existed; the pin-striped mayor of 1989 could no longer relate to the tough young black men with the high-op fade haircuts and angry eyes now on the street, nor they to him. He had lost control of the "home boys," as they called each other, and they had lost control of themselves.

In early 1989 the city faced other serious problems: a projected budget deficit of $175 million; poorly trained ambulance drivers who couldn't find the sick or injured people they were supposed to pick up (14 people reportedly died vainly waiting for them); hospitals so inundated with shooting victims some were forced to close their doors to new trauma patients; drug treatment centers similarly overwhelmed; juvenile criminals, including killers, walking away regularly from D.C.'s drug-ridden suburban detention center; a bloated bureaucracy so full of surly and incompetent workers Barry had been forced to initiate a special training program to teach them how to answer the phones without insulting the callers; courts and prisons choked with drug offenders while a $50 million federal grant to build a new 800-bed prison went unused because some neighborhood groups objected to its siting and the mayor lacked the resolve, and the political clout, to impose a choice on the city; more than 200 children shot or stabbed—some in front of their schools—and more black District children dying of homicide in 1988 than any other cause; D.C.'s swelling homeless population; its infant mortality rate of 20.3 deaths per thousand live births—like its murder rate, the nation's highest; taxes and real estate prices spiralling out of sight while one of every five D.C. residents lived in poverty; the loss of millions of dollars in federal grants because the city government had failed to act on time; a waiting list of 7,500 families for public housing in a system so disorganized a top official had described it as "total chaos."

Perhaps as a way of escaping the mess, at least temporarily, Barry—who increasingly had been retreating into his District Building office—disappeared from public view altogether in September 1988. He showed up a week later minus his moustache and 20 pounds lighter. Though he wouldn't admit where he'd been, reporters soon learned he'd visited a health spa in New York's Catskill Mountains, where he'd taken a series of upper colon enemas and learned to meditate. To throw reporters off, Barry had sent two of his bodyguards to a posh New York City hotel where they'd stayed for a week at a cost to D.C. taxpayers of $2,000. When questioned by reporters about this expensive subterfuge and other aspects of his secret vacation, Barry told them to mind their own business.

As it turned out, this was the mayor's final chance to thumb his nose with impunity at the white-controlled media and everyone else who, in his eyes, seemed intent on driving him from office. Less than three months later, Barry would shoot himself in the foot once more by risking a rendezvous with Chuck Lewis and getting caught.

Even after the Ramada story broke, however, Barry remained defiant. When the press revealed, for instance, in March 1989, that D.C. employees had testified before the grand jury that their superiors had told them to backdate subpoenaed records pertaining to the Virgin Islands personnel project, the mayor denied any personal or administrative wrongdoing. He had no comment when Department of Human Services director David Rivers resigned under pressure from the same federal corruption probe. (The man who replaced Rivers, Jerome Woods, was fired by Barry nine months later, after reporters revealed he was using city funds to buy groceries and pay rent for himself and his top aides.)

In September 1989, when hecklers in an ethnically mixed crowd booed him during an appearance at a neighborhood celebration in Northwest Washington, the mayor grinned and flipped them the bird, a gesture that was recorded by local television crews and broadcast to a citywide audience. Barry later publicly apologized, but he had again seriously damaged himself.

Despite his mounting troubles, in a year-end interview Barry incongruously boasted, "If I ran tomorrow morning, I could beat anybody in this town." He defied investigators to pin anything directly on him, asserting, "If all this corruption was going on, I should be in jail."

Barry wouldn't have long to wait. Meanwhile he seemed the worst possible leader for a city desperately in need of strong leadership and a positive example for its youth. The mayor hadn't ignited the inferno of drug violence sweeping the nation's capital in the late 1980s, but by polarizing the city along racial lines, he was fanning the flames.

Said Juan Williams in February 1990: "This city was racially divided before Marion Barry showed up. But what Barry has done is to really exacerbate those tensions—to the point where I think there is less communication, less of the kind of coalition-building so important to something like the quality of our public schools, the quality of our social welfare system, even the quality of our religious life. Things have become more and more split as black people have been put in the position of having to defend a man who in reality is indefensible."

The problems Barry faced, aside from the ones he created himself, were not much different from those faced by mayors of other large U.S. cities in the late 1980s. Besides the dramatic increase in drug use and violent crime, big-city mayors also faced chronic budget shortfalls brought about in part by a significant drop in federal aid. And, despite the media's tendency to point fingers and oversimplify, those problems couldn't all be blamed on the mayors. Eight years of benign neglect of the nation's poor and needy by Ronald Reagan also contributed greatly to the urban crisis. Hundreds of thousands of Americans now lived on the street, thanks in part to Reagan's budget cuts and to Jimmy Carter's well-meaning but misguided policy of deinstitutionalizing some of society's weakest elements. George Bush, the same man who used black convict Willie Horton to stoke white racial fears during his presidential campaign, now promised a "kinder, gentler America" brought about by voluntarism. But his nebulous "thousand-points-of-light" response to the urgent social problems of the late 1980s offered as real a solution as the fabled emporer's new clothes. The most important question in Washington, Chicago, New York, Los Angeles, Miami, Houston, and other big cities across the country was not whom to blame for the drift toward the powdery edge by what the media cynically called America's "permanent underclass," but how to reverse it.

In the nation's capital only one man had the wherewithal to answer that question, a man who had emerged from this so-called underclass himself. But Marion Barry was far too preoccupied with his own problems and his quest for illicit gratification to help anyone else.

As federal investigators closed in on the mayor, he beefed up his praetorian guard, which eventually comprised 37 District police officers. But while this well-armed phalanx was able to guard Marion Barry against potential outside threats, it could not protect him from himself. His bodyguards could not stop the mayor from going to the Vista International Hotel on January 18, 1990, for a surreptitious rendezvous with a former lover and a date with destiny.

Part Three: A Man, and a City, on Trial

16

UNITED STATES OF AMERICA V. MARION S. BARRY, JR.

The television crewmen hunched over their cameras like electronic marksmen, turning in unision to frame the blue Lincoln Town Car that pulled to a halt at the edge of the courthouse parking lot. They had come by the dozens from every major network and local station. Some even had come from overseas. They had come to cover Marion Barry's drug and perjury trial. Normally, they would converge on Washington's U.S. District Court only for crimes of a far graver nature: shooting a president, lying to Congress, sabotaging an election, subverting the U.S. Constitution. But that balmy Monday in early June 1990—Soviet president Mikhail Gorbachev had just departed the capital following his latest summit with President George Bush—they had come to take pictures of a man charged with more commonplace crimes—possessing cocaine and lying to a federal grand jury. They had come because the man was the black mayor of America's capital, a black-majority city besieged by drugs and drug-related crime. They had come because the federal prosecutor and most of the investigators were white, and the mayor's followers had made it clear that the trial would be a showdown between the two races. Some had warned that Washington would "burn" if the jury convicted Barry.

Inside a security booth at the edge of the street a deputy U.S. marshal pushed a button, lowering a metal barricade that allowed the mayor's car to pass. The limousine pulled right to the 3rd Street, NW, side entrance. The mayor, wearing his power outfit—dark suit, red tie, white shirt—got out of the car, followed by his wife Effi and his mother, Mattie Cummings, whom he'd flown up from Memphis. Despite the somber occasion both women wore bright summer dresses.

Barry smiled and waved, as if he were showing up for a routine fund-raiser instead of the worst personal, political, and legal crisis he ever had faced. Or perhaps he was just being smart, flashing his patented grin at the cameras, using the white-controlled media for his own ends.

If anyone knew how to manipulate the media, black or white, it was Marion Barry. Only six days earlier, on May 29, the embattled mayor had sat down with reporters from the *Washington Post* and predicted that no jury in the District would convict him. The paper ran the story on the front page under a banner headline the following day. Around the same time he had played tennis with some influential reporters, Michael York of the *Washington Post*, Del Waters of Washington's WJLA-TV, and Richard Kiel of the Associated Press. Two weeks earlier he even managed to praise the city's white-controlled media publicly as having been "unusually objective" since his March 13 return from substance abuse treatment in Florida and South Carolina.

Barry didn't need to win over the black media. Washington's five black-owned weeklies all had run stories and editorials highly supportive of Barry and reflective of the mayor's expected defense—that he had been set up by white prosecutors and members of the white media who didn't want a strong black leader to govern the nation's capital. Local black radio talk-show hosts such as WOL-AM's Cathy Hughes, WDCU-FM's Ernest White, and WPFW-FM's Jerry Washington hosted call-in shows or otherwise drew attention and sympathy to the mayor's plight. Why did they stick by a man who had embarrassed not only himself but the city he ran? In Washington's words, "He's *my* mayor, and I stand by him, right or wrong."

Barry knew that prospective members of his jury might read those papers or listen to those call-in shows, might even believe what they said. He knew that, given the facts in his case and the dozens of witnesses lined up to testify against him, his primary chance of walking free at the end of his trial depended on what legal experts call "jury nullification"—convincing the jury that even if he *appeared* to be guilty, because he had been entrapped, he deserved acquittal.

Barry also knew his trial would exacerbate already tense black-white relations in Washington. But that did not appear to concern him as much as beating the charges did. He had tried to strike a plea-bargain agreement with Jay Stephens, but talks between the U.S. attorney and Kenneth Mundy had broken down after Stephens insisted that Barry plead guilty to at least one perjury charge. In the District, perjury is a felony carrying a mandatory sentence of up to five years in prison.

When the elevator opened on the second floor, Barry came out first. He stopped a moment to eye the mob of mostly white reporters, temporarily barred from the courtroom, along with the general public, to allow hundreds of potential jurors to be seated instead. His half-smile seemed to tell them, Give me your best shot, I can handle it. Maybe he could. But the stakes for Barry, both personal and political, were now higher than they'd ever been before. If convicted on all 14 counts, he could face up to 26 years in prison and $1.8 million in fines.

Even if he were acquitted, Barry would win a Pyrrhic victory, his personal life, in all its sad and seamy detail, having been paraded before the world. As if sensing this, the reporters were unusually quiet. No one shouted questions at the mayor as he led his wife and mother down the hall to courtroom two, the same ornate chamber where some of the Watergate trials had been staged.

Inside the walnut-paneled courtroom, with its red, wall-to-wall carpeting and a beige marble inset behind the judge's bench, the mayor was relegated to a spectator's role. He sat silently at the defense table as silver-haired veteran jurist Thomas Penfield Jackson welcomed the unusually large pool of 250 potential jurors. (Normally, 40 city residents are called for a federal case and a jury seated in less than an hour.) Appointed to the federal bench by President Ronald Reagan in 1982, Jackson had presided six years later over the trial of former Reagan aide Michael Deaver, who was convicted of lying to Congress and a federal grand jury about his lobbying activities. Now he was overseeing an even more sensitive case. He began by splitting the jury pool into two equal-sized groups, each member of which he asked to fill out a 25-page questionnaire.

Some of the 69 questions—submitted by both sides in the case and ruled on by the judge—were routine: they asked about health, employment, education history, exposure to the case through the media. But many others were tailored to the Barry case: what political party did the respondents belong to; did they know any of the 48 potential witnesses; had they donated to Barry's mayoral campaign after his arrest; would "the defendant's religious beliefs, or the fact that a defendant had asked for Divine forgiveness" affect their judgment on his innocence or guilt; did they think race or politics played any part in the charge against the mayor?

Some questions seemed of dubious relevance, better suited for careful consideration by a philosopher, a sociologist, or a law or political science professor than a potential juror in a criminal trial. Jurors were asked whether or not they thought drugs should be legalized; whether they thought using concealed video- and audio-recording devices during an undercover investigation was "fair." Their opinions about politicians and high government officials in general were solicited, as were their opinions about the District of Columbia's form of government.

While the potential jurors wrestled with the ponderous form, some of the mayor's most vocal critics and supporters were gathering in a small park opposite the courthouse to strut their stuff for photographers and reporters. In their trademark red berets about two dozen Guardian Angels, the New York-based civilian crime-fighting group, circled a white marble statue of Civil War general George Meade. Several among the young, racially mixed group carried signs bearing such messages as "Barry Smoked Crack, We Don't Want Him Back," "Barry, Do the Right Thing, Resign!" and "Mayor Barry Goes Up In Smoke."

Soon they were approached by about 15 die-hard Barry supporters, playfully dubbed "Kool-Aiders" by Barry staff members, after the hundreds of followers of cult leader Jim Jones, who in November 1978, committed suicide in a Guyana jungle on Jones's orders by drinking cyanide-laced punch. One Kool-Aider carried a "Fight the Power" placard. Another distributed fliers that read, "D.C.'s Blacks Get Into The Act. And Get Those Racist Folks Off Our Mayor Marion Barry's Back. Don't We Know A Set Up When We See It?"

"We got some New York gays down here!" shouted Southeast Washington resident Florence Smith into the face of a young Hispanic Angel, who glared back at her but remained silent. "Go home!" she screamed.

Reporters and cameramen closed in on the made-for-television altercation, hoping to get something, anything, to feed the hungry news machines. With the cameras rolling, Curtis Sliwa, the sturdy, dark-haired young man who had founded the Guardian Angels, moved to the forefront. Was he going to use his martial arts on the woman? No. He merely grinned at her, making her even angrier.

"We are representing a national organization that has to deal with a stigma," Sliwa said cheerfully to the microphones being thrust into his face. "Washington is called the drug-crack-murder capital of America. With the mayor on trial for using crack, it just accentuates that fact."

"We are here to represent our Mayor Barry, which is one of the greatest men in D.C.," Smith retorted.

"We want *no* trial," said a man in dreadlocks. "We want it stopped today." He added, "You let them [television viewers] know we are for the black mayor of our city. We are not goin' with this racist bulljive."

"They been on Barry since the early eighties," said Donald Coble. "Anything they could find on Barry they were gonna use it against him." Then he made a prediction: "They're not gonna find a jury in Washington, D.C., that's gonna convict the mayor. You mark my words."

Barry had said it first.

Ed Hancock, a 91-year-old retired black federal worker, leaned on a pair of canes. "I was here before that man [Barry] came off the watermelon truck," he said, grinning defiantly at the Kool-Aiders. "That man is goin' down! They gonna be haulin' him down to Lorton [Reformatory]!"

"Uncle Tom! Uncle Tom!" shouted a young black woman standing next to Hancock. "You ain't nothin' but a blue-eyed devil."

"What have the white man done for *you*?" demanded a young black man wearing a sweatshirt and jeans.

"What have I done for myself?" Hancock asked, rhetorically, as he turned to face his tormentor. Then he added, defiantly, "I've got Marion in my sights. He's goin' down!"

No one came to blows outside the courthouse that morning. Tempers seemed to cool once the cameras were turned off. Yet no one could deny that the international media "circus" that D.C.'s nonvoting congressional delegate and mayoral candidate Walter Fauntroy had predicted would accompany Barry's trial was becoming a reality.

When court adjourned Monday, Barry slipped out of the courthouse, leaving his press secretary, Lurma Rackley, to deal with the journalists buzzing around a bouquet of microphones set up at the main, Constitution Avenue, entrance of the building. They were angry at having been kept out of the courtroom all day. They first asked bluntly who was minding the store while the mayor focused on his legal problems.

"The mayor will continue as usual," said Rackley, a delicately pretty 41-year-old former metro editor for the defunct *Washington Star* newspaper and an 11-year veteran of the Barry administration. "He's not out of town, he's not out of touch. He will continue governing."

Anyone who doubted that Barry was still in charge of the District government need only have talked to stunned city council members, who less than a week before had learned that the Barry administration had quietly and unilaterally executed a 20-year, $216 million, no-bid building lease with a group of investors that included Barry campaign contributor Richard A. Bennett, Jr. The mayor later backed off the move after several council members publicly challenged whether it was ethical or appropriate at a time when the city was more than $90 million in the red.

Meanwhile, asked how the mayor felt about his legal troubles, Rackley admitted, "Of course, he is nervous and afraid. He's a normal human being. Anyone would have apprehensions about going through a process like this." Then she added, "But the mayor is a very strong man."

The very next morning Barry got an opportunity to test that strength when 58 reporters from 43 different news organizations and half-a-dozen courtroom sketch artists were admitted to the courtroom. Taking up more than half the available seats, they scrutinized the mayor's every word and gesture. In addition to the capital's two major dailies, the *Washington Post* and the *Washington Times*, reporters had come from the *Washington Afro-American and Tribune* and *El Latino* ethnic weeklies, and from *Regardie's*. Every major U.S. television and radio network, every major U.S. wire service, and several out-of-town newspapers, including the *Baltimore Sun, Chicago Sun Times, New York Times, New York Daily News, Los Angeles Times,* and the *Philadelphia Inquirer*, had sent at least one reporter. *Time* magazine and the French newsweekly *L'Express* also were covering Barry's trial.

More than a dozen other reporters who had applied for passes, but were turned down because of limited seating, waited in the hall. Altogether the press took up six out of 10 benches, leaving only two benches for Barry's staff and supporters and two for spectators, some of whom had waited outside the courthouse since 4 A.M. for a chance to attend what the *Post* called "perhaps the most publicized trial in the city's 200-year history."

Just after 10 A.M., the mayor, wearing a red rose boutonniere, ambled into the courtroom through a side door, accompanied by his lawyers, R. Kenneth Mundy and Robert Mance. The trio sat down at the defense table on the right side of the courtroom. Barry's chief political advisor and campaign manager, Anita Bonds, sat at a small table behind them. Originally slated as a defense witness—to buttress an alibi defense for one of 10 cocaine possession counts against the mayor—Bonds, known as a shrewd judge of character, had been taken off the witness list to help Mundy and Mance pick the jury.

Mundy also had commissioned jury consultant Glenn R. Berlin to predict which jurors would favor Barry by running computerized analyses of the 250 potential jurors based on District census data and comparing that information to attitudes expressed by D.C. voters in past political polls. In this way Berlin could predict, for instance, that a blue-collar worker in Southeast Washington with two years or less of college would be far more sympathetic to Barry than, say, a white-collar worker in Northwest with a college degree. Mundy had not gained his formidable reputation by leaving anything to chance.

Seated at the prosecution table on the left side of the courtroom were Barry's opponents: assistant U.S. attorneys Judith Retchin, looking very businesslike with her short-cropped light brown hair and conservative suit; Richard Roberts, a tall, light-skinned black man whose rimless glasses and neatly trimmed Van Dyke beard gave him a scholarly air; and Albert Arrington, the bearded, balding, bespectacled D.C. police detective and sting team member who would aid the government in jury selection and presentation of evidence.

The government had another, more important reason for placing Arrington at the prosecution table: by doing so, they disqualified him from appearing as a trial witness. The defense wanted to question Arrington about an alleged drug tie between star prosecution witness Charles Lewis and Rayful Edmond, Jr. Edmond, a suspected cocaine dealer, was the father of Rayful Edmond III. The younger Edmond was a major cocaine trafficker in D.C. before his arrest and conviction for running a continuing criminal enterprise. Such a tie, if proven, could destroy Lewis's credibility.

Jay Stephens and his criminal division chief, Marshall Jarrett, had handpicked Retchin and Roberts from the U.S. attorney's staff of 250 lawyers. With a defender as tough as Mundy in Barry's corner, and Stephens's credibility on the line—not to mention the interest shown in the case by U.S. Attorney General Dick Thornburgh—the Justice Department obviously had to roll out its biggest and baddest guns.

Retchin and Roberts had been on the case since December 1988, when the Ramada drug allegations first surfaced. They had widened their probe to include D.C. government corruption after Charles Lewis revealed details of the joint D.C./Virgin Islands personnel project.

Aside from the job they shared, the two government lawyers could not have been more different. Judith Retchin was a foot shorter than Roberts, which gave them a Mutt-and-Jeff aspect in court. She also was sober and taciturn, her only known out-of-court diversions being gourmet food and tennis. Former U.S. Attorney Joseph diGenova, who had hired Retchin, called her a "superb lawyer." She had beaten Mundy in a high-profile case a year earlier, winning a conviction and mandatory life sentence against D.C. drug kingpin Michael Palmer for running a "continuing criminal enterprise" in the District.

By contrast, 37-year-old Richard Roberts was an outgoing, somewhat radical, graduate of Columbia University Law School by way of Vassar College (a member of the first co-ed class) by way of New York's High School of Music and Art. According to the *Post*, he still played a "hot" jazz piano. In college and law school, the paper said, Roberts had worn dashikis, taken up African causes, and studied socialism, traveling to Cuba to see the system firsthand. In the Justice Department, Roberts had teamed up with a federal prosecutor in Utah to win a conviction against Joseph Paul Franklin, a white man accused of the 1981 slaying of two black men whom Franklin had seen jogging with white female companions in Salt Lake City. When Franklin was convicted, the 200-pound defendant had called Roberts "a trained ape" and charged the prosecution table, upending a water pitcher before deputy U.S. marshals tackled him.

Both Retchin and Roberts were highly organized, methodical lawyers with excellent track records. But if they hoped to beat consummate defense master Mundy in a trial littered with racial and political land mines, they would have to reach further than they ever had reached before.

17

PICKING A PANEL AND
OTHER CRUCIAL BUSINESS

Only twelve jurors made it to the witness stand for questioning the second day, far fewer than both sides had
hoped. Of these, two were dismissed because of criminal
records. The extremely slow pace prompted reporters to
speculate, accurately, that the trial would run well past the
four-to-six weeks that pundits had predicted. *Voir dire* alone
would drag on for two weeks as lawyers probed one potential
juror after another. Despite the monotony, however, the legal
ritual offered a subtle drama that everyone knew could hold
the key to the outcome of the trial, and even occasional humor.
When a middle-aged black man was asked if he felt a person's
privacy would be invaded if he were secretly videotaped, he
quickly responded, "They do the same thing when you go
into the 7-11." The entire courtroom broke up.

As the opposing lawyers sparred over who would sit in judgment, Barry and his advisors, knowing that the jury soon
would be sequestered and thus out of media reach, stepped
up their public relations campaign. Anita Bonds mailed letters
to supporters comparing Barry's predicament to that of European Jews during the holocaust and the lynching of blacks in
the Deep South. The remarks, written by Bonds and published
in the mayor's campaign newsletter, "Friday Report," brought
an angry response from some prominent members of Washington's Jewish community.

David Friedman, director of the Washington area chapter
of the Anti-Defamation League, told the *Post*, "It's simply
ludicrous to link a drug prosecution to events as horrific as
lynching and the Holocaust."

However, William Cooke, president of the D.C. branch of
the NAACP, defended the newsletter. "I think what they're

trying to comment on," Cooke told the same newspaper, "is the severity with which he has been treated by the entire system, including the media.

"I don't know how the mayor can get a fair trial," Cooke added. "The press has already tried him."

In interviews with local media shortly before his trial, Barry himself was sometimes philosophical, almost resigned, and other times feisty and defiant.

"I've decided the only thing I can do is make my best effort," he said on "One Washington," a talk show aired during the first week of the trial. "If my best effort succeeds, fine. If it falls short, that's all I can do." He also predicted that "history will write at some point that we did more good than bad."

Meanwhile Barry desperately needed supporters right now. On the Sunday before his trial started, Barry reminded about 300 parishioners at the Metropolitan Baptist Church in Northwest Washington—he became a member of the church two weeks later—that he was still one of God's children, regardless of what happened at his trial.

"I've done some things I may not be proud of," admitted Barry, "some things I may be embarrassed about. But God is a forgiving God."

Somehow, even in a public expression of humility, the mayor could not admit, directly and unequivocally, that he felt badly about messing up. He said only that he "may" feel ashamed or embarrassed.

On June 4, the day jury selection began, the mayor appeared on the Cathy Hughes morning radio show, which on this particular day was videotaped and broadcast on cable television nationwide. He used the friendly forum to attack the U.S. government, which he compared to a "totalitarian" regime.

"It's frightening that since 1983 my family has had to go through my mail being opened, my bank accounts checked, my phones tapped," Barry complained, obviously playing to prospective jury members. "Can you imagine, you can't even have a conference in your bedroom with your wife for fear that they're listening to anything you say?"

Barry also told Hughes that "a local television station has gotten a copy of the [sting] tape from the prosecutors. They're trying to figure out now how to show it." He said it was part of a government campaign to "manipulate" him out of office.

Richard Roberts challenged that assertion in court the next day (June 5), accusing Barry of trying to turn the prospective jurors against the government. "His comments were, aside from being, we think, untrue, designed to attempt to infect the jury pool," Roberts charged.

When the facts were sorted out, it appeared that WRC-TV may have secretly copied the tape while being shown the *defense's* copy, not the government's, as Barry had charged. When this became clear, Barry quickly dropped his accusation. But potential jurors had no way of knowing which side was telling the truth.

Before the trial began, several black leaders tried unsuccessfully to stop it. D.C.'s nonvoting congressional delegate, the Reverend Walter Fauntroy, asked sympathetic federal lawmakers to talk U.S. Attorney General Dick Thornburgh into calling off his dogs in D.C.—at least long enough to strike a plea-bargaining agreement acceptable to Barry. He apparently failed. Near the end of jury selection, the embattled mayor tapped his old friend the Reverend Jesse Jackson to try to break the impasse in plea negotiations. Again, no deal. Finally, according to James Forman, publisher of the Washington-based Black America News Service, a high-ranking black leader approached President George Bush directly. The President had kept publicly quiet about the capital city's mayor, whose alleged drug habit was by now known to millions around the world. With his son Neil being investigated for his alleged role in the Silverado Savings & Loan scandal, Bush no doubt wanted to keep a low profile on criminal matters. In the privacy of the White House, however, says Forman, Bush told the black leader who approached him, "No, I'm not going to intervene. I *want* him to go to jail."

The President's refusal to help Barry was understandable. Long before the Vista sting, Barry's reported escapades—his alleged womanizing, his late-night car accidents, his visits to hospitals for treatment of his "hiatal hernia" (possible drug overdoses), his visits to his old friend Chuck Lewis at the

Ramada Inn Central in December 1988—had made him, in the eyes of the Bush administration, a national and international embarrassment.

On June 6, scores of local black journalists convened at Howard University to discuss the white media's coverage of the Barry trial. Several at the "open mike" forum, broadcast on local radio, accused the white media of symbolically "lynching" the city's black mayor by taking a purposely anti-Barry slant. In making their case they employed far more rhetoric than proof, but their high standing in the black community gave them credibility and clout among listeners, including potential Barry jurors.

Local black attorney and *Capital Spotlight* columnist Mary Cox, who each day sat in the front of the courtroom near the defense table, petitioned the United Nations Human Rights Commission in Geneva in Barry's behalf. Alleging that the trial was a racially motivated assault by the U.S. Justice Department on Barry's human rights and an "effort to drive the Mayor from office and ensure that he not seek re-election," Cox asked the commission to take up Barry's cause by sending an observer to his trial. (Six months later, Cox was still waiting for a reply from Geneva.)

A number of black D.C. clergymen also came to Barry's defense. In early June, two dozen ministers, led by the Reverend Robert Hamilton, Jr., gathered outside the courthouse to announce the formation of "Citizens for Barry," which Hamilton said represented around 75 local pastors.

"A bad dream is coming!" declared the Reverend James Bevel, a member of the ad hoc group who once had worked alongside Barry in Mississippi in the early 1960s and now was linked with the Universal Church of Christ in Northwest Washington. Like the other preachers Bevel realized that the U.S. civil rights movement was more or less defunct and that the struggle for racial justice in the nation's capital had deteriorated to a symbolic court battle. Bevel said he would convene a "People's Grand Jury" to investigate U.S. Attorney Jay Stephens. The public relations move was never completed, but Bevel's announcement struck a chord with Barry supporters who shared his outrage.

On June 14, with only two days of jury selection remaining, about 150 Barry supporters gathered in John Marshall Park next to the courthouse to decry the alleged U.S. government campaign to selectively prosecute black elected officials—a charge that Barry's attorney, Kenneth Mundy, later would make in court.

"If you have not yet been falsely accused, indicted, tried, convicted, or harassed in any way, just wait," black D.C. attorney Faye Williams warned. "As the Reverend Jesse Jackson has said, I cannot show you 'the Plan' in writing. But we all know the unwritten, often-denied policies and practices of our government, to stop the progress of our people."

The "Plan" to which Williams referred was a myth that had been kicking around since the latter days of the Reagan administration, when America's blacks woke up to the fact that the pleasantly smiling man in the White House had effectively abandoned them. Their disillusionment continued under President George Bush, who had continued Reagan's laissez-faire social policies and, after claiming it would lead to racial quotas in the workplace, had vetoed the 1990 Civil Rights Act that was passed by Congress. The myth, however, did have a basis in fact: under J. Edgar Hoover, the FBI had secretly investigated Martin Luther King, Jr., and other civil rights leaders whom Hoover suspected of being communist agents or simply didn't like. But no credible evidence has ever surfaced of any government conspiracy to selectively investigate or prosecute black elected officials, as some black leaders claim. In fact in 1990 there were more black elected officials than at any point in U.S. history, including the first post-Reconstruction black governor, Douglas Wilder of Virginia.

Barry's carefully orchestrated campaign to win the hearts and minds of prospective jurors and voters actually had started well before the trial. It had peaked in late May, when Barry visited one black D.C. church after another to plead his case and granted frequent interviews to the local black media, whose audiences most likely would include potential jurors. But in a telephone interview with Howard University's WHUR-FM radio a week before jury selection for his trial began, Barry went perhaps a bit further than his advisors had envisioned by admitting he had smoked crack at the Vista.

Or had he gone just far enough? By confessing to drug use he was effectively shifting the government's burden away from proving that fact beyond a reasonable doubt to demonstrating why such behavior mattered enough to indict a sitting mayor who still was supported by many of the city's black residents. Prosecutors got the message. During *voir dire* they asked each prospective juror if the mayor's confession to crack use would influence their judgment of his guilt or innocence.

On the same day he spoke on WHUR, Barry tried to downplay his stunning revelation by claiming in a *Washington Post* interview that the government, not he, was the culprit. "They had me ingest cocaine, crack cocaine, which could have killed me," Barry charged, implying that the government had somehow forced him to use the drug. "I could have been dead now, with 70, 80, 90 percent pure cocaine."

Barry also complained that he had been "hounded, harassed, vilified, slandered, and everything under the sun" by federal investigators and officials who had been "dipping and dabbling in the politics of Washington for a long time."

Ignoring the roughly one dozen members of his administration who had been convicted of corruption charges over the years as a result of that alleged "dipping and dabbling" by federal prosecutors, Barry declared: "They can't say we shot anybody, we robbed anybody, that we had a scheme to steal a million dollars from the D.C. government. That's why I feel good about proceeding ahead even in the worst case."

"What's the worst they [his former friends] can say," Barry scoffed, "that I used cocaine with them? I think if you talk to most Washingtonians—even my supporters have some inklings that I may have done that [used cocaine] because of all the deluge of information. So if they [the witnesses] testify I'd used cocaine with them before, that's not damaging. People already think that. A lot of people do."

Barry also asserted that a lot of people were taking his side in the legal contest.

"I hear it all the time," Barry said. "They think the government's gone overboard, overzealous in trying to bring a court of justice around something that, at worst, was harmful to me personally—if I did that."

Asked about the potentially harmful impact of his crack use revelation on the city's youth, besieged by a crack epidemic, Barry retorted, "I may be a poor role model, but being a poor role model is not a crime."

Finally, the capital's irrepressible mayor boasted that even if he did not win an outright acquittal at his trial, no 12 jurors in the District would vote unanimously to convict him.

"I think the prosecutors know," Barry asserted, "that in this town all it takes is one juror saying, 'I'm not going to convict Marion Barry. I don't care what you say.' "

A few days later, Barry followed up his provocative—and, as it turned out, prescient—claim by predicting on a local cable television show that if he sought reelection he would win the Democratic mayoral primary race the following September.

But on June 13, just five days before his jury was seated, Barry rendered the question of his political strength moot. During a lunchtime break from court he sped away in his Town Car, red light flashing and siren whooping, to secretly video-tape a surprising political message that would be broadcast later that night on Howard University's WHMM-TV (Channel 32).

"In my heart, I believe it's time for me to serve you, and God, in other ways," Bary proclaimed in an emotional, 15-minute statement replete with such divine references. "Therefore, tonight I'm announcing that Marion Barry will not be a candidate for reelection for my fourth term."

"I know many of you probably feel that my decision not to seek reelection is the wrong thing for me to do," Barry continued. He did not acknowledge that a far greater number of Washingtonians would have rejoiced if he had stepped down altogether—a move the mayor categorically rejected in his speech, contending that his resignation "would throw the city in such political turmoil and do violence to the [political] process, that it would take years for us to recover."

"I hope you will let go of your feelings and believe that my announcement tonight is the best thing for me personally, best for my family—that is, my wife and son," said Barry, "and also for my beloved city, that I respect so deeply."

"I've prayed on this," declared the born-again mayor, "and I think it's the best decision."

Although Barry stressed in his speech that his decision to take himself out of the 1990 mayoral race was "not related to my legal situation," the move reportedly had followed the collapse of plea negotiations with Jay Stephens.

In closing his speech, the mayor borrowed a line from Ecclesiastes. "For everything there is a season and a time to [every] purpose under the heavens," Barry paraphrased. "A time to get and a time to lose, a time to keep and a time to cast away." Then he added: "Tonight, it's time to cast away."

By giving Jay Stephens the prize he indirectly had sought without a fight—namely, his imminent departure from the District Building—Barry had skillfully outflanked his legal adversary. Now even the most skeptical potential jurors had a compelling reason to sympathize with him: a proud black politician had been forced to pay a huge price for his personal sins by giving up any future claims to the city's top job—so why punish Barry any further?

This very question, no doubt, was swirling through the mind of more than one of the 31 prospective jurors who filed into Judge Jackson's courtroom on Monday, June 18, and took seats on the long wooden benches in the spectators' section. They had been randomly selected by lottery from the remaining pool of 82 potential jurors. Eighteen were immediately moved into the burnished walnut jury box as the lawyers began to make their peremptory "strikes" or dismissals of unwanted jurors.

Dipping only once into the surplus pool of potential panelists, the opposing lawyers took just 36 minutes to choose the jury that would decide Marion Barry's fate. The final decisions came down, not unexpectedly, to race. Retchin and Roberts used seven of their nine permitted strikes to dismiss blacks they thought would be sympathetic to the mayor. Mundy and Mance, by contrast, used all but two of their 12 strikes to exclude whites they thought might vote to convict their client. Altogether, 13 black and five white Washingtonians were empaneled.

"Ladies and gentlemen," announced Judge Jackson, smiling pleasantly, "we have a jury seated." He added—perhaps he was unjustly sanguine—"I think the way in which *voir dire* has gone bodes well for a just and harmonious resolution of this case." Then Jackson read aloud the 14-count indictment, advising the jurors to listen with caution to the lawyers for both sides, explaining that they are advocates who will try to persuade them that their view of events is the correct one. Finally, he reminded the jurors that when all the evidence had been heard and they went into the jury room together, the verdict will be "yours and yours alone."

Jackson purposely did not reveal who the six alternate jurors were, a move aimed at keeping everyone focused on the testimony, which was sure to be both long in duration and often complex or controversial in content. He placed all 18 jurors in the custody of deputy U.S. marshals, who took them home to pick up clothes, then drove them to the Holiday Inn in nearby New Carrollton, Maryland, where they would live for the next six weeks.

In many ways the jurors, who lived in seven of the city's eight wards, were a classic cross-section of the city. More than two-thirds were black in a capital 70 percent black. One out of three worked for the city or the federal government, which are the primary D.C. employers. Three other jurors worked at hospitals. One taught private school. Two jurors were unemployed and two were retired. Four worked for private concerns. Ten had a relative or close friend with a drug or alcohol problem—not surprising in a city besieged by drugs.

In other ways the jurors did not reflect the general population. All but three of the jurors, who ranged in age from 22 to 70, were women. Ten had been born outside the District. Two out of three had attended college, five at the graduate level—a much higher level of education than the average Washingtonian. Thirteen of the 18 attended church regularly, and several of the regular churchgoers were Baptists, the mayor's newly chosen denomination.

Feelings about the defendant seemed to depend not only on race but on the age and religion of the juror and in what region of the country he or she had grown up. Four middle-aged black, churchgoing jurors, like the defendant, had been reared in the Deep South and tended to identify with and support Barry. Of this quartet two admitted before the trial that the experience had made them wary of whites.

"I was brought up in the South, and I know what [racial] prejudice is," wrote 61-year-old Alabama native and unemployed juror Johnnie Mae Hardemann on her questionnaire.

Hilson Snow, Jr., 49, also a native of Alabama, cited "various incidents of difficult treatment over the years" in answering a question about whether he believed himself "to be a victim of prejudice of any sort."

Forty-eight-year-old Doris Hawkins-Whitehead, a manpower development specialist for the D.C. Department of Employment Services, said in court she had "felt saddened" to learn of Barry's indictment. But Hawkins-Whitehead also said she could find the mayor guilty if the evidence so indicated.

Valerie Jackson-Warren, a 40-year-old secretary for the D.C. Department of Corrections, said she found undercover surveillance operations "an invasion of privacy." Her skepticism was shared by seven other black female jurors. Only one black panelist, 34-year-old Deborah Noel, a clerk at Howard University Hospital, said she favored undercover operations, "because it helps the police and the FBI catch criminals."

Although most of the jurors said they had no opinion on whether race played a role in the government's prosecution of Barry, two, including Harriedell Jones, a 58-year-old accounting assistant at the U.S. Department of Housing and Urban Development, said it did.

"I felt, and I think most blacks feel," said South Carolina native Jones during *voir dire*, "that they're trying to get him out of office."

Tonna Norman, a 30-year-old records manager for the federal Defense Mapping Agency, admitted that she harbored ill feelings toward Hazel Diane "Rasheeda" Moore, the black former model the government had used to bait the Vista trap.

In response to a question whether "race or politics played any part in the charges against Mr. Barry," Norman wrote on her jury form, "yes and no," explaining, "I question whether or not the Government would have taken the same steps against a less public figure and why they took the degree of action [that they did] against Mr. Barry."

The youngest black juror, 22-year-old Marsena Hall, an office assistant for the Hearing and Appeals Board of the D.C. Public Schools, wrote on her questionnaire: "At the moment, I feel the mayor is innocent, because I really don't know the evidence." However, she added: "I do feel, if I had to, I could make a fair and impartial judgment."

Two of the white jurors also seemed to lean slightly toward the defendant.

Fifty-four-year-old Edward Eagles, who would be chosen jury foreman, expressed reservations about government sting operations on the questionnaire. Eagles, coincidentally, taught history at St. Albans School for Boys, the same elite preparatory school in Northwest Washington where the mayor's nine-year-old son, Christopher, had just finished the fourth grade. (Barry reportedly withdrew Christopher at the end of the year because of classmates' taunts.) But Eagles also indicated, in a written response, that he did not condone lying under oath.

Anne Douglas Freeman, a 28-year-old office manager for the upscale Middendorf Art Gallery in Northwest Washington, responded thus to a question about whether a person is ever justified in lying under oath: "In the case of someone who is mentally or physically ill, lying under oath may not have been intentional, rather an act that was 'uncontrolled.'"

Freeman answered a question about alcoholism by describing it as "a degenerative disease." Since she shared the widely held clinical view that substance abuse, including alcoholism, which Barry had publicly admitted to, is an illness—a view promoted almost daily by Barry since his return from substance abuse treatment—she conceivably could condone Barry's alleged lies to a federal grand jury by perceiving them as the unintended acts of a man made "ill" by his alcohol dependency rather than as intentional lies.

Several other jurors also said they viewed alcoholism as a disease.

There were, however, a few skeptics representing both races on the panel.

Forty-five-year-old Marilyn Thomas, a black secretary at the U.S. Holocaust Memorial Council, wrote on her questionnaire: "I feel from reading the newspaper headlines on May 31, when Mayor Barry acknowledged he had taken crack cocaine before the Vista incident, that he should have admitted [to authorities] that he used a [controlled] substance before." But she also said, "I cannot state that he is guilty of the Vista [cocaine possession charge] because he has not had an opportunity to present his case to the citizens of the District of Columbia."

Sheila Kern, a 40-year-old white government relations manager for Motorola Incorporated, said she was confused by press reports saying that the mayor had admitted smoking crack at the Vista, because those reports did not "square with [Barry's] not guilty plea." Kern called the publicity surrounding Barry's arrest and trial, "Unfortunate for the city, embarrassing."

Joseph Deoudes, a 23-year-old white college student and co-owner of District Courier Service, wrote on his jury form that he could "absolutely" presume Barry's innocence in judging the case. But he also wrote, in answer to a question about lying under oath, that anything other than the truth, under oath, would appear to be perjury."

Barry was charged with three counts of perjury.

The oldest juror, 70-year-old Margaret Batson, a retired white railroad employee, wrote on her form that "too often, our politicians are not honest." But when questioned in court, she conceded, "Everyone is innocent until proven guilty."

Prosecutors Retchin and Roberts knew that if they hoped to win a conviction they had to convince the panel that the government had played fairly with the defendant and that the mayor not only was guilty of the charges beyond a reasonable doubt, but that he *deserved* to be convicted, and punished, for his misdeeds. They would have to make the jury believe, finally, that Marion Barry had been hoist by his *own* petard, not the government's.

But as Barry left the courthouse after the final day of jury selection, he made it clear that he was not going to make the prosecutors' job easy.

"The canaries [stool pigeons] are coming," he announced, using street slang to describe dozens of his former close friends and associates whom the government planned to put on the stand to testify against him.

18

ENTER THE "CANARIES"

On Tuesday, June 19, the first day of actual testimony in the mayor's two-week-old trial, Marion Barry strode purposefully into the courtroom, wearing a dark suit, a red carnation, and a self-confident smile. Ignoring his legal nemesis, Jay Stephens, sitting in the front row, his suit freshly pressed, every hair in place, the mayor strode to the defense table, sat down, and joked with his co-defender, Robert Mance. If the mayor was scared, or even nervous, he didn't show it.

Barry's wife, Effi, wearing a stylish summer dress, her hair, as always, fixed in a perfect, helmetlike coiffure, was back in court for the first time since the start of *voir dire*. She sat next to Lurma Rackley in the second row, grimly hooking a multicolored rug, like a twentieth-century Madame Defarge.

At 10:17, Richard Roberts stood up to speak for the government. "This is a case about deceit and deception," he said, "designed to keep the public, the police, and the grand jury from discovering the unfortunate but seeming truth that the defendant, Marion Barry, had been snorting cocaine and crack for years all over D.C and elsewhere.

"During the course of this trial, you will learn that while the defendant preached to our community, 'Down with dope!' he was putting dope up his nose."

Crisply, succinctly, without fanfare but with withering detail, Roberts laid out a pattern of executive lies and drug abuse stretching over six years. He told the jurors they would see Barry smoking crack on the Vista videotape, then mimicked what they would see by lifting an imaginary pipe to his mouth, lighting it, inhaling the crack smoke, holding his breath for a full 10 seconds, then, finally, exhaling as the jury watched, enthralled. Then he repeated the pantomime. Barry leaned back in his chair, appearing almost to doze.

"Every person has two sides," Roberts continued. "Well, this case is about the other side, the secret side of Marion Barry."

Roberts said the evidence would show "beyond a reasonable doubt" that Marion Barry had possessed and/or used illegal drugs with 10 different people in 20 different places—hotels, offices, business establishments, and boats—over a six-year period starting in 1984. He said Charles Lewis had started the cards falling for the government in December 1988, when he had offered cocaine to a Spanish-speaking maid at Washington's Ramada Inn Central, hoping to engage her in sex but instead prompting an investigation that led quickly to the mayor. He noted that the trap finally had slammed shut 13 months later when Barry was arrested at the Vista.

Roberts said Barry had compounded his troubles by lying to a federal grand jury in January 1989, after eliciting pledges from Charles Lewis and James McWilliams—a D.C. employee who had been with Barry and Lewis at the Ramada—to back up his lies.

Roberts said that the "defendant's deception began to unravel when Charles Lewis was caught in the Virgin Islands" in an FBI drug sting in March 1990 and then turned state's evidence a few months later. Adding a bit of spice to the proceedings, Roberts said, "Evidence will show that the defendant enjoyed a torrid relationship with Miss Moore for three years." He told how cocaine dealer Lydia Pearson, down on her luck, had "handed him [Barry] the crack cocaine with one hand and her 171 job applications with the other" when visiting the mayor at his satellite office in the Reeves Municipal Center.

Drawing another indelible word picture, Roberts told the jurors how former Youth Pride, Incorporated, worker Darrell Sabbs had, in recent years, seen Barry "use the corner of a business card to scoop up some of the cocaine powder and raise it up to his nostrils and inhale it." He said Washington restaurateur Hassan Mohammadi would describe how he saw the mayor "snort cocaine off a desk through a rolled dollar bill" at his Georgetown restaurant and that other witnesses "will tell you how the defendant was fond of preparing cocaine-laced cigarettes," which Barry called "M.B. specials."

Finally, Roberts advised the jury to "pay attention, keep an open mind, and, above all, use your common sense. If you do those things, both sides will receive a fair trial."

The mayor's chief attorney, R. Kenneth Mundy, began the defense case by keeping the pledge he had made several months earlier to put the government, rather than his client, on trial.

"This is a case," said Mundy, pacing before the jury box, "about deals the government made with the devil. For over a year and a half [since the Ramada Inn story broke] this case has been tried in the newsrooms, but now it is going to be tried in the proper place, in this courtroom.

"Approximately seven years ago, the government made a determination that it was going to *get* Mr. Barry, and that it was going to be prepared to go to any lengths and to any extremes to accomplish that—to make a case against Mr. Barry."

Mundy was risking a judicial rebuke with this claim. Judge Jackson had ruled in a written order that the defense "shall not refer to the matter [of the cost and duration of the investigation] in opening statement, nor shall it offer affirmative evidence without prior leave of court." He wanted to keep the jury's attention trained on the evidence, rather than Barry's claim that he was the victim of an elaborate and expensive scheme to bring him down. But Jackson permitted Mundy to take a swipe at the government in his opening statement, despite the order.

"The evidence will show," said Mundy, "that in that quest [to "get" Barry] they reached into the inner recesses of humanity and brought forth three notorious drug dealers, Mr. [Hassan] Mohammadi, Mr. Charles Lewis, and Mr. James McWilliams."

To drive home his message, Mundy belittled the state's star witness, calling Charles Lewis a "man for all seasons for the government, their man Friday," who was "willing to put any music and any lyrics to whatever tune the government wanted him to say," and who, along with another key witness, Rasheeda Moore, had already shown a serious lack of credibility by lying repeatedly to a grand jury investigating Barry. Mundy pointed out that the FBI had gone all the way to California to bring Moore back to D.C., that agents then "babysat her children, gave her money for shopping." He said that for the Vista sting, the government "provided the atmosphere, the accommodations. It provided the bait and it provided the booze. It provided the pipe and it provided the drugs. It provided the know-how in Ms. Moore showing Mr. Barry how to light the pipe and how to work the pipe, and it provided the fun. The evidence will show, ladies and gentlemen, entrapment, pure and simple."

Again, Mundy was skating dangerously close to the edge judicially by implying that the government had induced Barry to smoke crack at the Vista. In the same official order in which he had strictly limited any testimony about the cost and duration of the Barry investigation, Jackson had written that "the issue at trial in this case is not, as the defendant suggests, the government's 'integrity and humaneness,' but is instead whether the defendant committed the acts alleged in the indictment, as related by witnesses for the prosecution. That those witnesses (or others) may have supplied defendant with potentially dangerous substances is of no moment, and would not render their testimony any less believable."

Regarding the government's most dramatic piece of evidence, Mundy said, simply, "You watch the [Vista] videotape. You see who brings up the subject of drugs."

He called Iranian restaurateur and former embassy official Hassan Mohammadi, who would testify to using cocaine and opium with the mayor, "a professional snitch" who had escaped conviction in this case and in two earlier criminal cases by pleading guilty to lesser charges and turning state's evidence. Mundy asserted that Mohammadi had done this to avoid being deported back to his native Iran where, as a former consular official at the Iranian embassy in Washington under the Shah, he could count on being treated harshly by the Islamic fundamentalist government.

Mundy concluded: "I ask you to listen carefully to the evidence which you will receive and from the evidence and the cast of characters the government put together, you will see that there is reason not to believe, there is reason to discredit."

Ramada Inn Central general manager Sukhjit Singh was the first government witness to take the stand. The tall, bearded hotelier, wearing a dark suit and a white turban, cleared up one mystery of the Barry saga: it was *he*, not a D.C. police commander, who had called back the vice squad detectives on their way to Charles Lewis's hotel room to make an undercover drug buy from Lewis on December 22, 1988. Using a walkie-talkie, Singh had urged the detectives, who were disguised as hotel maintenance men, to abort their mission when he realized, that a "government official was in the hotel." The government's lead-off witness, whose sole purpose was to confirm Barry's presence at the hotel, spent only 10 minutes on the stand.

Next the government rolled out its biggest gun, in the unlikely person of Charles Lewis, the pudgy, baby-faced former D.C. employee and confessed drug dealer whom another government witness would later describe as "a dollar short and a day late for 20 years" and "50 going on 12." But on this day the prodigal son of a prominent Virgin Islands family, dressed in a cobalt blue, three-piece suit, brought anything but a smile to the defendant's face.

Each time Lewis mentioned a different time or place where he had allegedly used drugs with Barry, Retchin walked to one of two magnetized charts set up behind the defense table where the jury could see them clearly. They showed the dates and locations on which Barry allegedly had used cocaine with the 10 unindicted co-conspirators, including Lewis. To indicate the month and year of the alleged drug use, Retchin would remove a small, magnetized cardboard strip opposite the co-conspirator's name. Underneath was a scarlet patch. To indicate locations, she would place a magnetized card with the name of a hotel, boat, D.C. government building, or residence named in the testimony. By the end of the trial the dates chart had become a patchwork of red; the location chart was covered with scores of magnetized cards.

Lewis's drug odyssey with Barry had started, said the witness, in June 1986, when he had met Barry, and the mayor's security guard, Ronald Harvey, at the airport in St. Thomas, U.S. Virgin Islands. On the drive to the luxurious Frenchman's Reef hotel, Lewis said he had pinched his nostrils together to indicate cocaine use and asked Barry in coded language if he happened to "need anything special" during his trip.

According to Lewis, Barry had understood the gesture but declined his offer on that particular occasion. However, said Lewis, the mayor had taken Lewis up on his offer on subsequent occasions, including a drug-filled weekend in March 1988, when Lewis, Barry, and a Virgin Islands woman had consumed $300 worth of crack cocaine together while the mayor, according to trial witnesses, had tried, mostly without success, to drag a succession of island beauties into his bed.

"He asked me if I could get some rocks [of crack cocaine]," said Lewis in a softly weary voice that matched his appearance. "I told him 'yes,' because that's what I was using."

Lewis, who back then had represented the Virgin Islands government in a joint personnel project with the District government (he was fired in April 1988 by Alexander Farrelly, the islands governor, for gross "incompetence"), recounted how Barry had given him money to buy crack. Lewis said he had purchased about two dozen packets of the drug at a St. Thomas housing project during the mayor's four-day stay in 1988 and at various times had used crack, powder cocaine, and/or marijuana with the mayor in rooms at the Frenchman's Reef and Morningstar Beach hotels in St. Thomas and on chartered sailboats with the memorable names of the *Brigadoon* and *Ocean Fantasy*. The witness got a laugh when he described the skipper of the *Brigadoon* who, he said, after serving lunch during the June 1986 cruise, had come out of the galley with a covered tray, lifted the top to reveal several marijuana joints, and exclaimed, "Wait'll you see the dessert!"

Mundy objected, pointing out that his client had not been charged with using marijuana or, for that matter, with using any drugs outside the District. Jackson overruled him on the grounds that the testimony showed a pattern of chronic drug abuse by the defendant, part of the government's attempt to prove both "predisposition" (in order to negate defense charges of entrapment related to the Vista sting) and perjury (alleging that Barry knew about Lewis's drug activities).

Lewis said he had smoked one of the joints with Barry and "R.C." in the 36-foot sailboat's cockpit while Barry's police bodyguard was on the bow, and that the three of them had gone below to do some cocaine powder out of sight of the bodyguard, crew, and other guests.

Lewis also recounted a March 1988 visit Barry had made to the Virgin Islands in which he had brought along his son, Christopher, and Christopher's friend, Jonathan Miller. He said the mayor had stayed at the Morningside Beach hotel while the boys, along with one of Barry's bodyguards, stayed at a Sapphire Bay condominium owned by Washington millionaire and former Barry campaign donor John Hechinger. Lewis said Barry's legal counsel, Marlene Johnson, also had joined the mayor on that trip and that she too "had drugs at her hotel." He said that while he was getting high with the mayor and island resident Wanda Stansbury in Barry's hotel suite, he had expressed concern to Barry that Barry's bodyguard, Ronald Harvey, who was staying in a nearby hotel room, might learn about the illegal activities. Lewis said Barry told him "not to worry" about the D.C. police detective detailed to protect him.

Then Lewis, just released from jail after serving more than a year on drug charges related to the 1988 Ramada Inn incident, but still facing sentencing for his 1989 drug sting conviction in the Virgin Islands, was asked about the mayor's four admitted visits to the Ramada, each of which formed the basis for a count in Barry's indictment. In addition, three felony counts for lying to the grand jury were based on the Ramada Inn visits. Lewis recounted several visits by the mayor to the Ramada Inn Central in December 1988 and said that D.C. Public Works Department employee James McWilliams had joined them on one of those occasions. Contrary to what Barry had told the grand jury—that he had visited Lewis because his old friend was out of work and "sort of down, you know, sort of depressed"—Lewis said the mayor had brought him crack at the Ramada at least twice—once in a matchbox and once concealed in Barry's trouser cuff.

"When he [Barry] was in the Virgin Islands, I took care of him," explained Lewis. "When I was in Washington, he would take care of me."

The witness said that on one of Barry's Ramada visits he and Barry found themselves with crack but no way to smoke it, so the mayor had fashioned a makeshift pipe out of tinfoil, a hotel sherbet glass, and a rubber band and used it to smoke crack.

If Lewis was telling the truth during even part of the three hours he spent on the stand, Washington's mayor was not only a cocaine user, but a liar, since Barry had told a grand jury in 1989 that he had never seen Charles Lewis possess or use drugs. It was a subdued-looking Marion Barry who drove away from the courthouse at the end of the first day of testimony Tuesday.

Still the government had to prove that Lewis was a reliable witness. Because of the mayor's popularity and the way the government had bagged him, proving every "fact" in the case was going to be an uphill struggle. Knowing this, Jay Stephens gave a brief statement on Tuesday afternoon, hoping to dispel any remaining confusion about why the government was prosecuting Barry.

"In doing this," Stephens told reporters outside the courthouse, "we are seeking to fulfill our obligation to hold the defendant accountable for the criminal conduct charges in that indictment, based on the evidence, not on some irrelevant factors such as politics, or race, or the status of the defendant. Let me assure you that in this case we have sought to do that because justice demands no less."

When Stephens had finished so eloquently setting himself up for what very nearly became the worst debacle in his two-year reign as D.C.'s chief prosecutor, he turned on his heel and walked briskly away, taking no questions. His assistant, Judy Smith, a tall, strikingly attractive young black woman, broke the tension when she cheerfully began displaying some of the day's evidence for the press. Like Vanna White unveiling a new convertible on "The Wheel of Fortune," she laid out on a small table the hotel sherbet glass Lewis and Barry allegedly had used to smoke crack at the Ramada and taped to a board a glossy color photo of Barry on the deck of the *Ocean Fantasy*. In that picture the mayor is wearing a white sport shirt, slacks, and sunglasses, and holding a drink. He appears to be talking to a woman in a bathing suit reclining on the deck of the sleek, black-hulled vessel.

Charles Lewis returned to the stand on Wednesday, June 20, but before proceedings got underway the mayor strode cockily over to where the press was seated. He smiled when he saw WUSA-TV's Bruce Johnson.

"I see you got your protégé with ya," said Barry, referring to Jackie Hamilton of National Public Radio, who was seated next to Johnson. Both reporters are black.

"That's right," retorted Johnson, smiling.

"Miss Hamilton," said Barry, "where were you yesterday? I didn't see you in court."

As Hamilton explained, nearly 60 other reporters listened intently. Barry was letting them know two things: first, that he could and would ignore the white reporters whose stories angered him, and second, despite his seeming nonchalance, he actually missed very little of what went on in the courtroom—including the absence of a single black reporter.

"You missed the canaries singin'," Barry told Hamilton, who smiled back at the mayor. "They're comin' in droves, gettin' ready to land."

"Some of them have landed already," retorted Bob Strickland, another black WUSA-TV reporter.

"Yeah," Barry shot back, "but some of 'em crippled."

Nevertheless, Charles Lewis did a lot of singing Wednesday. He was on the stand the entire day. Retchin finished walking him through the litany of his alleged drug use with Barry and the mayor's subsequent attempt to cover up his activities at the Ramada by allegedly encouraging Lewis and James McWilliams to lie to the police and press about what really happened there.

"Did you reach an understanding with Mr. Barry as to what you were going to tell the police?" asked Retchin.

"Yes," replied Lewis. "My understanding is that I would tell the police the same thing I told the *Post* reporter. I told the *Post* reporter a lie and, therefore, I would be telling the police a lie."

Then Retchin asked Lewis to list the reasons he had decided to turn state's evidence, obviously hoping to head off any attempt by Mundy to discredit him on cross-examination. Lewis said he felt "uneasy" and "uncomfortable" at having lied to the federal grand jury in Washington, that his subsequent arrest and conviction in the Virgin Islands in a drug sting engineered by Ronald Stern "was like a wake-up call to myself." Then Retchin turned Lewis over to Mundy, the former lightweight boxer who came on like a heavyweight.

"The pangs of conscience for your conduct weren't so great that you didn't go back and start selling drugs, selling crack cocaine, were they?" asked Mundy. "You really didn't wake up and start cooperating until you got convicted in the Virgin Islands, is that correct?"

"Both things happened at the same time," parried Lewis.

"You went on trial and you were convicted and you were facing big time, weren't you?" retorted Mundy, not willing to let the witness off the ropes.

"The reason I waited—"

"Is that a yes or a no?" snapped Mundy.

"Yes," admitted Lewis.

Mundy then asked the witness if the U.S. attorney's office in Washington had agreed to ask for leniency in his behalf when it came time to sentence him in the Virgin Islands drug case. When Lewis tried to assert that he was merely trying to tell the truth, Mundy jeered, "You got a pretty sweet deal, didn't you?" He noted for the jury that the U.S. attorney's office had dropped drug distribution, fraud, and perjury charges against Lewis that could have put him behind bars for up to 50 years.

"I don't know," Lewis countered. "I don't have anything to measure it by."

Mundy asked Lewis about the powder cocaine he had admitted bringing from Florida to D.C. for James McWilliams and two other Washington friends during the fall of 1988, a drug connection Lewis had admitted Barry knew nothing about. Mundy also got the witness to describe the lies he had told to a federal grand jury in January 1989, lies that Lewis had retracted during a subsequent grand jury appearance. Mundy was trying to make Lewis look like a pawn in the government's master plan to "get" the mayor.

"My [trial] testimony," explained Lewis, "isn't to convict the mayor. "My testimony to the grand jury wasn't to indict the mayor, I was a witness [asked] to testify truthfully and completely."

"Mr. Lewis," demanded Mundy, "was it conscience or was it a desire to help and save yourself which primarily prompted you to start cooperating with the government?"

"Self-preservation is always first on anyone's mind," Lewis admitted.

Only once did Lewis get the better of Mundy. After testifying that Barry had become so paranoid while visiting him at the Ramada that he had unscrewed lightbulbs over the bathroom vanity mirror and placed them in his pocket—apparently to take home to check for listening devices—Mundy asked Lewis why the mayor would do such a strange thing.

"I says 'You know, what is with this bulb?' " replied Lewis, explaining that he'd asked the mayor the very same question.

Lewis's one-liner broke up the courtroom, which in turn reduced the tension and encouraged the incipient comedian.

"At the end of the night," Lewis offered, "he [Barry] would go to the bathroom, you know, prep himself, wash his face, and I'm not lookin' to see if he is stealing light bulbs or soap, you know."

Despite such rare countershots, however, by the end of his second day on the stand the government's star witness was reeling.

On Thursday, June 21, Mundy tore into Lewis again. Using transcripts of Lewis's previous trial testimony and his January 1989 grand jury testimony, he pointed out inconsistencies, which he then challenged Lewis to explain. But before the witness had a chance to respond, Mundy would hit him with another question. While jurors gave no sign of how they felt about Mundy's rough interrogation of the witness, Judge Jackson made it clear where he stood.

"You haven't touched on a substantive issue yet with respect to this testimony," Jackson admonished Mundy during one of the day's frequent bench conferences, which followed equally frequent lawyers' objections.

"The jury will be the judges of the effect of the testimony," Mundy shot back.

"What you have touched upon is his [Lewis's] credibility," allowed Jackson, "and you have effectively placed his credibility into question. But you haven't dealt with the substantive issues in the case."

Barry's chief defender wrapped up his cross-examination of Lewis by challenging two of Lewis's earlier assertions—that he had lied to the grand jury to "protect" the mayor and that the mayor was not really a particularly "close" friend of his.

"If you would lie in January of 1989 to protect Marion Barry, a man who wasn't a particularly close person to you, you would sure lie in August 1989 [to the grand jury] and on to the present to protect Charles Lewis, James McWilliams, and other persons much closer to you, wouldn't you?"

"No," answered Lewis, who then was excused by Judge Jackson. But the damage had been done.

The day ended on a light note. When the next witness, Orlando Berrios, a former bellman at the Ramada Inn Central, was asked to identify the mayor, he pointed to Barry sitting at the defense table, prompting a spontaneous smile and wave from Barry. The move drew a sympathetic laugh from the jury. But by the end of the third day of testimony, it was Barry, not Lewis, who appeared to have been hurt the most. Although Mundy had effectively challenged Lewis's credibility, he had left basically unchallenged Lewis's allegations of specific dates and places where Barry had taken drugs with him, received drugs from him, or where Barry had provided them to Lewis. If other witnesses were equally specific and convincing in this regard, Barry's only hope for acquittal would have to come from jury nullification.

Three more government witnesses testified on Friday, June 22, the fourth day of testimony: D.C. Public Works Department official James McWilliams, who had visited Lewis's Ramada Inn Central room on Monday night in December 1988, hoping to lobby the mayor for a job change; Barry security guard Fred Gaskins, who had delivered some papers (and allegedly some money) to the Ramada room the same evening McWilliams had visited; and Office of Personnel Management senior management analyst John Olsen, a longtime friend of Charles Lewis who had given him shelter at his suburban Falls Church, Virginia, home after Lewis had fled the Ramada. Of the trio, only McWilliams spent much time in the witness chair, and only he appeared to significantly damage Barry, a man he described ironically as "someone who I respect and whose services to the city and work in civil rights was something that I considered important."

McWilliams, who six months earlier had pleaded guilty to aiding and abetting the possession of cocaine at the Ramada had initially used the Fifth Amendment before the grand jury to keep from having to tell what he had seen at the Ramada. He had cooperated with the government only recently, because he had been paying too high a price in terms of legal fees and a disrupted life during the past 15 months by being "a loyal soldier." He had finally decided to "make a clean breast of what I had done" by telling the truth.

In court that day, "the truth" included a detailed description of McWilliams's unsuccessful attempt to lobby Barry for a job change while the mayor sat in the tiny bathroom at the Ramada, apparently high on crack.

"He was sitting on the commode [fully dressed] and he was just sort of slumped over a little bit," said McWilliams, who said he had seen white smoke pouring over the top of the bathroom door and smelled something "unusual" after Barry and Lewis went into the bathroom. But he said he saw neither Barry nor Lewis actually ingest any drugs. "I kept makin' my pitch about the job," said McWilliams. "And he looked up at me and said, 'You know, you look a lot like Santa Claus.'"

Laughter filled the courtroom as a somber-looking Barry, dressed this day in a grey, double-breasted suit with a red rose boutonniere, looked down and adjusted his shirt cuff.

"We were watching the [Monday night football] game," recalled McWilliams, when asked what he and the mayor did while Lewis went off in search of more drugs. "He said to me he knew a young lady that likes to make love for two or three hours, and he would introduce me."

Roberts elicited this rather cheap shot against Barry to show the jury not only how the witness spent his time alone with the mayor, but to make him look virtuous by comparison. Later Roberts ended his questioning about the Ramada by asking McWilliams if Barry had attempted to influence him after the police investigation began.

"We greeted each other very briefly," said McWilliams, explaining how he had run into the mayor at a holiday function a few days later, "and he asked whether everything was all right, and I said, 'Yes.' I took that to mean that neither Mr. Lewis nor I had caused him any problems."

During cross-examination, Robert Mance tried to discredit McWilliams by questioning him about the cocaine powder he said he had procured from Lewis on several occasions for a D.C. government employee McWilliams supervised and whom he described as "like a daughter."

"As part of your agreement for testifying in this case, they agreed not to charge you with those felony charges of distribution, isn't that right?" asked Mance.

"Part of the [plea] agreement was that if I testified truthfully, they would not prosecute me for other activities such as receiving small amounts of cocaine and giving it to a friend of mine," retorted McWilliams, deflecting Mance's attempt to portray him as a drug dealer.

D.C. police detective Fred Gaskins, part of the mayor's security detail, spent only a few minutes on the stand, enough to describe an errand Barry had sent him on: to bring an envelope full of papers—and, the government alleged, five $20 bills for Lewis to buy drugs—to the Ramada. Gaskins said he handed the envelope not to Lewis but to McWilliams, who answered his knock at Lewis's hotel room door that night. He said he had seen the mayor put some papers into the envelope in his limousine, but nothing else, including money. Although Roberts got Gaskins to admit that he did not see what else Barry may have placed in the envelope before he stuffed some paperwork inside, the government probably lost this round because it failed to prove conclusively that Barry put money in the envelope. It was Gaskins's word against Lewis's.

Friday's final witness was John Olsen, a bearded, heavyset white man with a booming voice, who described the sudden arrival of Lewis at his house. He called Lewis an inveterate "free-loader" but said he was not without a certain charm. During Lewis's brief stay at Olsen's suburban Virginia home, Lewis had made a phone call—apparently to the mayor—using the pseudonym "Alexander Farrelly," the Virgin Islands governor who two years earlier had fired Lewis from his government consulting post for incompetence. Olsen didn't know for a fact that Barry was on the other end of the line, but Lewis told whoever it was, "Don't worry about anything, I have got things under control. I will take care of business, there is nothing to worry about. I'm going in tomorrow to meet with the authorities."

Olsen said that after Lewis had hung up the phone he had turned to him and said, melodramatically, "Something's going down with me and the mayor and the ball is in my court. It's up to me to take care of business and that is what I am going to do tomorrow." Olsen also testified that James McWilliams had made repeated calls to Lewis at his house that weekend.

At the end of the first week of testimony, Barry and Mundy appeared at "Barry Beach," the name reporters had given to the main courthouse entrance at Constitution Avenue, NW, because of the shirtless cameramen, female production assistants in shorts, and the explosion of colorful golf umbrellas to shield them all from the sun. Mundy wore a straw boater, one of the many hats the flamboyant lawyer would don during the trial in an effort to play along with the intense media scrutiny, perhaps mock it a little. Barry stood behind his lawyer, wearing a silly grin.

"Every day the press keeps asking how we think we did with witnesses," said Mundy. "We are not keeping a scorecard." Then the former boxer used a fight analogy. "Everybody keeps looking for a knockout with witnesses. I remind you that you win fights also on points, by nicking and bruising."

19

BARRY TAKES A BEATING

When testimony resumed on Monday, June 25, it was the government, not Mundy, doing most of the nicking and bruising. The punishment was inflicted by four Virgin Islands women who told the jury about the mayor's alleged drug use and his often clumsy attempts to seduce them during trips to the U.S. territory in June 1986 and March 1988.

Barry was not on trial for sexual crimes, but Judge Jackson apparently allowed the testimony as to Barry's sexual conduct because, in each instance, it was linked to his alleged drug abuse.

Jonetta Darden Vincent, a "disaster specialist" for the territorial government, said she had seen Barry smoking marijuana with "a young lady" (Rasheeda Moore) on the bow of the *Brigadoon* during a June 1986 cruise. She said she could smell the marijuana smoke—a claim Mundy challenged, given wind conditions on a boat at open sea and the fact that Vincent said she was sitting near the stern. She also admitted that she had smoked marijuana during the cruise and had tried to snort cocaine, but her sinuses swelled up when Charles Lewis placed some powder in her nostrils in the head of the boat. Prodded by Mundy, she also conceded that she was unable to identify the *Brigadoon* when shown photos of it more than three years later by the FBI. Although she saw the "young lady" and Barry go below deck, she said she didn't know what they did down there. Nor could she recall the captain coming up from below with a platter of marijuana joints as Lewis had testified.

In a recorded statement, Virgin Islands businesswoman Dixie Lee Hedrington—who had told the court by way of her attorney that she was "too pregnant to travel"—said she met Lewis when he hired her secretarial services company to type job descriptions for the D.C./Virgin Islands joint personnel project.

She said Lewis offered to introduce her to the mayor, a man he "always referred to as his buddy." The introduction took place in March 1988, when Barry was staying at the Morningstar Beach Hotel in St. Thomas. She described entering Barry's room wearing a dress slit high up on both sides. Barry, she said, was lounging in his robe on one of two double beds with a woman named Wanda.

"[Barry]" started talking about my legs and what he could do with me, and I became annoyed," said Hendrington. He said he "likes women with long legs and he'd like to be between my legs. I was just totally irritated with his approach. I told him something to the effect that, 'I really don't appreciate your tone. I'm here with Charles.' Wanda was the mayor's local girlfriend, so I thought it was kind of rude of him to be talkin' to me that way while she was there."

Hedrington said Lewis pulled out a marijuana joint, lit it, and passed it to her. She partook, she said, only after Lewis reassured her it was not laced with cocaine powder or crack. She said everyone, including Barry, smoked the marijuana. Then, Hedrington recalled, Lewis said to Barry, "Buddy, I got something for you." She said Lewis showed Barry how to use a bong (drug pipe) he had brought, then "they went into the bathroom and they giggled, talked." She said she saw neither Lewis nor Barry smoking crack, a drug whose odor she was familiar with ("it smells like a really cheap perfume"), but "I saw smoke coming over the door, and I smelled it, so I just drew my own conclusion—that they were smokin' crack."

Her bottom line on Barry? "He was a pig, in my opinion."

Schoolteacher Zenna Mathias was more charitable. An attractive, short-haired woman wearing a cobalt blue dress with white polka dots and a white jacket, Matthias said she had gone to the Morningstar Beach Hotel with her old friend Charles Lewis in March 1988 and found the mayor of America's capital city "reclining on his bed" while watching an X-rated movie. She said Lewis left after introducing her to Barry and handing the mayor a small glass vial of cocaine powder.

"Why don't you be comfortable, take your shoes off?" Matthias recalled Barry asking her the moment Lewis left. "Why don't you come and look at the video with me?"

The married mother of three had replied, "Oh, I'm used to the human anatomy, I don't need to see that."

She said she had gone to Barry's room not for sex but because she was planning to attend law school in Washington and thought he might be able to help her. She took a seat near the door and heard "two sharp inhalations" behind her, but never actually saw Barry taking any drugs. Then she used a straw to snort cocaine offered by the mayor. (She didn't explain how taking drugs was related to her networking mission).

Matthias said Barry made a number of suggestive remarks to her during the movie but that he lightened up after it ended, although "on the way to the bathroom, he did try to grab me around the waist, but I just kept on going." She said the mayor seemed "relieved" after she made it clear she wasn't interested in sex.

Following an afternoon break, Barry cut some of the mounting tension by testing all the black leather swivel chairs at the defense table in a futile attempt to find one that didn't squeak. When the jury returned, Virgin Islands native Linda Creque Maynard took the stand. A tall, thin, plain-featured woman with short-cropped hair who wore an olive dress and glasses, Maynard would give some of the most controversial and potentially damaging testimony of the three-week-old trial. But before Judith Retchin began questioning her, the prosecutor asked for a bench conference.

"I wanted to alert the court and remind counsel that this witness, if asked about it, will testify that Mr. Barry forcefully overcame her sexually, that she believes she was raped by Mr. Barry," said Retchin out of earshot of the jury. "I do not intend to elicit that on my examination. What I am asking for is permission from the court to lead her around the topic."

After consulting with Barry, Mundy told Jackson, "We prefer that it not be brought out, and we will not bring it out."

Maynard testified that she knew she was in trouble the moment she entered Barry's hotel room because the mayor, lounging on the bed in his robe, said to Lewis, "Ah, this one is for me."

"No, this one is not for you," she said she had replied. But while smoking crack in the bathroom with Charles Lewis, who soon left, she said the mayor was "behind of me, leanin' against me, touchin' on me."

"Did you think that Mr. Barry's sexual advances were appropriate?" asked Retchin.

"No, I don't think so," replied Maynard.

"Did you feel humiliated?" Retchin pressed.

"Yes, I did," answered Maynard.

During cross-examination, defense counsel Robert Mance tried to discredit Maynard, but while doing so he inadvertently elicited testimony of the alleged sexual attack.

"Did you mention to Mr. Lewis anything about money?" asked Mance. He and Mundy were trying to paint all four island women as whores.

"No," Maynard replied.

"What happened when you left?" Mance demanded.

"I got down in the car and I found $50 in my pocketbook," Maynard answered.

"Who put money in your pocketbook?" asked Mance. He had just made a big mistake.

"It had to have been Mr. Barry," replied Maynard. "He was offerin' me money all the time and tellin' me he can give me anything I want, while he was making his advances."

"Did you tell Mr. Lewis what had taken place in the room?" asked Mance.

"No," replied Maynard, "I just wanted to forget all about what happened." Then the witness began to cry. As she took off her glasses, Judith Retchin asked prosecution tablemate Albert Arrington for his handkerchief, which she brought to Maynard on the witness stand. As this transpired, Barry somehow managed a tight smile, but several black female jurors glared at him.

During redirect, Retchin asked Maynard if the mayor had "put any limits on himself with you at that point?"

"No, he didn't," replied the witness.

"Objection," interjected Mance.

At a second bench conference, Retchin told Mance she was trying to be circumspect but that he had given away everything else except what really happened at the hotel.''

Judge Jackson overruled the objection, telling Mance, "For everything except possibly the word 'rape,' I think you have opened the door. You suggested this lady was a complying person who had no inhibitions about remaining on the property, she had the wherewithal to depart, and when she left, she found $50 in her pocket.''

Retchin, who had been icy at the bench, gently but bluntly rephrased her question to the witness.

"Did you and Mr. Barry have sexual relations in the hotel room?''

Maynard hesitated. Then, in a tremulous voice, she answered, "Yes.''

"Did you want that to happen?'' Retchin asked.

"No,'' said Maynard. Then she removed her glasses and began to sob.

"I'm sorry ma'am,'' said Retchin.

Judge Jackson called a 10-minute recess. In the jury room Deborah Noel and Margaret Batson also cried. At the end of the break Barry came in smiling. He stopped to share a joke with Lurma Rackley in a transparent attempt to appear unworried about the devastating testimony. Mignon Mundy, Kenneth Mundy's wife, who sat next to Rackley, turned away, unwilling to look Barry in the eye. Jackson came in red-faced and glared at Mundy.

Later that evening Barry appeared on Washington's WJLA-TV (Channel 7). In a live 10-minute interview with black news anchor Renée Poussaint, the sweating mayor deflected a direct question on the subject of Maynard's testimony, saying only, "God has blessed me to relax, to feel strong, and to bless the victims [a.k.a. "canaries"]. The government witnesses were pressured, pushed into this.''

He told Poussaint he was "not worried at all about this testimony. The public should not take all these statements as an indication of anything.''

Barry then lambasted the media for being "disrespectful, crude, discourteous and just classless''—as if the media, rather than his own actions, the government's decision to elicit testimony about his alleged sexual indiscretions, and a crucial slip by his lawyer in court, had brought this terrible embarrassment down on his head.

Barry came into court on Tuesday, June 26, for the sixth day of testimony, wearing a yellow rose corsage on his lapel—in recognition of "the canaries," he said—and a multicolored West African "kente" cloth scarf in honor of Nelson Mandela's visit to Washington. Effi Barry, who had skipped Monday's X-rated testimony, reappeared, wearing a white embroidered dress and a yellow rose corsage to match her husband's. Barry greeted her with a hollow smile and a peck on the check.

Even before Barry's legal crisis, their union had been marked more by ceremony than passion. Effi Barry confirmed this in an extraordinarily candid newspaper interview published during her husband's trial.

"Our entire marriage has been in public life," she told the *New York Post*'s Cindy Adams. "And, unfortunately, he's an alcoholic. Our marriage never really had a chance to jell."

Effi Barry told Adams she knew about her husband's drinking problem from day one of their marriage and soon suspected that Barry was "a womanizer" too, but accepted these imperfections because "I love him," and because she wanted to hold the family together, such as it was.

Effi Barry said she had warned her husband repeatedly that he was "going to be set up with a woman," and that her only question upon learning of his arrest was, "Who was she?"

The women the mayor dallied with, she scoffed, "were just used, because my husband came home to me every night."

Yet Effi Barry implied that her own personal ties to the mayor were largely symbolic, that they had stayed together primarily for the sake of Christopher, now 10. She told Adams she and Barry had eaten family-style dinners at home together "maybe five, six times" in their 12 years of marriage.

Washington's First Lady described her husband as "naive, not a judge of character," a "street dude" with a damaged ego and problems with self-esteem that had resulted in part from "growing up poor and black in the South." She said the mayor's alleged friends "have turned out to be hangers-on," and without her he would be alone. Asked whether she would "grow old and gray as Mrs. Barry," she told Adams, "I wouldn't say that." She quickly added, "I mean, one never knows."

Meanwhile, prosecutors were homing in on the three perjury charges against Barry, which were based on his alleged lies to a federal grand jury. As the opposing lawyers, jurors, judge and defendant listened over headsets, audiotapes were played aloud of Barry's grand jury testimony of January 19 and 24, 1989, in which he apparently told one lie after another— if the testimony of Charles Lewis, James McWilliams, and the four Virgin Islands women could be believed. Barry told the federal grand jury that he had never seen Lewis with drugs, given Lewis drugs, or given him money or anything else of value with which to buy drugs. He also denied receiving drugs from Lewis at the Ramada.

Some of the mayor's apparent lies were clever, some clumsy, some downright embarrassing, as when he was asked if Lewis ever had given him cocaine.

"Not unless he put it in a drink or something and I didn't know it," Barry replied with aw-shucks ingenuousness.

On the tapes, the mayor sounded surprisingly relaxed; he even joked about his predicament. When asked about his relationship with James McWilliams, for instance, Barry had responded, "I've had affairs at his house," He added: "I've had *political events* at his house. Correct that very quickly."

The grand jurors had found that remark hilarious.

But no one in the grand jury room had laughed at his best material, which concerned his 1988 Virgin Islands junket.

"I took three suitcases of D.C. government work down there," Barry could be heard saying on the audiotape, "and I did a lot of reading, lot of perusing of materials that were informational for me and probably wrote eight to 10 memos to my staff about various things."

He was so determined to give the taxpayers back in D.C. their money's worth for his trip, the mayor had told the grand jurors, that he even had taken a "suitcase of D.C. government business" on a daysail, "went down in the cabin part of the boat and worked on some business."

On Tuesday night a man who had helped lead a social revolution in the American South arrived late and unexpectedly with his wife at the Washington Convention Center and took a seat behind Nelson Mandela, who was leading a political revolution in South Africa. The African National Congress leader gave a fiery speech that brought the fist-waving, foot-stomping audience to its feet several times and filled the hall with wild cheering. Mandela had met privately with the mayor during his historic visit to the capital and discouraged Barry from attending the rally. He knew how much Barry had done in the past for his fellow American blacks, but he was politically shrewd enough to keep his public distance from the scandal-tainted Marion Barry of 1990. Mandela invited Jesse Jackson, Barry's old friend and possible future mayoral rival, to introduce him on the podium, although Barry had requested the honor. Mandela's rebuff was a sadly accurate indicator of how far Barry had fallen from grace.

On Wednesday morning, June 27, *The Witness*, the one everyone had been waiting for, finally arrived.

"Your honor, the government calls Rasheeda Moore," announced Judith Retchin.

A side door of the courtroom opened and a light-skinned 39-year-old black woman, dressed in black except for a pair of long, gold, cluster earrings, rambled into the courtroom on high-heeled shoes. Was she dressed for Marion Barry's symbolic funeral? Star witness Rasheeda Moore looked every bit the former model with her high cheekbones, full mouth accentuated by bright red lipstick, penetrating eyes, stylish clothes, processed hairdo, and confident carriage; but she also looked tired and overweight. She had lived life hard and it showed.

Effi Barry took one look at her husband's chief accuser and former lover and shook her head. Could this really be the woman for whom Barry gave up his future?

In a husky voice Moore took the oath and settled in for a long and devastatingly productive day on the stand. Directing her testimony to the jurors for maximum effect, Moore said she had taken drugs—marijuana, cocaine powder, crack, and opium—and/or had sex with Barry "over 100 times spaced over a three-year period" at 22 locations in and around the District and in the Virgin Islands starting in the spring of 1986. She said the mayor frequently gave her money to buy drugs and was a sophisticated enough user to be able to "freebase" cocaine powder into rocks of smokeable crack by mixing it with water and baking soda and cooking it over a flame. He could also construct a makeshift crack pipe with tinfoil, water, and a jar when no other smoking implement was available, she said.

She said that on frequent occasions Barry had acted paranoid when he was high, complaining to her that he thought he was being followed. She said on one such occasion, when he looked out the window of her 16th Street, NW, apartment and saw "a light blinking," he hid in the bathroom telling her he feared the light was a surveillance camera. On another occasion, Moore said, after smoking crack at a friend's Northeast Washington home, Barry became so afraid that police were closing in on him that he hid his remaining "rocks" in a vacuum cleaner bag until she finally reassured him that no one was after him. At that point, Moore said, he retrieved the drugs, dusted them off, and smoked some more.

As Barry sat, chin in hand, glaring at Moore, and Effi Barry hooked her rug with studied pruposefulness, the witness described multiple trysting spots ranging from her 16th Street, NW, apartment, to the mayor's home, on Suitland Road, SE, to the McLean, Virginia, residence of African American Episcopal bishop H. H. Brookins, who, she said, was asleep in a nearby bedroom when she and the mayor smoked crack in a second-floor bathroom. Moore said she also had smoked crack with Barry in his satellite office at the Reeves Municipal Center and, on another occasion, in the basement of her mother's Northwest Washington home. On that occasion, Moore recalled, the mayor had nearly passed out after taking a huge hit off the crack pipe.

"He took a very big hit," said Moore. "He consumed a lot of smoke and held it for a long time. When he let it out, his body started shaking and he almost fell and I grabbed him and said, 'Are you okay?' And I said, 'Stay focused.' So he focused his eyes, got his composure.''

After Barry recovered, said Moore, "He said, 'That was a really great hit.' ''

Moore said that when they went upstairs, her mother, Mary, served the mayor tea and sandwiches.

Moore said she and the mayor had met so often at the Gold Coast home of D.C. advertising executive Jeffrey Mitchell that "there was a [bed]room there that was kind of a standing joke—that it was our room."

She said she and Barry had watched Fourth of July fireworks for two consecutive years (1986 and 1987) from the balcony of a room at the L'Enfant Plaza Hotel, across from the Washington Mall. On those occasions, she said, as a precaution, Barry hid the cocaine powder they used in rolled-up currency under the bathroom sink in their hotel room.

Moore said that during her more than three-year relationship with Barry his police bodyguards frequently gave her rides in the mayor's limousine, sometimes to pick up drugs. On one occasion, she said, Sergeant James Stays even babysat her children while she and Barry went out for the evening.

'' 'I hope you're not gonna be bad tonight and go down to Florida Avenue [an open-air drug market],' '' Moore said Stays had teasingly admonished them as they left. Stays, a 30-year D.C. police veteran, would later deny virtually everything that Moore said about him.

She said that she and Barry had tried several times to quit using drugs but never seemed able to stay away very long, especially when they were together. She said that from the start of their extramarital affair she had "tussled with" her guilt feelings, but that Barry had convinced her to continue seeing him. Once, at the Channel Inn on D.C.'s Potomac River waterfront, she said, "he told me that it was divine providence that we were together. I told him that I believe divine providence is a very strong word. He was playing with God's divinity. But at any rate, I did continue with the relationship.''

When she finally worked up the nerve in June 1988 to tell Barry, during a rendezvous at the Hyatt Regency Hotel near Capitol Hill, that she wanted to break off the sexual relationship, she said the mayor did not take it well.

"He asked me if he could make love to me," she said, and when she refused, "He slapped me." She says she slapped Barry back, and "he slapped me back and I ended up on the floor. He said, 'I haven't hit a woman in twenty years. You have been the worst of them, man. Just get out, get out!'"

Moore said she left the room, briefly, then came back and apologized.

"I said, 'Don't worry. It's probably for the best.' I was bein' eaten up with guilt because of the adultery and everything."

Effi shook her head at Moore's belated guilt pangs. Several female jurors looked at Barry with apparent disgust. The mayor was spared even greater embarrassment when his lawyers successfully blocked an attempt by Judith Retchin to lead Moore into a detailed description of an assignation with Barry at the Vista International Hotel nearly two years before the sting operation.

At the bench Retchin proffered to Jackson that Barry had threatened to cut off funding for her "Project Me" contract if Moore did not perform fellatio on him. The prosecutor said she was willing to forgo the sexual allegations and have Moore testify only that Barry said to her, "If you give up on me, you lose everything that comes with me." Mundy understandably objected: the government was entering dangerous territory by implying that Barry had tried to exchange a city contract for a sexual favor—an allegation which, if proven, would constitute a separate, indictable crime. Jackson ruled that Retchin—who agreed to temporarily drop the line of questioning—could revisit it during her redirect examination of Moore, since it could, in his words, explain "why she [Moore] is prepared to testify against him."

Moore also testified that she had not seen Barry snort cocaine during a June 1986 sailboat ride with Barry in the Virgin Islands, although she had shared a marijuana joint with him. Her testimony refuted that of Charles Lewis, who said Barry had indulged in both cocaine and marijuana aboard the *Brigadoon*.

Finally, Moore said that she had agreed to cooperate with the government after joining a church in Los Angeles and "tusslin' with the lies" that she had told to many people, including federal grand jurors in D.C. inquiring about the mayor's alleged drug activities.

When Moore finally strode out of the courtroom Wednesday afternoon with a determined, even jaunty, gait, Barry was left reeling. He had been hurt badly. Spectators and reporters could only wonder what had motivated Moore to become, in Barry's words, the government's chief "canary." Although she had revealed on the stand that the government had decided not to prosecute her for her admitted crimes of possessing cocaine and lying to a grand jury about Barry's drug use and said she had rediscovered God while living in Los Angeles, even such powerful incentives did not seem enough to motivate the streetwise former model to play Delilah to Barry's Samson. One was almost forced to conclude that, as she later testified, Moore truly believed she was the only one who could stop Barry from killing himself with drugs, and that having him arrested was the swiftest, surest way to do that.

On Wednesday night Barry returned with his wife to the Washington Convention Center, this time to attend a kick-off rally for local political candidates slated by the Nation of Islam. On the dais the mayor embraced the group's 57-year-old leader, Louis Farrakhan. The controversial black separatist, born in Boston as Louis Eugene Walcott, grabbed Barry's hand and raised it in the air.

"I don't want the mayor to stop," Farrakhan told the cheering crowd of 17,000. "I want the mayor to run, Barry, run."

As the mayor's battered ego soaked up the applause, Farrakhan called Barry a "repentant soul" who is "under attack" by federal prosecutors. Echoing more mainstream black leaders such as NAACP executive director Benjamin Hooks, who had accused the government of selectively targeting black elected officials for investigation, Farrakhan charged that Barry was only the latest victim of a national campaign to harass and discredit black elected officials.

"Is his prosecutor sinless?" the provocative Black Muslim minister asked rhetorically. "Is the attorney general sinless? Is President Bush sinless?"

Farrakhan said that Barry "deserves our forgiveness." Finally he asserted, "We stand with those who stand with us."

During Barry's political heyday, he would not have shared a podium with a man who stirred national controversy with his virulently anti-Semitic remarks, his calls for a separate black nation, and his contention that the AIDS and drug murder epidemics sweeping America's cities were genocidal conspiracies launched by whites. Some of Barry's most generous campaign supporters were white businessmen and developers, including Jews, who would not take kindly to Barry's embrace of a man who had called Judaism "a gutter religion," described Adolf Hitler as "wickedly great," and accepted financial donations from Libyan dictator Muammar Kaddafi.

Barry had other, more personal reasons to avoid Farrakhan. During a May 1990 campaign appearance at Washington's Mayfair Mansions housing project where unarmed "Fruit of Islam" patrollers in bow ties and suits had driven out heavily armed drug dealers, Farrakhan, in a pointed reference to Barry, had publicly castigated morally corrupt black leaders, urging the Mayfair residents to replace them with Muslim candidates.

"You can't offer them a strange woman because they have their wives," Farrakhan had asserted about the Muslim candidates. "There is not going to be any back-room smoking and drinking. And you can't serve them any drugs."

Normally Barry could have been expected to indulge his penchant for political paybacks in return for this slight. But on this night Barry needed a lift, not another fight. He was seeking approval anywhere he could get it, circling the wagons of racial solidarity, even if that meant embracing a man who was, in his own way, no more tolerant than the white racists against whom Barry had struggled much of his life.

20

THE STING UNREELS

On Thursday, June 28, came what every juror, spectator, and reporter had been waiting for: the Vista sting videotape. But before they got a long-awaited glimpse into what prosecutor Richard Roberts had termed Marion Barry's "secret side," Judith Retchin tried to put a government spin on the tape by walking Rasheeda Moore step by step through her role in the events of January 18, 1990. Retchin was concerned about the hostility many of the jurors had expressed toward undercover operations in general and Rasheeda Moore in particular. She also knew that Kenneth Mundy would try to sway the jury in Barry's favor regarding any ambiguous actions or dialogue on the tape—there were plenty—and to discredit a woman who had turned against her lover. First, Retchin asked Moore why she had agreed to join forces with the government.

"I wanted to cleanse myself," said Moore. "It is getting rid of a lot of things, putting it out in front, exposing myself and becoming transparent. It is a personal cleansing."

As Moore elaborated on her cathartic motives for setting Barry up, explaining that she hoped to save the mayor and herself from the deadly curse of drugs, her voice began to falter, and she appeared near tears. Barry sat chin in hand, glaring at her. He did not look grateful.

Retchin asked Moore who first mentioned drugs at the Vista.

"The mayor brought it up," replied Moore. "He asked me if I had 'been good.' And he answered the question: 'Of course not.'"

Moore explained that Barry was asking whether she had been taking drugs. She said he asked her several more times about her drug use before Wanda King, the FBI undercover agent, produced the crack. She said that Barry also had asked

267

if Wanda "messed around," which she took to mean did Wanda use drugs. Moore told him "she toots cocaine" occasionally.

Finally, Retchin asked Moore why she had screamed when the FBI agents burst into the hotel room.

"I didn't want him to think that I was involved in the operation," confessed Moore. "It was trying to release some of the pain—for him. It was a frightening situation and that is when I saw his expression on his face, an expression I had not seen in the past. I reacted to that expression by saying, 'Where is the mayor? Where is the mayor? Where is Wanda?' and it was just a way of trying to help him through the process."

Several jurors laughed.

As Retchin continued to quiz Moore about her role in the sting, outside the courtroom Minister Louis Farrakhan showed up with 10 bodyguards, all wearing bow ties and carrying walkie-talkies. Barry had given the Nation of Islam leader one of the defense's courtroom passes. However, Judge Jackson ordered that Farrakhan be kept out.

After lunch, technicians wheeled out five television monitors—one each for the judge, the jury, the government, the defense, and, finally, the public and the press. The mayor, wearing a dark, double-breasted suit and a yellow rose corsage, walked in jauntily, flexing his jaw muscles, rocking from side to side like a boxer entering the ring. He stopped a moment before the five rows of reporters and sketch artists on the left side of the courtroom. Napoleon-like, he stuck his right hand inside his suit jacket and scanned the sea of scribes. One out of seven reporters was black, with a sprinkling of Hispanics. The rest were white. Barry knew many of them, including tall, blonde, athletic Jan Smith of Washington's WTTG-TV (Channel 5). She could backpedal in her high heels as surely and quickly as a football safety covering a pass receiver. The skill was invaluable in the quick-strike interviews she did with her television crew whenever Barry or some other key player in the courtroom drama left the federal courthouse at the end of the day.

"Mr. Barry, is the videotape another canary?" Smith shouted above the din.

"I hadn't thought about that," grinned Barry, who earlier had characterized the tape as "just another tool in the U.S. government's conspiracy." He added: "Very interesting."

The tape began to roll at 2:05 P.M. Spectators and reporters craned their necks and shifted in their seats for a better view of the screen as a middle-aged black man entered room 727 of the Vista International Hotel, casually greeted his former lover and her "friend," removed his suit jacket, and sat down next to her on the bed. The picture was grainy and under-exposed, the soundtrack occasionally unintelligible. One observer likened the tape to old television footage of the astronauts landing on the moon. But there was no mistaking the identity of the man who, only minutes after entering the hotel room, reached over and grabbed his former lover's right breast.

Barry's 83-minute strut upon the world's stage was far more sad than dramatic. As Tom Shales of the *Post* so aptly put it, the public airing of Barry's dirty laundry "made possible a new kind of global and communal embarrassment." He added: "As television, the videotape was grimly compelling. The encounter between Barry and Moore seemed joyless and furtive and there was no evidence of any euphoria produced by the drug. As for the bust, it had little resemblance to the glamorous arrests in cop shows and action movies. This was not exciting. This was degrading and pathetic."

Because of the tape's poor technical quality, the jurors spent more time following the dialogue in transcripts the government provided than watching the monitor. But when the large-screen television showed Barry lifting the glass pipe stem to his lips, tilting his head back, firing up the crack with a lighter, and taking a huge hit, the 18 federal panelists watched in rapt silence.

When the FBI agents were shown bursting into the room to arrest Barry a minute or so later, even the stoical Effi Barry grimaced. In a back row Kool-Aider Patricia Little, who attended the trial daily, began sobbing, prompting her removal by marshals.

At the very end, however, the video became almost humorous. As he was being searched, Barry kept repeating variations of "That goddamn bitch set me up!" Later a paramedic said to him, "I understand you've been under quite a bit of stress," while in the background the robotic voice of the cardiac monitor kept chanting, "Check electrodes! Check electrodes!" There was also pathos—the mayor of the nation's capital sitting on a hotel bed in his shirt-sleeves and suspenders, his hands cuffed behind him, talking quietly to men who called him "sir" and "Mr. Mayor" and all but apologized for arresting him.

In the 20 minutes left after the tape played and before court adjourned, Mundy tried to reverse the negative momentum. He tore into Moore. He dredged up the illegitimate children she had had with two different men and their alleged criminal records. He attacked her credibility by pointing out apparent inconsistencies in her testimony, grilled her on dates of Barry's alleged drug use that she was unclear about, and tried unsuccessfully to get her to admit she'd introduced Barry to crack in the spring of 1987.

At times Moore managed to parry Mundy's thrusts, but he was quickly scoring points with the jury. At one point she was near tears when Mundy pressed her about her drug use in April 1990—three months *after* the Vista sting.

"This is something I have to deal with every day," she said of her fight against cocaine addiction.

Barry sat at the defense table nodding, a slight smile on his lips. But his satisfaction would be fleeting: by the time court adjourned for the day, he had been hurt far worse than the government's star female witness. And the damage was not limited to the courtroom.

The sting videotape—because it was evidence and thus in the public domain—was released and broadcast, in whole or in part, on every local station and national network, and, via satellite, to the world. The next day newspapers as far away as London, Johannesburg, and Bogota ran front-page stories on the Barry trial. Within the week, D.C. street vendors were doing a brisk business in T-shirts reading, "I Saw The Videotape" on the front and "The Bitch Set Him Up!" on the back. Johnny Carson, Jay Leno, and the "In Living Color" television comedy ensemble did Barry jokes or skits. Other than former president Richard Nixon during the Watergate scandal, no U.S. politician had ever been so publicly vilified.

On the evening of June 28 Barry returned to the Washington Convention Center for another shot of ego-fixing applause. This time he was joined on the stage not only by Minister Louis Farrakhan but by two other controversial black leaders—the Reverend George Augustus Stallings, Jr., a renegade Catholic priest who had started his own church, and Illinois representative Gus Savage, the Chicago-based Democrat the *Washington Post* called "a master at race-baiting politics."

Savage told the crowd he was concerned that no local politicians had turned out to support the mayor. "We need a change in your elected representation," he said. "You need to elect some representatives who are more afraid of you than they are of white Americans and Jewish Americans."

Having tarred the city's elected representatives, its whites, and its Jews in a single stroke, Savage sat down and let a more creative speaker address the forum.

"The trial," asserted Farrakhan, "bears witness to the wickedness of the United States government. The government of the United States of America has always been against strong black men and women who will lead their people where they don't desire."

Comparing Barry's plight to that of Jesus Christ, the Islamic minister said the mayor had his own Judas [Rasheeda Moore] who betrayed him "for thirty pieces of silver" and freedom from prosecution. "They [federal prosecutors] are so afraid that you love the mayor that they want to crucify him!"

Then Farrakhan made an observation that even Barry might not agree with: "This is good for the mayor," he said. "The holy Koran teaches us that hell is meant for purification. God is going to use the mayor to bring down the government. God is going to use the weakness of the mayor to bring down the strong."

Finally, the controversial Islamic minister told his audience that, "There's going to be a worldwide revolution, and it's on its way to the U.S.A."

As cheers filled the auditorium, Barry smiled gratefully. It didn't seem to matter that he was being used to send Farrakhan's revolutionary message to his followers. The beleaguered mayor had found in this tiny, radical subset of black Washingtonians someone to applaud him, someone to take the sting out of his global humiliation.

21

"PEOPLE ARE ANGRY"

On Friday, June 29, the Reverend Stallings attempted to enter the courtroom but was blocked by marshals at Judge Jackson's order. Jackson had ruled that Stallings, like Farrakhan, might intimidate jurors and disrupt the proceedings.

"We are going to have hell on Earth," warned Stallings, if the judge did not change his mind.

Stallings did not have to wait for Armageddon. The American Civil Liberties Union petitioned the District of Columbia Court of Appeals in behalf of Stallings and Farrakhan. Out of apparent deference to Jackson, the appeals court threw the matter back to the federal judge on a technicality, after noting pointedly that although judges have broad leeway in maintaining order inside their courtrooms, no spectator should be barred from a public trial "simply because his presence is thought to send an undesirable message to the jurors."

A week later, Jackson relented and let both men in.

Before he did so, however, Barry and his followers milked the issue for potential sympathy. Outside the courthouse on the day Stallings was banned, Barry told reporters, "I think we are in a totalitarian situation where Bishop Stallings or Minister Farrakhan" cannot attend the trial. "It's like Nazi Germany." Then, the mayor asserted, "This trial is not just about some alleged criminal act on the part of Marion Barry; it's a larger issue than that."

In fact Barry and his followers *were* turning Barry's trial into a "larger issue."

Later that evening, radical black lawyer and newspaper columnist Mary Cox during an interview on WJLA-TV claimed that "All African-Americans are on trial."

273

"At no time since Reconstruction has there been a comparable period of incessant harassment of black elected officials," asserted the NAACP's Benjamin Hooks, although he provided no concrete evidence. More persuasively, Hooks compared the alleged fortune spent on the Barry investigation—a rumor that had been elevated to "fact" by repetition—to the government's relatively lackadaisical response to the villains of the savings and loan industry.

"Something is wrong with our system of justice," observed Hooks, "when more than $40 million is spent and over 70 FBI agents assigned to trail and monitor one black elected official, to set up a sting operation to bring him down, and then to have America's chief law enforcement officers say afterwards that due to limited resources, no criminal investigations will be launched against 1,600 greedy savings and loan bank officials who have stolen $500 billion."

The Reverend Stallings invited Barry to his Southeast Washington church on June 30 to help celebrate the first anniversary of the founding of Imani Temple African-American Catholic congregation.

Calling Barry "the greatest mayor this city has ever had," Stallings said the mayor was "in trouble right now because he is too smart, too intelligent, and too black." He charged further that Barry's trial had stemmed from "the demonic and evil mind of the government. They [federal officials] figured that since Marion Barry couldn't get bought, he had to get caught."

That same weekend D.C. Council member H. R. Crawford told the *Washington Times* that because of the trial, race relations in the city had "reached a very, very explosive point. Any little thing, the least little insignificant incident, can touch off a major incident of significant proportions that can be avoidable if we all use level heads."

On Monday, July 2, 2,000 people—including about 500 members of the mayor's Youth Leadership Institute and scores of senior citizens bussed in for the occasion—gathered in Freedom Plaza in downtown Washington to hear such newly converted Barry supporters as local Nation of Islam leader

Dr. Alim Muhammed rail against the federal government's attempted "lynching" of the mayor.

To a chorus of cheers and raised fists, Dr. Muhammed assailed television stations and networks for playing the Vista sting videotape, calling them "no better than some gang of rednecked, tobacco-chewing Ku Klux Klan" members. "This is not the kind of country where some judge and some hangman that's called a U.S. prosecutor can subvert the political process, because that's really what [the Barry trial] is all about," declared Muhammed.

Then he articulated the belief of at least 20 percent of the D.C. electorate who, according to voter surveys, still supported Barry: "They [federal officials] know they could never defeat the mayor at the election place. They know they could never defeat him by running a candidate against him. What we are witnessing is a subversion of democracy, a subversion of the process of government."

As the rhetoric on the street grew more heated and far-fetched, inside the courtroom Kenneth Mundy and Rasheeda Moore were captivating jurors and spectators with their *ad hominem* exchanges.

Pressed by Mundy about why she set Barry up, for instance, Moore explained: "I agreed to participate in the sting because the Lord put it in my heart to participate in the sting."

"When did the Lord visit your heart?" Mundy asked.

"The Lord visits my heart all the time," Moore replied.

"To put that [the decision to cooperate with federal lawmen] in your mind, I mean?" Mundy clarified.

"The Lord visits my heart all the time, okay?" Moore retorted. "As I was saying, if I could complete [my answer], Mr. *Monday*,"—she seemed to delight in mispronouncing the defense attorney's name—"I am a born-again Christian and I do believe in the laws of the land and the laws of God. And God has given me in my spirit to do this, and I can only speak what I feel, and the consequences of exposing myself and exposing the mayor are not very good for me, nor do I enjoy doing this. But it is the only thing that I could have done."

Finally Mundy hit Moore with the question he had been building toward.

"When you were visited by the Lord," he asked with pointed sarcasm, "were you visited only in part of your heart so that you continued buying and using drugs after you had this great visitation?"

"Objection!" said Retchin, as several jurors chuckled.

"Sustained," said the judge.

But Mundy had already scored, as he did again in revealing Moore's vagueness about the dates on which she and Barry had allegedly used drugs together.

"Can you give me a month, a day and a year for any of these incidents?" Mundy demanded.

"No, I cannot," Moore admitted, amazingly, even though she had named scores of locations during direct examination by Retchin and had given precise details of what happened at each one.

"For all of these 100 or more episodes?" Mundy asked, incredulously.

"No, I cannot," Moore repeated. She appeared to have surrendered. Or was she belatedly trying to protect the mayor, trying to soften the blows she had delivered at the Vista and in her earlier testimony by suddenly playing dumb on the stand? There was no way to know.

Mundy grilled Moore about everything from her admitted lies to a federal grand jury, to her drunk driving arrest in Los Angeles, and the drug and perjury charges that federal authorities in the District agreed not to press after Moore began cooperating. In reviewing the sting videotape, which he played frame by frame at times to back up his inquiries, Mundy got Moore to admit that she had asked Barry seven times if he wanted drugs during their brief Vista encounter and that he had said no each time.

He asked her if she didn't think she had exceeded her written "mandate from the FBI not to influence, not to persuade, not to invite" the mayor to use drugs.

"I did," Moore surprisingly confessed. "I did get overwhelmed and carried over." But she quickly added that her actions were not out of a "zeal to get Mr. Barry," as Mundy had just suggested.

Mundy pointed out that telephone records showed that Moore had called Barry outside of office hours no less than 224 times between June 1986, when she first started seeing him, and June 1988, and that she had tried to reach him more than a dozen times after she moved to California a year later, but that the mayor had rebuffed her, talking to her only once during that period. Mundy drew a picture of a desperate, insecure woman who had reason to feel rejected and perhaps to seek revenge. "Why did you shout, 'Maria, Maria!' just before the police broke in [to the hotel room]?" Mundy demanded. "Was that supposed to be the signal?"

"I would have to read the transcript again to tell you why," Moore countered dryly. She wasn't giving anything up without a struggle. But neither was Mundy.

"You say you had no vengence on your mind against Mr. Barry because of Maria McCarthy?" the defense counsel asked. He knew Moore had found her girlfriend and the mayor *in flagrante delicto* shortly after introducing them.

"I have no idea," Moore stonewalled. "I wish I could figure out why I said it. I have no explanation."

Questioning the witness about Barry's claim that he did not know how to use the crack pipe Moore had brought to the Vista, Mundy asked Moore if she thought that the mayor somehow knew he was under surveillance.

"I felt from the very beginning," replied Moore, "that he felt something, was suspicious of something."

"Ma'am," replied Mundy, "if that is true, why did Mr. Barry go on a few moments later and hit the pipe?"

It was the question at the heart of the trial.

"Because he had a desire to," replied Moore, summing up the truth in six short words.

Score one for the government.

Mundy stung Moore again when he asked her about the $32,000 in cash payments and benefits he estimated she had received from the government during the previous six months, especially the $1,700 a month she was being given in the Federal Witness Protection Program.

"When was the last time you worked and earned that much money?" Mundy demanded.

"I can't be sure," replied Moore. "Probably when I was working the 'Project Me' program, working for the District government."

"When did you make the deal with the government for this amount of money?" Mundy asked with audible disgust.

"I never made a deal with the government," Moore protested. "I went into the Witness Protection Program based on this operation, so I never made a deal with the government, Mr. Monday."

Mundy had inadvertently opened a Pandora's box. On her redirect questioning of Moore, Judith Retchin elicited testimony about why Moore had entered the Witness Protection Program.

"My life had been threatened," said Moore. "There was a $100,000 contract on my life." She claimed the threat came from someone who knew her in high school.

After Moore dropped her bomb on the startled jurors, Retchin stated that nothing indicated Barry had any part in the threat.

But when Mundy asked Moore during recross-examination if she remembered who had sent her the alleged death threat letter, and whether she had ever seen it, she replied no each time. Jurors were left to guess whether she had ever been threatened at all.

Mundy had scored again.

Occasionally, however, his aggressiveness backfired. When he tried to paint Moore as a sexual opportunist for allegedly trading sexual favors in return for the "Project Me" contract, she stung Barry with her reply. "He said if I turned my back on him, I turned my back on the program," said Moore, describing a rendezvous in May 1988 during which she said Barry had asked her oral sex and she had refused. "So the program was cut that summer," Moore said.

As court adjourned for the day only minutes later, Mundy and Anita Bonds began gathering their papers together. Barry stood next to them, his hands thrust into his trouser pockets, looking downward, his face a study in dejection, his eyes glazed over. After keeping up such a defiantly positive public demeanor through a month of trial proceedings, was the

defendant finally starting to feel the sadness and embarrassment the trial's revelations were visiting upon so many others
in the city, including his wife and son? Barry was such a good
actor, it was impossible to tell, but the emotions certainly
appeared genuine.

Later, outside the courthouse, Kenneth Mundy summed up
his impression of Moore.

"She was intelligent and resourceful," he deadpanned. "She
made up things as she went along. I guess she told the truth
when she gave us her name. I think most of everything else
was a lie."

Frances Murphy, publisher of the *Washington Afro-American
and Tribune*, lumped Moore together with the Virgin Islands
women who had preceded her on the stand. "They have put
on nothing but prostitutes," said Murphy at the end of Moore's
testimony. "They're gonna have to do better than that [to
convict him]. People are angry. If the jury reflects the people
in this city, they're angry, too."

22

PILING UP EVIDENCE, OR PILING ON?

Marion Barry's trial lasted five more grueling weeks. After Rasheeda Moore stepped down, the government put 21 more witnesses on the stand, bringing its total to 32. The new witnesses added to a litany of mayoral abandon that eventually included more than 200 instances of alleged cocaine use over a seven-year period starting in 1983. The government also introduced more than 100 exhibits, from the tiny rock of crack cocaine found in Barry's suit jacket after the Vista sting to an elaborate chart illustrating the scores of locations where Barry allegedly had used drugs with 10 unindicted co-conspirators. Some of the additional evidence the government introduced seemed designed more to shame than to prove a legal point. On July 5, for example, prosecutors played for the jury a videotape of a 1986 news conference in which Barry, himself the target of previous drug investigations, vigorously defended the D.C. police department's "Operation Clean Sweep," aimed at street-corner drug dealers.

"With this drug epidemic," Barry told reporters in the tape, "got these crybabies who say, 'What about the rights of those who are going out to buy drugs?' As far as I am concerned, they ought not to be out there buying drugs in the first place, and there would be no question about their rights. We will use every legal means that we can. We want every drug buyer to know that the next drug buy may be from a police officer."

Other prosecution evidence was startling in what it revealed about the mayor. Telephone logs showed more than 26,000 calls made to Barry's command center and from his limousine between June 1986 and January 1990. Of these 2,690 were placed to or from 10 of the mayor's 19 unindicted co-conspirators. Barry, a self-described "phone junkie," had placed the highest number of calls—573—to 27-year-old administrative secretary Theresa Southerland, a.k.a. "Miss T."

Southerland, who testified only after being arrested on a bench warrant, told the jury of sex-and-drug-filled assignations with a man who, she said, had subsequently "loaned" her money for Christmas presents or to help her with bills. She said she usually supplied the drugs but during one encounter the mayor had surprised her with cocaine in a folded dollar bill.

"I was there maybe half an hour," said Southerland in a breathy, little girl's voice, "we had a coupla drinks, we talked and we listened to music. I excused myself. I went to the bathroom, and when I came back cocaine was on the table."

Canary food.

On that occasion, said Southerland, Barry had used the corner of a business card to scoop the drugs up to his nostrils.

Another government witness, D.C. attorney and Barry friend Lloyd Moore, Jr., whose firm, Leftwich, Moore & Douglas, reportedly has received millions in city contracts, testified on the same day that he had provided both cocaine and a trysting place for Southerland and Barry. He said they would disappear into an upstairs bedroom at his Northwest Washington home, sometimes for hours at a time. Rasheeda Moore also had described drug-filled assignations with Barry at Moore's.

At least one government witness, admitted cocaine addict and dealer Lydia Pearson, seemed more helpful to the defense, despite her testimony about delivering a job application and crack cocaine to Barry at the Reeves Municipal Center in September 1988. During cross-examination by Mundy, Pearson testified that Rasheeda Moore had told her in June 1986, after learning of Barry's dalliance with Rose Marie "Maria" McCarthy, that she "was gonna get him." Pearson's testimony substantiated Mundy's claim that Moore cooperated with the government out of revenge.

There were occasional touching moments. When Jeffrey Mitchell, a D.C. advertising executive and longtime Barry friend, was asked to explain his relationship with Barry, he cleared his throat and in a voice near breaking, said, "Over the years I have grown to know and develop feelings for Mr. Barry, very close to that of a brother. I love Marion Barry, just like he was in the [same] womb." According to the witness, Barry would stop by his home in Northwest Washington about twice a week. Mitchell said they occasionally used cocaine together, but most of the time they didn't do drugs.

"He'd just come and we'd have a couple of drinks, and just cool out," Mitchell testified. "He would grab a bowl of soup or some beans."

Another reluctant prosecution witness, Montgomery, Alabama, financial consultant Doris Crenshaw, described a relationship with Barry that dated back to the civil rights era. The two had enjoyed, said Crenshaw, "a very close friendship. We confided in each other. He comforted me after the death of my mother. He's a very kind and understanding and sympathetic person."

But the bespectacled, short-haired, frumpy, and highly accomplished woman, who had worked for the Democratic National Committee, for the 1980 Carter-Mondale reelection campaign, as deputy director of minority affairs for Action, the federal volunteer agency, and as national field director for the Reverend Jesse Jackson's Operation Push, also testified that she had used cocaine with Barry dozens of times, starting in 1984 at her former Capitol Hill home. She was the 10th female witness to describe a drug and/or sexual relationship with the mayor.

Like several other prosecution witnesses, Crenshaw testified that Barry would phone her before stopping by her house. She said he wanted to make sure she had drugs but didn't want to say so on the phone, so he used coded language.

"Now, how, if at all, would the defendant ask you if you had any cocaine before he visited your home," asked prosecutor Roberts.

"He would say something like, 'Do you have any refreshments, any cognac? What is happening?' " replied Crenshaw. "Or 'Is anything happening?' Or something like that."

"And what did you understand that to mean?" queried Roberts.

"Did I have any drugs," said Crenshaw.

"Any particular type of drugs?" Roberts asked.

"Cocaine, sir," replied Crenshaw.

Crenshaw also testified that she had used drugs with Barry at Washington's Park Hyatt Hotel along with another Barry friend, Willie Davis, on the evening of December 22, 1988, only hours after Barry had visited Charles Lewis at the Ramada Inn Central.

Although Crenshaw could not recall exactly what date she had used cocaine alone with Barry in November 1989—the basis of count 12 in the mayor's indictment—she testified that Barry had visited her sometime that month at the Mayflower Hotel wearing a jogging suit and that they had taken drugs together as she packed her suitcase for the trip home.

After her brief testimony Crenshaw issued a statement through her lawyer, expressing her deep "regrets" for any "improper" activities she engaged in with her old friend Marion Barry. "Some of us did not make the transition from the sixties that we should have," Crenshaw wrote, "as far as the casual use of drugs is concerned."

Her statement spoke volumes about the situation in which the mayor, Crenshaw, and perhaps millions of other middle-aged Americans now found themselves.

Yet another reluctant prosecution witness, Darrell Sabbs, the first director of Barry's Youth Leadership Institute in 1979, described a "very close, almost father-son relationship" with Barry. Sabbs spoke of his shock when he arrived in Washington in January 1990 "to be with a friend who was announcing his re-election," only to discover that "there had been this entrap-sting, whatever you wanta call it."

With his perhaps not-so-accidental verbal slip, Sabbs had come closest to expressing what many of the other unindicted co-conspirators clearly felt: that the government had set Barry up and then leaned on them unfairly to seal his legal fate.

Sabbs, who had taken the Fifth Amendment during his first appearance before a grand jury investigating Barry and subse-quently displayed a conveniently porous memory for dates and details of Barry's alleged drug use, said he had contacted

Barry after the mayor's January arrest and "told him I was concerned about him, and thinkin' about him, and that I loved him and to take care of himself."

When asked why his memory was suddenly so bad when he had testified with relative clarity during a second grand jury appearance, Sabbs replied, revealingly: "The criminality and the politics have been so intense in this case, my response only reflected the kind of emotional distraction—and distress— that I was under, and still am."

While Sabbs may have been the most defiant prosecution witness, potential witness Rose Marie "Maria" McCarthy took the prize for being the most reluctant. She chose to spend a month behind bars for contempt of court rather than testify.

Former D.C. official and financial advisor Bettye Smith checked herself into a mental hospital in Chattanooga, Tennessee, a week before she was scheduled to testify. Smith's psychiatrist, A. Lee Solomon, wrote a letter to her lawyer, Paul Friedman, which Friedman quoted in part at a hearing before Judge Jackson: "Her thinking, which is being clouded by her mood, is that her testimony will destroy her in the eyes of her parents. She currently finds suicide to be more acceptable than testifying."

Jackson said he believed he was "being played with" and ordered Smith arrested in Tennessee on a federal bench warrant and flown to D.C. by U.S. marshals. She took the stand in tears on July 17. But after only a few minutes she became increasingly animated and soon told jurors about the 15 or 16 occasions when she had shared drugs with the mayor.

The final flurry of prosecution witnesses also brought some welcome humor to the rather grim proceedings. Iranian restaurateur Hassan Mohammadi, who referred to Barry as "Mr. Mayor" and testified about a sycophantic relationship with Barry in which he supplied drugs, gambling money, and trysting places to the mayor—a "privilege" that eventually cost him three months in jail—described a visit in December 1988 to the Washington home of another Barry friend, black developer R. Donahue Peebles. Mohammadi, whose company, Media Productions, Inc., had received a $195,000 contract from the District lottery board in 1988—an award that reportedly prompted a federal investigation—said that he had joined Barry, Barry friend Willie Davis, and Davis's girlfriend in a bathroom of Peebles's home to snort cocaine when Barry became paranoid.

"What happened after you saw them in the bathroom?" asked prosecutor Roberts during direct examination.

"Mr. Mayor came outside and they were just checking windows, just wanted to make sure there was nobody watching us," Mohammadi replied.

"Who was checking the windows to see if anybody was watching you?" queried Roberts.

"Mr. Mayor," said Mohammadi.

"How was he dressed?" asked Roberts.

He had his pajamas on," answered Mohammadi.

Roberts also quizzed Mohammadi about a night he had spent with Barry and "Miss T" (Theresa Southerland) playing blackjack at a Bahamas casino. Mohammadi said he had lent the mayor between $3,000 and $4,000 in cash, which Barry lost at the gaming tables that night and never repaid. He said the mayor had sought comfort instead in the arms of his curvaceous Miss T.

The next morning, said Mohammadi, "I asked him if he had a good time, and he said, yes, he did, he had a good time. And he said, 'She killed me.'"

"Who killed him?" asked Roberts.

"Apparently, Miss T," replied Mohammadi.

On the "Insight" talk show on Howard University's WHUR-FM radio, Barry summed up his impressions of the "canaries."

"Basically, what the government has done is find people, some of whom were associates of mine, who have a lot to lose," said Barry. These witnesses, he said, "engaged in activities that could be criminal, or could be charged, or they faced deportation or other kinds of strenuous consequences. And they paraded them out."

In another radio interview Barry went even further, charging that the FBI had cynically used black women to "bait" its honey trap.

"If you notice," Barry said on WDCU-FM's "Crosstalk" show, "in this whole operation, it has been the FBI's strategy to use black women from the very beginning. You found black women being used as pawns and victims too, to some extent."

Sometimes Barry fought with humor rather than accusations. During a trial recess Barry picked up the sketchbook of a startled female courtroom artist, scrutinized the image of him, and said to the woman, "Don't make me white." Getting a laugh from reporters, Barry took the sketchbook over to his wife and showed it to her. Effi broke into a rare, warm smile when she saw the silhouette of Barry, drawn against a white background, which had not yet been filled in by the artist. Then the mayor handed the sketchbook back to the artist. "Darken me up now," he quipped as he strode out of the courtroom.

Despite all the damning evidence, Barry kept up his feisty facade throughout the proceedings. In late July after a day of testimony he announced that he would throw his political support behind *no* Democratic D.C. mayoral candidate—"I think the citizens are capable of deciding for themselves," he said about the primary race. Barry noticed a photographer shooting him as he mopped his face with a handkerchief.

"You got it?" Barry quipped. Then he wiped his face again. "One more time," he said, grinning, and did it again. It was vintage Barry, pinned against the ropes but still taunting his "persecutors" as he called the white media-white governmental types he claimed were plotting against him.

23

CIRCLING THE WAGONS

A s the government piled up additional evidence against Barry, the mayor drew the wagons of racial solidarity more tightly around him. He gave exclusive interviews to black journalists, attended rallies organized in his behalf by black constituents, and publicly embraced black leaders. Besides Farrakhan and Stallings, former comedian and political activist Dick Gregory, who had rushed to Barry's side after the Vista sting, also made a brief appearance at the federal courthouse, "to show my outrage for this corrupt and vicious system that is racist and sexist." Even D.C.'s nonvoting congressional delegate, the Reverend Walter Fauntroy, who had publicly criticized Barry for trying to turn his drug and perjury trial into a racial showdown, made an appearance.

Barry welcomed all but Fauntroy with a hug.

But when the Reverend Al Sharpton came down from New York to lend his support, Barry finally drew the line. He ducked out a side door of the courtroom to avoid the heavyset Brooklyn preacher with permed hair and Fu Manchu moustache who had stirred the fires of racial discord in New York around other controversial trials. Sharpton ignored the mayor's snub and picketed outside the courthouse, making the six o'clock news.

Barry's own public relations moves included weekly visits to at least two black churches, where he found material as well as spiritual sustenance: by mid-July, parishioners reportedly had donated more than $100,000 into a blind trust to help defray the estimated $500,000 cost of his legal defense. In a remarkable show of support for the mayor and his family, parishioners and other Barry friends also set up trusts for the education of Barry's son, Christopher, and to cover the cost of Barry's seven weeks of addiction treatment. On July 29, Effi Barry's friends held a $25-a-cup benefit tea at the University of the District of Columbia's Carnegie Library. It drew 1,000 people.

Even without Barry's generous friends and supporters, Mundy's law firm, Reynolds and Mundy, would not go bankrupt. A few months before the Ramada Inn incident, Barry presciently had designated the firm the city's minority counsel for the preparation of general revenue bonds. As such, Reynolds and Mundy was guaranteed the right to create 35 percent of all such bonds, which generally bring the firm that prepares them up to one percent of their face value. A week after Barry's trial started, the D.C. Council approved the sale of $120 million in revenue bonds to finance the construction of a Washington Hospital Center addition. Reynolds and Mundy would make up to $420,000 on that move alone.

On Thursday, July 19, Barry co-counsel Robert Mance led off the defense case—which Kenneth Mundy had promised would be "full of thrills and surprises"—by calling to the stand D.C. police detective James Stays, an 11-year veteran of the mayor's security detail. On direct examination Stays denied ever seeing the mayor use drugs and refuted Rasheeda Moore's earlier testimony that he had babysat her children and driven her to open-air drug markets in D.C. to buy drugs for the mayor.

A broad-shouldered, affable man, Stays kept up his entertaining answers for about an hour, telling the enthralled jurors, among other things, about the night, at a Virgin Islands hotel where he was staying with Barry, that prosecution witness Dixie Lee Hedrington allegedly entered his room and, with barely a word of explanation, removed her dress and plopped down on his bed in her underwear. During her cross-examination of Stays, however, co-prosecutor Retchin quickly broke the spell when she asked Stays if he ever had told another Barry bodyguard, Detective Warren Goodwine—whom Retchin had interviewed—that Barry's friend Willie Davis, a former aide to Birmingham, Alabama, Mayor Richard Arrington, had supplied cocaine to Barry.

"Me? No, ma'am," Stays blurted before Mance or Mundy could object.

In a bench conference Retchin told Judge Jackson she also had evidence of alleged drug use by Stays—an allegation that would impeach his credibility, to say the least. Jackson overruled the objection.

A recess was called to give Stays a chance to confer with a lawyer. When he retook the stand he tried to parry Retchin's questions about cocaine use. But despite his denials, the government had rocked the defense just as it was getting underway. Stays was suspended from the mayor's security detail and stripped of his police powers a few days after his testimony pending a police investigation of his alleged drug activities.

Retchin's ambush of the mayor's loyal protector so angered Barry he told reporters during a recess that the government had "tainted [Stays's] reputation. They are backed up against the wall and using these Satanic, dirt-like tactics."

Mundy was less colorful, but in his description of the morning's events, he conceded that the drug-use allegations against Stays were damaging. "We were not aware of the allegations. Nobody has ever mentioned them to us."

It was the first time during the trial Mundy had been caught with his guard down, and he admitted it. For the rest of its first day the defense didn't fare much better. Defense witness Darrel Hardy, for example, who heads the city's summer youth employment programs, testified that when Rasheeda Moore and her two "Project Me" partners presented their proposal to him in June 1986—months after the deadline for submission of such proposals—his office nevertheless had approved the $47,000 request within days.

"You had the clear impression Mr. Barry wanted this program funded, didn't you?" asked Richard Roberts.

"That was the impression that was given us," said Hardy. who also testified that Moore's company, Designer's Goldfinger, Inc., had received a $120,000 contract award the following year—nearly double the $63,000 the proposal had called for. He said his superiors had indicated the mayor wanted the funding doubled.

When Detective Warren Goodwine took the stand, the former bodyguard revealed in cross-examination that he had requested a transfer from the mayor's security detail following the Ramada Inn incident.

"I felt like the mayor is entitled to his privacy," said Goodwine, who would not be more specific.

The next day, Mundy tried unsuccessfully to get the mayor's defense case off the ground by revealing a trio of "surprises." The first one even angered the judge. Was it not true, Mundy asked FBI special agent Michael Mason, that Charles Lewis was "hooking up with a very notorious D.C. drug dealer?" He knew that the jurors would want to know more about this allegation. "I would use the name but—"

Jackson interrupted Mundy and called him to the bench, where the defense counsel said he could impeach Charles Lewis's credibility by showing that Lewis once had tried to introduce a friend, Sonny Watley, to Rayful Edmond, Jr., the father of convicted drug lord Rayful Edmond III, allegedly to help Watley set up a cocaine network in D.C. Mundy cited as his source notes taken by D.C. police detective Albert Arrington, Jr., during an August 1989 interview Arrington and Mason had conducted jointly with Lewis. But Arrington could not testify in the trial since he had heard other testimony while sitting at the prosecution table. Nor would Jackson allow Mundy to question Mason, who had taken the stand, about the alleged introduction to Edmond by Lewis, since that would require Mason to testify second hand about notes Arrington had taken. However, Jackson said he would allow Mundy to recall Lewis to the stand.

Unflapped by the failure of this "surprise," Mundy pushed for another. He asked Special Agent Mason if his notes taken during an interview with Lewis indicated that the prosecution witness had asked him about "the reward range" he could expect from the government in return for his cooperation. Mason, a black G-man, answered that Lewis may have used those words, but that the government's key witness was referring to the plea-bargain agreement he hoped to conclude with the government, not money, as Mundy claimed.

Finally, Mundy asked the judge to let convicted felon Roscoe Jackson, husband of government witness and former Rasheeda Moore business partner Carole Bland Jackson, take the stand. Mundy said Roscoe Jackson would testify that he had overheard Rasheeda Moore offer his wife money to confirm that Barry had taken drugs at the Tiber Island apartment complex in Southwest Washington in June 1986. Retchin, caught off guard perhaps for the first time in the trial, stalled by asking for an opportunity to examine Jackson's criminal record. But it turned out to be an unnecessary move. Judge Jackson would not permit Roscoe Jackson to testify, but he allowed Mundy to recall Carole Bland Jackson, who denied that Moore had offered her a bribe.

Mundy also marched out a third mayoral bodyguard. D.C. police detective Ulysses Walltower said he had never seen the mayor use drugs, but he conceded that during a 1988 trip to the Virgin Islands the mayor had been out of his sight for many hours, so Barry could have been doing drugs without his knowledge.

The day clearly went to the government, yet at its end the beaming defendant appeared on the courthouse steps hugging supporters and sparring playfully with reporters.

"This is the end of the seventh week of our trial," said Barry, using the royal plural. "I'm now wearing [a] white [rose corsage]. Yellow represents the canaries, and they're gone now. White represents purity and truth."

Then the mayor once again portrayed his situation in biblical terms.

"We're up against an awesome power of government," he said. "They have all the resources and all the technology. It's like David and Goliath. Our strategy is to convince the 12 jurors that the government has not proved me guilty beyond a reasonable doubt."

Barry did not comment on another controversial case decided in the U.S. District Court that day (July 20). A three-judge federal appeals panel overturned one of three convictions against Iran-Contra defendant Lt. Col. Oliver L. North—for destroying government documents—on the highly technical grounds that the judge in North's case had not properly instructed the jury. It set aside North's two remaining convictions—for obstructing Congress and accepting a bribe—after concluding that North's immunized testimony before Congress may have been used improperly by a federal grand jury to indict him. The decision, understandably, brought fresh cries of outrage from Barry backers at the latest instance of "white man's justice."

24

WHAT "THRILLS AND SURPRISES"?

Six of the next seven defense witnesses were used for a single purpose: to buttress Barry's alibi for count three of the indictment, alleging that around 10:15 A.M. on September 7, 1988, Lydia Pearson had brought three $30 bags of crack cocaine and her application for a city job to Barry in his office at the Reeves Municipal Center.

Barry staff member Clifton Roberson told the court he had personally accepted the job application from Pearson that morning, although he couldn't remember the exact time. He identified a copy of the typed job application he allegedly had received from Pearson, which was entered as a defense exhibit.

A Safeway Stores manager and a D.C. community activist both testified that Barry had attended a ribbon-cutting ceremony for a new store in Northeast Washington the same morning, arriving around 9:30 or 9:40 and leaving about 45 minutes later.

Barry's chauffeur, Walter Bracey, said he had driven Barry directly from the Safeway opening to D.C. Fire Department headquarters at the former Gremke School building in Northwest Washington, without stopping at the Reeves Center. Under cross-examination, however, Bracey seriously hurt his credibility when he claimed he could remember no other destinations, other than the District Building, where he had taken the mayor during 12 years as Barry's chauffeur.

Joseph Yeldell, a former director of the city's Office of Emergency Preparedness, and D.C. fire chief Ray Alfred testified that Barry attended a meeting at Gremke on the morning in question. The meeting, to discuss the city's trouble-plagued ambulance service, had begun at 10 A.M., which would have given Barry an airtight alibi. But under cross-examination both men admitted that the perennially tardy mayor had arrived late for the meeting and had spoken to the group for just over an hour. They testified that they had viewed a 71-minute videotape of Barry's speech at the meeting that showed the clock reading 11:52 at the time of the mayor's departure. That would put Barry's arrival at fire department headquarters sometime around 10:40 A.M., nearly half an hour after two other defense witnesses said he had left the ribbon cutting.

The 10:40 A.M. arrival time also would jibe with Judith Retchin's assertion during a bench conference that phone logs showed that the mayor's car phone had been used to place a call at 10:42 A.M. that day—a fact that Mundy tried to minimize by saying the logs did not show who had used the mayor's car phone. In any case, Mundy dropped his plan to play the videotape of the fire department meeting in court. Still looking to score his first real points for the defense, he called D.C. Public Works Department employee Charles Mason to the stand. Mason refuted government witness Hassan Mohammadi's testimony about using cocaine with Barry at Mohammadi's Georgetown apartment, which Mason also had visited the night in question. But under cross-examination Mason admitted that Mohammadi and Barry had excused themselves at one point and disappeared into a downstairs bathroom, where, Mohammadi had testified, he and Barry had snorted cocaine.

By July 23, four days after starting the defense case, Mundy had gone through half his 17 witnesses and not yet produced a single "thrill" or "surprise." But he finally scored some points when he brought Charles Lewis back and asked him point-blank if he had a "working relationship" with the four Virgin Islands women who had testified for the prosecution. "Were these young ladies that you would customarily provide or make available to dignitaries or persons visiting the Virgin Islands?" Mundy inquired.

Lewis responded indignantly that he "didn't entertain any dignitaries." A moment later, however, Lewis offered testimony that could help the mayor. Asked about Barry's alleged sexual assault on Linda Maynard, Lewis testified that he had walked with Barry and Maynard from Barry's St. Thomas hotel room to the parking lot immediately after her visit. Barry, said

Lewis, gave Maynard "a little peck on the cheek." He said Maynard did not appear upset, nor did she tell him she had been attacked. Lewis said Maynard told him, simply, "The mayor is something else."

Score one for the defense.

Mundy's primary reason for recalling Lewis, however, was to ask Lewis about his alleged attempt to introduce Sonny Watley to Rayful Edmond, Jr.—an allegation that certainly would discredit Lewis in the jury's eyes. But when Mundy asked the court for permission to ask Lewis about the alleged ties, Jackson again barred such testimony, ruling, "The name Rayful Edmond has such a cachet today in the city and in the present circumstances, I find the prejudicial effect [against Lewis] is far in excess of any probative value" of the testimony.

So much for Mundy's biggest, most thrilling "surprise." It was back to "nicking and bruising."

On Wednesday, July 25, Mundy recalled FBI special agent Frank Steele to the stand in an attempt to show a break in the chain of custody of the business cards taken from Barry during the Vista sting. An FBI chemist had testified that he found traces of cocaine on the cards. Mundy was trying to get the card evidence thrown out because no itemized list ever had been made of the cards and they were not tested for cocaine residue until five months after they were seized.

The balding evidence agent responded to Mundy's half-hour grilling with exaggerated politeness, often punctuating his pithy answers with a grin. Reaching for some way to discredit Steele, Mundy pointed out that the time sequence in Steele's notes did not coincide with the times written down by other law officers involved in the sting.

"Was your watch 15 minutes off during the course of this activity?" asked Mundy.

"I don't know, sir," Steele replied, poker-faced. He glanced down at his watch, then looked up innocently. "My watch is just one I got at [J.C.] Penney's. It wasn't synchronized with anything."

Several jurors laughed.

Judge Jackson, however, was not amused. During a bench conference he scolded Mundy for wasting so much time. But like a pit bull in a fight, Mundy wouldn't let go of Steele. He kept peppering the FBI agent with questions about who had custody of the cards, until he finally got Steele to admit that he had incorrectly noted in his evidence report that he had received Barry's business cards at the Vista from Special Agent Peter Wubbenhorst rather than from Special Agent Ronald Stern, as he had noted.

"I made a mistake, Mr. Mundy," Steele confessed.

"Did you make any other mistakes while you were the property seizing agent?" Mundy demanded.

"No, sir, no other mistakes," Steele replied.

"I have no other questions, your honor," said Mundy.

The defense counsel had nicked the government by disparaging a minor player in the sting, but it was hardly a major victory. Mundy seemed to score a few more points when he called to the stand Albert and Carmen Benjamin, a respectable, middle-aged Virgin Islands couple who had gone sailing with Barry and several others, including their old friend Charles Lewis, in June 1986, and who had then invited the group back to their home afterward to sample Mrs. Carmen's bull-foot soup, known in the islands as an aphrodisiac. Both testified they had seen no drug use by the mayor on the *Brigadoon*.

Their testimony conflicted with that of Rasheeda Moore, Charles Lewis, and Jonetta Vincent, who said they had used cocaine or marijuana with Barry on the boat.

Mundy also questioned the Benjamins about whether FBI agents and D.C. police detectives who flew the couple to Washington in October 1989 had come down a little too hard on them. Mundy was trying to prove, as he had asserted in his opening argument, that the government would "go to any length and any expense" to "get" Barry.

The law officers, said Albert Benjamin, "kind of kept driving home the point that I *had* to know, I *had* to see, I *had* to be aware of [Barry's alleged drug use], and just getting right down on top of you and just crowding you to the point that one time—and Officer Pawlik knows this, I told him in no uncertain terms—'Mister, you have pushed your luck too far,' because it was too much pressure."

Carmen Benjamin testified that the lawmen, who questioned husband and wife separately, "were cordial, but they were [also] kind of aggressive with us." She said that at one point she banged her fist on the table and demanded an end to the five-hour grilling. The lawmen apparently relented only after she offered to take a polygraph test to show she had not seen drugs on the cruise. They also had taken the Benjamins out to an expensive dinner following the interrogation.

But during cross-examination the government effectively counterpunched. Richard Roberts got Carmen Benjamin to admit that she did not see everything that took place on the boat because she spent nearly an hour in the water snorkeling. Roberts elicited testimony from Albert Benjamin that he purposely had averted his eyes from the scene taking place on the ship deck only a few feet away, where he said Barry was cavorting with Moore in a way that, as Benjamin had earlier told the grand jury, "annoyed me to the max."

"What else made you feel disturbed or uncomfortable once the boat ride began?" queried Roberts. "Would you tell this jury?"

"Yes, well, overexposure," answered Benjamin, "probably, of a woman, of a brassiere under the top of the cabin."

"When they were on the boat and she was in the fashion as you described her, were they together?" asked Roberts.

"Yes," the witness replied.

"What did you see him doing?" asked Roberts.

"He was making advances toward her and she was accepting."

"In other words, they were fondling each other?" asked the prosecutor.

"Right," said Benjamin.

Roberts also got Benjamin to admit that he had become "suspicious that there was something out of the ordinary going on on that boat" when he saw Barry, Moore, and Lewis go below "quite repeatedly" during the four-hour cruise. When asked how he reacted to their unusual behavior, the 55-year-old retired army sergeant explained that he did nothing because "I was not interested in trying to find out" what they were doing.

By showing the jury *why* the Benjamins hadn't seen Barry using drugs on the *Brigadoon*, Roberts had vitiated the couple's usefulness to the defense.

Later the same day Jackson bluntly warned the lawyers for both sides that the jurors were becoming restless and he was losing patience with the *ad hominem* exchanges between them at the bench.

"Don't argue about it," an exasperated Jackson lectured the sparring lawyers during one of the frequent bench conferences. "I want to get this case over with."

Indeed, by the end of the seventh week, the jurors, like most everyone else in the courtroom, looked both restless and tired.

The defendant, for his part, sought refuge in the "People's Prayer Tent," a bright yellow-and-white-striped canopy set up near the federal courthouse by a group of local black ministers. Trailed by scores of cameramen and reporters, Barry joined a handful of preachers and supporters in singing "I Shall Not Be Moved" (to the tune of "We Shall Overcome"), then bowed his head as the Reverend Willie Wilson prayed for a man Wilson called "a prime example of what prayer can do."

"We pray that You move on this system perpetuating all manner of evil and wrongdoing," Wilson implored.

A few moments later a quietly smiling Barry clapped and sang, along with others, several verses of the spiritual "This Little Light of Mine, I'm Gonna Let It Shine." A teenage boy stood nearby with his hand on the mayor's shoulder. Then the Reverend James Bevel offered a closing prayer.

"Lord, we thank you for those who came along in the sixties," intoned Bevel, who had served in the trenches with Barry in Mississippi. "People like Martin Luther King, Jr., and Marion Barry."

The pinstriped mayor stood, head bowed, unable to stop pursing his lips in an unconscious gesture of distress. Marion Barry clearly was *not* the same man that Bevel had met three decades earlier. Yet somehow, despite the steep price he was paying for holding on, a month and a half of highly damaging and embarrassing testimony had still not made Barry a man ready to give up the fight against what he clearly perceived as official injustice.

25

FIGHTING THE FEDERAL GOLIATH

On Thursday, July 26, before calling his final witness—
FBI special agent Ronald Stern, who had led the Vista
sting—Mundy made perhaps the most extraordinary
proffer at the bench of any trial in the city's history. From the
start Mundy had sought to tie Barry's prosecution into an
alleged FBI plot to selectively prosecute black elected officials
across the country. Mundy wanted to put the allegations on
the record to build a case for a possible appeal on racial
grounds. Judge Jackson had denied a pretrial defense motion
to raise the issue as part of Barry's trial defense. Jackson also
had denied dozens of other defense motions launched by
Mundy, in the defense attorney's words, as a "flotilla" aimed
at the government.

"Your honor," said Mundy, "I will not raise this [federal
conspiracy allegation] with agent Stern because I understand
the court's preclusion of these questions would keep me from
making these declaratories. But we were also prepared to
show, and I put on the record, that we received from three
sources information that, prior to coming here to organize and
orchestrate the sting against Mr. Barry, Mr. Stern had been
in Atlanta trying to set up a sting of [former Georgia state
senator] Julian Bond, [former Atlanta Mayor] Andrew Young,
and two other black politicians and public figures in Atlanta."

Mundy went on to assert that Stern had orchestrated a sting
against black elected officials in Chicago and that the same team
of FBI agents, though not including Stern, had previously tried
to work a sting against two black elected officials in California.
Mundy claimed that he had information from "very reliable
sources" that Stern, in effect, moved around the country as
the head of an FBI "assault force." He asserted that he could
call "a string of witnesses" to "verify these facts."

301

"We are prepared also," Mundy continued, "to show that prior to Miss Moore agreeing to the sting that there had been approaches made to six different persons, women, in the life of Mr. Barry who had turned down [a request to participate in a sting], and money was offered to them." Furthermore, he claimed, several black female agents had turned down Wanda King's part because they considered it to be morally repugnant.

"All right," Jackson calmly replied. The white Republican jurist, who projected a warm but reserved persona from the bench, had been given perhaps the most politically loaded case the District had seen in decades. He didn't need more trouble. "I will accept your proffer and I accept your assurance that you will not raise [the allegations] because they are to be excluded," he added.

Judith Retchin was not quite so imperturbable.

"I would note that I think the allegations are outrageous," declared Retchin, who proferred in a subsequent bench conference that no witness ever had been offered money and that Wanda King was the first black female FBI agent offered the assignment. "But regardless, given the inflammatory nature of them I would ask that these proceedings be sealed."

Mundy objected. Even if the court sealed the record, he argued, the allegations would become known to the public. Jackson agreed.

"All this court has to do is protect from the jury what it considers to be appropriate," lectured Mundy. "The court has done that. I disagree with some of the court's rulings, but I will respect them and I will not go beyond them. But I do not believe this court should be a party to what appears to be excluding information that will ultimately end up in the public well anyhow."

Again Judge Jackson agreed and said he would not seal the record.

This was all too much for Retchin.

"I would note that if allegations are going to be made that are not appropriate for a jury to consider," said the prosecutor, "it should be done outside the court, and that this forum should not be used as a way of airing things—"

"But," Jackson interrupted, "he has to make a proffer on the record in order to—"

"The record will remain here and it can go to the [D.C.] Court of Appeals," asserted Retchin, "but it should be sealed because this court should not be used as a forum to make allegations against people's reputations." She was referring to Ronald Stern.

"I agree with that, Ms. Retchin," said Jackson, "but I also agree there is no way to keep this from the public domain, and there is no point in my trying to keep it from the public domain." He added wearily: "Your motion to seal is denied."

The judge never asked Mundy to name his sources of information or to name any of the black elected officials the defense counsel claimed had been targeted outside Atlanta. Nor did he ask Mundy to explain his charge that the government had tried to bribe witnesses to testify against Barry, or any of his other allegations. Jackson left that inquiry to an appeals court, if the occasion should arise.

If Jackson had allowed Mundy to present his information on the alleged "assault force" to the jury, it may well have discovered that Mundy's "very reliable sources" were actually pretty nebulous. They included, Mundy said, two attorneys for Barry prosecution witnesses, a "well-known figure" who was convicted in the HUD scandal, a source from "a Congressional office," and "a former FBI informant." But Mundy failed to name any of these sources.

A source familiar with Mundy's strategy said Barry's chief defense counsel got much of his information on the alleged FBI assault force from radical black attorney Mary Cox, who each week during the trial took Uncle Sam to task in her *Capital Spotlight* column, and from the office of Rep. Mervyn Dymally (D-Ca), a former chairman of the Congressional Black Caucus who for years has waged an unrequited campaign to prove black elected officials are being "unduly harassed" by the federal government. (In the January 1988 *Congressional Record*, Dymally cited a former FBI official in alleging selective targeting of black elected officials in Atlanta and charged that "such a policy represents the ultimate abuse of power and places at risk more than 6,700 elected officials mandated to serve the people of this Nation.'')

Mundy's "assault force" allegations also sounded suspiciously similar to charges made by Birmingham, Alabama, Mayor Richard Arrington, Jr. After being investigated for his alleged link to a bribery scandal involving city zoning changes, Arrington had charged that the FBI had a hit list of black elected officials. Other nationally known black elected officials under federal investigation also had cried foul, including Detroit mayor Coleman Young, who charged that the federal government had a vendatta against him and his administration after a long FBI probe of alleged misuse of a secret police fund in the city failed to implicate him. But no black elected official, including Marion Barry, had ever been able to prove any conspiracy theory.

Finally, according to federal law enforcement officials interviewed by the *Post*, Mundy had his facts wrong about Ronald Stern. The officials told the paper that although Stern had been an FBI agent in Atlanta as Mundy claimed, he had played only a minor role in the investigation of former Atlanta Mayor Andrew Young for alleged obstruction of justice and of former Georgia state senator Julian Bond for alleged cocaine possession. No charges were ever filed in the 1987 probe based on allegations made by Bond's estranged wife. Regarding Mundy's proffer that Stern had participated in a sting operation against Young and Bond, Robert Barr, the U.S. attorney in Atlanta in charge of the investigation said, simply, "That's absolutely false."

Instead, the FBI told the *Post*, Ronald Stern had played a key undercover role in the FBI's "Operation Nickelride," which resulted in the drug conviction of Leroy Stynchcombe, the *white* chief deputy sheriff of Fulton County, Georgia. They said he also had helped bring down several other corrupt white officials in the Peach State.

Moreover, Stern had been a deputy U.S. marshal in Chicago, not an FBI agent. The 35-year-old Stern was a relatively new agent, and Atlanta had been his first FBI assignment. He had been transferred to the Washington Metropolitan Field Office in 1987 to join the public corruption unit, primarily to investigate abuses at the U.S. Department of Housing and Urban Development. Regarding Mundy's most controversial accusation, FBI spokesman Jim Mull said, "Any allegation that the FBI has a team of agents moving throughout the nation targeting black officials is unfounded and is categorically denied."

Either the federal law enforcement officials were lying, or Mundy was bluffing. In either case, based on the public record, Judge Jackson apparently did the mayor's chief legal defender a favor by denying his request to use his information on the alleged FBI "assault force" as evidence in Barry's trial.

At another bench conference that same day, Mundy proferred that the defense could introduce evidence "indicating the length, the intensity, and the expensiveness" of investigating Mr. Barry.

Had Jackson permitted Mundy to introduce this evidence, the defense counsel would have faced some additional hard contradictory facts. The $42 million figure he and others had so often cited as the cost of the Barry investigation was, at best, fictitious. In a pretrial motion filed to counter Mundy's claim of astronomical government spending on the Barry case, federal prosecutors in the District wrote: "Any claim that this office spent around twice its annual budget in conducting its investigation of defendant's activities over a 13-month period, while at the same time prosecuting over 22,000 other cases annually, is absurd on its face."

The prosecutors put "the cost of pursuing 10 complex investigations involving Barry or his subordinates from 1982 to 1990, including the January 18 sting at the Vista International Hotel, [at] between $2 million and $3 million." The federal corruption probes included contract steering, expense account irregularities, and contract fraud cases brought against top Barry administration officials, and they resulted in at least 10 convictions or guilty pleas, excluding Barry's case. (After the trial, Jay Stephens finally laid the matter to rest when he announced that the total costs of the Barry investigation and prosecution, over a 13-month period, starting in December 1988, was approximately $250,000.)

Finally, Mundy made one last proffer, referring to Jackson's pretrial ruling that the defense counsel could not attempt to show any government endangering of Mr. Barry's health or life, or to make any attack on government drug distribution in sting operations.

Judge Jackson's rulings, which basically prevented Mundy from putting the government on trial, as he had hoped to do, could not stop Barry's lawyer from trying to make Ronald Stern personally the fall guy for an alleged racially inspired entrapment. But when the tall, boyishly handsome Stern, in a blue suit, white shirt, and red tie, strode briskly into the courtroom, it was clear he wouldn't make Mundy's job easy. For the next four hours Mundy used every courtroom trick he knew, from humor to intimidation, to try to discredit Stern. He began by asking the witness if Rasheeda Moore was given specific guidelines for how far she could go in encouraging Barry to join her at the Vista.

Picking up a thick set of "operational instructions" that had been prepared for the sting, Stern read: "It is anticipated that the cooperating witness will have a telephone conversation with Mayor Barry and invite him to the hotel room." He added: "She was instructed that, if Mr. Barry suggested an invitation, that Rasheeda was to invite him over."

"If you were aware that Mr. Barry in a telephone conversation with Miss Moore previous to him actually coming to the hotel was suggesting and indicating that they should meet in the lobby for a drink and a talk, would you have encouraged her to invite him up to the room?" Mundy probed.

"Well, Mr. Mundy," retorted Stern, "that didn't happen, so I don't know what I would have done at the time."

"It didn't happen?" countered Mundy.

"It didn't happen," Stern repeated.

"What do you mean it didn't happen?" Mundy demanded.

Back and forth they went, Mundy trying to get an admission that Moore was to press the mayor to come, and Stern maintaining Barry had come of his own free will. All afternoon they continued, one temporarily gaining the upper hand only to be knocked down by his opponent a few moments later.

For example, they fought over the interpretation of Barry's comment to Moore when he first entered the hotel room, a comment that Stern later said Moore had told the FBI agents to expect from Barry.

"Initially, when Mr. Barry arrived, he did ask Rasheeda if she has been good," said Stern, insisting that Barry's question meant what Moore had told him it meant: had she stayed away from drugs?

"We are back to that?" Mundy asked sarcastically. "That [interpretation of Barry's remark] is the whole linchpin [of the sting operation], isn't it?"

"It is part of it," Stern responded. "I believe it is a very important part."

At the very least, Mundy had demonstrated that there was more than one way to interpret Barry's comment. And in further go-rounds with Stern, he focused on the many times that Barry had suggested during the encounter that he wanted to "make love" to Moore, an action not necessarily connected to drug taking. But when Mundy pressed Stern about the instructions the FBI had given Moore on keeping Barry in the hotel room, Stern stung Mundy.

"So, she was supposed to keep him there because it was there that the trap was supposed to spring, right?" Mundy queried.

"She made an effort to keep him there," Stern replied. "But I don't think she threw her body across the floor."

Interpretation came up again when Mundy asked, "Well, now, sir, 'Does your friend mess around,' that connotes drugs to you instead of sexual promiscuity?"

Stern answered that Moore had never explained to the FBI just what "messing around" meant to her, but he assumed that Barry was again referring to drugs.

"To you as a man, if someone were to say, 'Have you been messing around lately,' that could mean sexual promiscuity, couldn't it?" asked Mundy.

"It could," Stern conceded as jurors and spectators laughed.

In another exchange, when Mundy implied that the government had too vigorously played the role of drug pusher to

Barry at the Vista, Stern said, dryly, "We were affording Mr. Barry an opportunity to violate the law."

Asked why the agents didn't enter Moore's hotel room and arrest the mayor immediately after he received the drugs from Moore, and clearly was in possession, Stern explained: "There were too many plausible questions that he could have raised at that time. Number one is, we could have walked into the room to take custody and he could have called his security people and said, 'This lady wanted drugs. Have her arrested.' "

That was the "reverse sting" described in the FBI's operational guidelines.

Stern said the sting team moved only after receiving the go-ahead from Assistant U.S. Attorney Daniel Bernstein, who was in the room with them. The sting team leader also revealed that Barry almost eluded the sting. When FBI special agent Wanda King failed in her first attempt to sell Barry crack, Stern said they were ready to pack up and go. But then Barry told Moore to " 'go get some, go get it!' " Stern said.

Unable any longer to deny the mayor's role in his own downfall, Mundy demanded to know why the FBI, the D.C. police, and the U.S. attorney's office had allowed Barry to smoke the crack, an act that could have endangered the mayor's life.

"I didn't permit him to ingest the drugs," countered Stern. "He permitted himself to ingest the drugs."

By the end of the afternoon, after multiple bench conferences, Judge Jackson was holding his hand to his forehead, as if nursing a migraine. The jury looked tired. It had been a long day and a very long trial. Everyone seemed anxious to have it end. When Mundy informed Jackson that Barry would *not* testify in his own behalf, signaling the end of the defense case, there was an almost palpable sense of relief in the courtroom.

"I'm not going to do it [testify]," Barry had told Ernest White on WDCU-FM's "Crosstalk" the day before. "The government has a responsibility to put on evidence to prove me guilty beyond a reasonable doubt. We're under no obligation as [the] defense to put on any evidence at all."

Barry conceded, however, "There was some discussion about me going on the stand. Some of the people said we should get on so we could have a good tug-of-war between the U.S. government and the mayor. Well, you know, that's like David and Goliath; the U.S. government is Goliath."

26

PEOPLE DO LIE

A visibly nervous Darcell Walker took the stand Friday, July 27. The young D.C. government secretary, the first of four surprise prosecution rebuttal witnesses, had been subpoenaed by the government less than an hour earlier. Walker told the jury she had typed an "absent without leave" slip for her boss, key defense witness Clifton Roberson, who had testified that he, rather than Barry, had met with prosecution witness Lydia Pearson at the Reeves Center the morning of September 7, 1988. Pearson had testified that Barry bought crack from her that day at the Reeves Center. Darcell Walker said she had typed an AWOL slip showing Roberson missing from his job from 4:30 to 6:30 P.M. on September 7. But when she gave Roberson the form to sign he became upset, drew a line through those hours, and wrote in "8:30 to 10:30 A.M." instead.

This slip, introduced as government exhibit 104, also contained a handwritten note reading: "Laying gravestone for my father's grave. Turned in leave slip, which was rejected. Signed under protest. CR."

The government, unimpressed by Roberson's sentimental excuse, backed up its attack on his credibility with the testimony of D.C. personnel office employee Eugene Bowers, who said that official time and attendance records also showed Roberson absent from 8:30 to 10:30 A.M. on September 7, 1988.

In a rare comment from the bench, Judge Jackson called the new prosecution evidence "a rather startling revelation. I think it reflects badly on Mr. Roberson."

Delois Anne Mise testified she had used cocaine with mayoral bodyguard James Stays at a cookout in Kettering, Maryland, in August 1985. A former civilian D.C. police department employee, Mise said in 1983 she also had seen Stays enter a room at the Omni Shoreham Hotel in Washington, where she saw on a table a plastic baggie full of white powder, which she took to be cocaine. She said Marion Barry was standing next to the table.

Mundy got Mise to admit during cross-examination that she had no way of knowing what was in the baggie at the Omni Shoreham, but she stuck to her account of snorting cocaine powder with Detective Stays at the Maryland barbeque.

The last trial witness, Terry Lee Brenay, looked and spoke as if he had just stepped out of "Gilligan's Island." A former Michigan policeman, Brenay had moved to the U.S. Virgin Islands in 1979 and had worked there ever since as an outboard motor repairman and as skipper of the *Brigadoon*, on which he once took a party that included Marion Barry on a daysail.

Brenay, who said he was known as "First-Pull" in the island's outboarding community because of his skill at fixing engines, said at one point during the June 1986 cruise that he smelled marijuana smoke wafting from the boat's main salon. He went below to investigate and found Barry, Charles Lewis, and a Virgin Islands woman whose name he couldn't recall sharing a joint. Did he ask them to put it out? No way. He joined them.

"Now, after the second marijuana cigarette was completed, what happened next?" prosecutor Richard Roberts asked him.

"Well, it wasn't very good marijuana," Brenay recalled and then added, "I had a joint that I brought along with me."

"Did you say anything to Mr. Lewis when you gave it to him?" Roberts inquired.

"Yes," answered Brenay. "I said, 'Here, try this, It's home-grown. It's much better quality than what you have.'"

Brenay kept up his one-liners during cross-examination by Mundy, who at one point asked the former skipper where exactly he had sailed the *Brigadoon* that day. "Now, you are able to recall on this particular trip that you were somewhere between Congo and Lobango?" Mundy asked. "Am I pronouncing it right?"

"It is an old island called Love-and-Go," quipped Brenay, who added: "[There] used to be a whorehouse on the island."

The courtroom exploded into laughter while the red-faced Judge Jackson, in an effort to maintain his decorum, hid his smile behind a fist. Before he let this final witness step down, however, Jackson, a sailing buff, asked Brenay how much water the *Brigadoon* displaced, and other nautical questions which the bearded, blue jeans-clad witness cheerfully answered.

The following Monday, July 30, both sides formally rested their cases. On Tuesday, Judge Jackson heard arguments on suggested jury instructions. According to veteran trial observers, most jurors pay scant attention to such precepts, relying primarily not on what the judge says but on common sense, instinct, values, and memories, even television- and movie-viewing experiences, to guide them during deliberations. But this was no ordinary trial. The Barry jurors, caught up in a political and racial vortex, would probably be grateful for any help they could get.

The government, ever sensitive to the unspoken but crucial racial dimension of the trial, had asked Jackson to instruct the panel not to consider any alleged "racial motivation" the government may have had for prosecuting Marion Barry. It also asked Jackson to make it clear that when a person is predisposed to commit a crime—such as using illegal drugs—he or she cannot use entrapment as a legal defense.

The defense, on the other hand, focused primarily on witness credibility. It asked the judge to remind jurors that they should "take into account any evidence that witnesses who testify may benefit in some way from his or her testimony." In an obvious reference to Rasheeda Moore, the defense also asked Jackson to instruct the jurors that the testimony of any witness "who provides evidence against the defendant for pay or immunity from punishment, or for personal vindication or advantage, must be examined and weighed by the jury with greater care than testimony by an ordinary witness."

While Jackson and the lawyers worked on final jury instructions, Barry took his last public shot at the government. In an interview outside the federal courthouse, the embattled mayor, surrounded by reporters and well-wishers, reached a new rhetorical high, calling the federal corruption probe of him and his administration the "$50 million Jay Stephens folly."

Challenged by a reporter about the astronomical figure he had just used—$10 million higher than the figure cited by Benjamin Hooks and other black leaders—Barry retorted, "It is not for me to prove. It's for Jay Stephens to disprove."

Months earlier the U.S. attorney *had* factually countered Barry's claim. But that did not keep the mayor from issuing the racially inflammatory statement. Even if the jurors could not hear his message, the voters would. Barry was considering a run for an at-large D.C. Council seat, and playing the racial card could pay handsome dividends in some quarters of the city.

The mayor did, however, concede that "I've made my share of mistakes, no question about that. I certainly have done some things I'm not very proud of." But he quickly added, "That was private conduct" for which he was not on trial. "I've not looted the treasury," he insisted. This assertion, of course, was debatable—particularly in light of the conviction of two former deputy mayors for stealing hundreds of thousands of dollars from the city. But that was ancient history. Technically, however, Barry was right: the government had never charged him personally with corruption.

"The city would not be going through this trauma and drama," the mayor asserted, "if not for the zeal of the federal government."

Then Barry delivered one of his more ludicrous rationalizations: "If you look at the whole array of crimes in America, most of them are committed in private from time to time." If other people were breaking the law and getting away with it, why shouldn't he?

The mayor said the most upsetting aspect of the trial for him personally was seeing some of his "close friends pressured, pushed, coerced, or whatever into not speaking the truth."

When asked about a *Washington Times* story saying that members of the Metropolitan Police civil disturbance unit were gearing up for a possible riot, should he be convicted, Barry dismissed the report, saying, "I've not heard serious considerations by anyone of that kind of setback."

To the mayor's credit, he finally found something—his supporters' anger—too potentially destructive to exploit for his own selfish ends. But then Barry took his habitual shot at the "racist" media: "When people in media talk of rioting or violence, they're usually talking about the African-American community. Let me remind you that white people can riot too; but we're not talking about that among any community, white or black. You obviously don't realize that we have grown as a people the last twenty years. We will not destroy that which we have worked so hard to build up." He added, "Those who would even talk about that don't represent me, don't represent what I stand for."

In fact, some black leaders staunchly in Barry's camp, D.C. Council member H.R. Crawford and the Reverend Jesse Jackson among them, had warned of the unrest building in the black community because of the trial. Crawford had described the situation in some neighborhoods as "explosive." In a veiled reference to Barry's predicament, Jackson had told the D.C. Democratic Women's Club that the perception of government entrapment of black elected officials takes on "big overtones" to blacks who themselves have been victims.

Finally, the mayor was asked what the jurors should consider while deliberating his fate.

"I would like for them to—those who are Christians—to pray hard and to remember that God is a forgiving God."

Then Barry made an amazing statement for a man laboring under the weight of triple perjury charges. "Also," he said, "I'd like [them] to remember that people do lie—under oath, in public, and on the stand."

27

THE FINAL ROUND

On Wednesday, August 1, at 10:16 A.M. the bell rang for the final round of the legal slugfest. In addition to the mayor, the U.S. attorney, and their entourages, Courtroom two at the U.S. District Court held scores of reporters and sketch artists, a dozen courthouse employees, relatives and political backers of the defendant, 18 members of the public, and 18 jurors, six of whom, perhaps signaling the solemnity with which they viewed the occasion, perhaps in mourning for their lost summer, wore black.

Judith Retchin rose from her seat at the prosecution table. At the end of a trial, when summary arguments are heard, it is customary for the government to strike the first blow. For her most important day in court, the mayor's co-prosecutor wore a blue pinstripe suit and gold earrings. Uncharacteristically, she also had placed a blue-and-white silk handkerchief in her breast pocket. Perhaps it wasn't too late to show the federal panel a persona less grim and businesslike than the one she had maintained during six-and-a-half weeks of grueling testimony. Playing the heavy in the mayor's scenario of racial victimhood had taken its toll on Retchin. She looked tired. She could see that the jurors looked tired. It was time to wrap this up and go home.

"May it please the court," said Retchin, in a traditional bow of politeness to the bench.

Judge Jackson, expressionless to maintain his neutrality, nodded ever so slightly in response.

Retchin turned to the jury box. "Ladies and gentlemen, when we began this case several weeks ago, we told you that the case would show deceit and deception, the deceit and deception of the defendant, Marion Barry." Retchin swept an arm toward the defense table where the mayor sat with his hands folded, staring innocently at the jurors. "And, ladies and gentlemen, that is exactly what the evidence has shown in this case. The evidence has shown that for years Mr. Barry chose a select group of friends and associates and wrapped himself in this group, in this web of deception, so that Mr. Barry could possess and use cocaine.

"The web of deception began to unravel December 22, 1988, at the Ramada. And the web continued to unravel from that point, ladies and gentlemen—and what did it reveal?" Retchin pointed to two large, magnetized charts bearing the names of the 10 people who testified they had used cocaine with Barry, and the dates and locations of the alleged drug offenses. "You saw that [through] the years, not only has Mr. Barry been using and possessing cocaine in every quadrant of the city—in hotels, on boats, in private homes—he has been doing it with the protection of some of the members of his own executive protection unit."

Because of his high office, said Retchin, Barry "had to cover up what was really going on. It is not easy for a mayor of a city to use drugs, ladies and gentlemen. Do you think Mr. Barry could walk out onto 14th Street and buy drugs from someone on the corner? He can't do that, ladies and gentlemen, especially when he is holding himself out as the person who is leading our war on drugs."

Precisely, methodically, ticking off points on her fingers, Retchin walked the panelists through the government's case. She reminded them of key testimony, and of the lies Barry had allegedly told to a federal grand jury, lies that, if proven, could bring the mayor up to 15 years in prison.

Retchin spoke for two-and-a-half hours. She called the evidence against Barry "overwhelming," not without justification. Forty-eight times, she referred to alleged lies told by the mayor. Most important, she tried to convince the jurors that, regardless of what Kenneth Mundy had said, and probably would say in his closing argument, Marion Barry was no "victim" being picked on by the U.S. government; instead, she suggested, he had used his office and perquisites of power to exploit the weak and the vulnerable, to "ensnare" them in his "web of deception."

Of her witnesses, whom Mundy had impugned as coming "from the inner recesses of humanity," Retchin contended, "if [the defense] counsel wants you to believe that, well, ladies and gentlemen, then Mr. Barry is right with them. It was Mr. Barry who gave us our witness list, when he chose to have Thanksgiving dinner with these people, travel with them to the Bahamas, call them from his car phone, take them on boats, visit them in hotels.

"Now, some of you might not like Rasheeda Moore," Retchin allowed. She had seen the way certain jurors watched the government's star female witness. She had read the angry comments on the jury questionnaires and the newspaper accounts about the hostility many blacks felt toward the woman who had set the mayor up. She knew Rasheeda Moore was not the most popular woman in Washington. Since Retchin also knew that jurors tend to believe witnesses they like, and were skeptical of those they did not like, she had to make them at least tolerate Moore. "Some of you might think, well, I don't like the idea that someone who had a close relationship with anyone else would come in here and spill their guts and tell everything about what happened," Retchin continued. "Ladies and gentlemen, you don't have to like Rasheeda Moore. You don't have to invite her home for dinner."

Several jurors smiled.

"What we are asking you to do," said Retchin, "is look at the testimony of Rasheeda Moore and see whether or not it is truthful."

Using the charts to jog their memories, Retchin reminded the jurors that several other government witnesses had confirmed parts of Moore's testimony; she asked the jurors not to allow the defense counsel—whom she called "a very, very skilled lawyer—probably one of the best cross-examiners in this jurisdiction—to leave them with a "false impression" of the allegedly differing testimony of those witnesses.

Retchin then briefly reviewed the 14 counts of the indictment, starting with the four misdemeanor drug possession charges and the three felony charges that arose from Barry's four admitted visits to his friend Charles Lewis at the Ramada Inn in 1988.

She said Lewis's testimony was full of concrete details such as the brown matchbox in which Barry had allegedly brought Lewis rocks of crack cocaine, that his testimony was not the kind one would expect from a man the defense had made out to be a "facile liar" and a "notorious drug dealer."

She used the testimony of James McWilliams, a far more stable figure than the peripatetic Virgin Islander, to back up Lewis.

"What did they [Barry and Lewis] say when they came out of the bathroom?" Retchin asked, referring to McWilliams's testimony about seeing Barry and Lewis disappear into the Ramada bathroom, from which he'd seen clouds of aromatic white smoke emerge. " 'Wow, that was great shit!' " The prosecutor stretched out her hand to the smiling jurors. "What do you think they were talking about, ladies and gentlemen?" she asked.

The defendant joined in the laughter, but his wife, one hand in the lap of her white embroidered dress, one propping up her chin, sat motionless, staring icily at Retchin.

On Effi Barry's right, Mattie Cummings, Barry's mother, pursed her lips, a nervous habit she shared with her son. The former Mississippi sharecropper and housemaid, in her mid-70s, always had been Barry's number one fan, cheering from the sidelines as he won one unexpected trophy after another: a scholarship to college, a master's degree in chemistry, leadership of the first national student civil rights group in U.S. history, a seat on the D.C. school board and city council, and finally, the mayor's job. "He never was a quitter," she once had said proudly of her son. But on this day, as she sat ramrod straight on the hard wooden bench in her bright red-and-white print dress, listening to Retchin's litany of accusations, Cummings looked as if she might have wished that her son the battler had given up just this once, plea-bargained or whatever it took to avoid the humiliation of the trial.

Judith Retchin walked over to the defense table and pointed at Mattie Cummings's son. "He himself corroborated [his four visits to the Ramada Inn Central in December 1988] in his grand jury testimony," said Retchin, trying to nail down the perjury charges. Then she took off her gloves. "Evidence goes to show you, when Mr. Barry went into the grand jury, he lied. He lied. The ultimate deceit. The ultimate cover-up.

"Ladies and gentlemen, our government can't work well when the chief executive officer charged with enforcing all the laws goes into the grand jury and shows his utter contempt and disdain for the [judicial] process."

Then Retchin all but apologized for putting Linda Maynard on the stand. Did she regret the move?

"Some of you may have been offended by what you heard," Retchin offered, "[but] whatever your personal opinions are, put them aside." She reminded the jurors, "It was Mr. Barry [not the government] who connected cocaine and sex, and that is why you heard the evidence."

After a lunch break Retchin continued her relentless summary. In an attempt to explain the most confusing charge, count one, conspiracy to possess cocaine, the prosecutor likened Barry to the "hub of a wheel" from which emanated many "spokes," leading to the mayor's alleged friends and lovers.

She told the jurors that if they found that any one of these unindicted co-conspirators had supplied drugs to or were given drugs by Barry, "that would be a crime."

"Conspiracy does not mean that people went into a dark room and signed an oath between themselves written in blood," she explained sardonically. "It can be the wink of an eye," she said, winking at the jurors; "a nod of a head," she nodded; "a signal, an unspoken agreement."

Mimicking the testimony of witnesses who had spoken of "codes" Barry used to ask for drugs—often from his car phone—Retchin asked: " 'Is anything happening? What's happening?' "

Her rendering of Barry's street slang was stiff, inauthentic, a graphic reminder of the wide gulf of language, culture, and experience that separated the world of the accusers from that of the accused.

Knowing how much time her opponent had invested defending against count three, which alleged that the mayor had received crack cocaine from Lydia Pearson at the Reeves municipal center on September 7, 1988, Retchin devoted special attention to attacking Barry's alibi. "The glue to the alibi was [Barry's chauffeur] Walter Bracey," she said. "Do you remember Walter Bracey? Ladies and gentlemen, Mr. Bracey is probably not one of the most sophisticated people we're going to meet, and you should not hold that against him." A few jurors smiled. Bracey had testified that he couldn't remember a single destination in his 12 years of driving Barry around the city other than the Safeway store in Northeast Washington where Barry had attended a ribbon-cutting cere- mony on September 7, 1988, and the District Building, where Barry had his main office. "But even though Mr. Bracey is not sophisticated, he should know the difference between the truth and a lie. Ladies and gentlemen, was his testimony believable? Mr. Bracey was trying to say whatever he could to help the defendant. He was a good soldier to the last moment."

Retchin told the jurors that Barry aide Clifton Roberson, the defense witness who had testified that he, not Barry, had accepted a job application from Lydia Pearson on September 7, "was not even *at* the Reeves Center on September 7th. Darcell Walker [Roberson's secretary] remembers typing out the [absent without official] leave slip. Maybe he was confused, because he certainly did not see [Lydia Pearson] on September 7th."

Once again ridiculing the defense claim that all the govern- ment witnesses had come from "the inner recesses of human- ity," Retchin asked the jurors to recall the testimony of Darrell Sabbs, the former leader of the mayor's Youth Leadership Institute, a man "who said he had a father-son relationship with Mr. Barry." If the jurors believed his testimony, she said, they would be obligated by law to convict Barry on count 11, which alleged that Barry had used drugs with Sabbs at a Washington hotel on August 26, 1989.

About Doris Crenshaw, the witness from Montgomery, Alabama, whom Barry had known since their civil rights days together, Retchin said, "It's hard to imagine a witness with more credibility." Retchin asked the jurors to recall Crenshaw's testimony about using cocaine with Barry on "numerous occasions," including November 1989, when Crenshaw said the mayor had stopped by her room at the Mayflower Hotel in downtown Washington. The visit was the basis for count 12, alleging that Barry had possessed cocaine in the District between November 7, 1989, and November 10, 1989. Retchin explained that in order to convict Barry on count 12, they did not need to pinpoint the exact date of the alleged drug offense. She said they just needed to find that Barry had used cocaine "on or about" the date or dates in question. She said such temporal flexibility applied to all the other counts as well.

Finally, Retchin explained, in a simple, yet powerful parable, why the government had gone after Barry. "Imagine that you were at war," she said, in a thinly veiled reference to the crack wars raging on the city's streets, "and there was a general who was leading your war, and the general was a very smart general, a very popular general."

The jurors looked at the defendant, who stared back at them impassively.

"When he was with his troops, most of his troops," Retchin continued, "the general usually said the right thing. He usually inspired the troops to fight the war. But then you got allegations, you heard that the general was helping the other side, and you started to investigate and you called the general into the grand jury and said, 'General, is it true, are you helping the other side?' The general took an oath and said he was not helping the others, but you continue to get more allegations.

"You talked to the general's friends," she said, once again pointing to the chart. "You talked to the general's associates, and they told you that, yes, the general was helping the other side. He was helping the other side in hotels, in boats, in private homes. He was helping the other side in 1983, '84, '85, '86, '87, '88, '89.

"Ladies and gentlemen," said Retchin, looking directly at the jurors' faces, "what would you do? Wouldn't you want to tell the general, 'You can't help the other side?' How can we win the war when the general is helping the other side?" Evoking Lincoln's Gettysburg Address, she added, "You can't win a war with a camp divided."

Then Retchin connected her parable to the most important, but also the most controversial aspect of the government's case, the Vista sting.

"Wouldn't you want to give the general an opportunity to show he was not helping the other side?" she argued, standing near the jury box, holding out her hands in supplication. "That is what the undercover operation at the Vista was about, ladies and gentlemen." Retchin began to pace. "In a perfect world you would not need an undercover operation." She stopped and looked directly at the jurors. "Unfortunately, we do not live in a perfect world.

"Some of you might have thought it a good idea to have the undercover operation," Retchin continued, staying in close, giving the jurors a chance to see that she wasn't really so heinous, she, the representative of the white-dominated federal government, the lady with the sporty blue-and-white handkershief jutting out of her breast pocket. "It [the sting] is a good idea because seeing is believing and 'I wanted to see for myself,'" she suggested.

Retchin threw out reason after reason why the panelists should feel that the undercover operation was not only appropriate, but a fine idea. But, she noted, "Whatever you feel, his honor [Judge Jackson] will tell you you must put aside if you thought it was a good idea or a bad idea. Write us a letter after the trial, but it has nothing to do with what happened. [Your personal feelings] should not affect your deliberations at all.

"His honor will tell you that none of the defendant's constitutional rights were violated, that the installation of the cameras and the microphones was legal, that you must consider the evidence that was obtained from that sting operation just as you would any other evidence in this case."

Retchin urged the jurors to play the videotape until they were sick of it. "You'll learn a lot about the defendant. The most telling thing on that tape: Marion Barry goes into his pocket, he gets the money and he gives it to Rasheeda. 'I don't smoke anymore, honey.' And he asked for [cocaine] powder. That's not saying no to drugs, ladies and gentlemen. That's saying he had a preference for cocaine powder instead of crack."

"Mr. Barry's habit was breaking the law and getting away with it," said the prosecutor, once more pointing to the defendant, who ignored her. "He thought he could get away with it again. Mr. Barry smoked the crack from the stem as though he had done it all the time, and we know he has done it often." She added, "No one forced Mr. Barry to do anything. When you listen to Mr. Mundy tell you about entrapment, see if Mr. Mundy is able to show you where on the [sting] tape anyone was holding a gun to Mr. Barry's head."

Retchin walked to the large magnetized chart showing the names of the 10 government witnesses who said they had used drugs with Barry and/or provided him with drugs between 1984 and 1989: Charles Lewis, Rasheeda Moore, Lydia Reid Pearson, Hassan Mohammadi, Theresa Southerland, Lloyd Moore, Jeffrey Mitchell, Darrell Sabbs, Bettye Smith, Doris Crenshaw. Each small block of red on the chart represented one month. Next to Rasheeda Moore's name was nearly a solid red line for the years 1986 to 1988.

"Each time the strip was taken off here," Retchin said, pointing to the chart, "that is predisposition. The government would just have to show one [such incidence of] predisposition," she asserted, to prove the conspiracy count. "You have heard testimony that approximates 200 times of Mr. Barry using cocaine, of the general working for the other side.

"Ladies and gentlemen, there is no entrapment here. If anything, all it [the evidence] shows is compulsion.

"When he is caught," said Retchin, sweeping an arm toward Barry, "he tells a lie. The first thing out of his mouth, a lie. And what does he do? He blames someone else. On the tape he is blaming Rasheeda. It is not taking responsibility. There is no shame."

In closing, the prosecutor made a calculated bow to her rival's exceptional courtroom skills. "I don't intend to compete with Mr. Mundy," she confessed. "There is no way I would win any contest like that. But don't get distracted by smoke and mirrors. Focus on the evidence, and use your common sense. The evidence will add up.

"Ladies and gentlemen," she said, stealing her punchline from the title of a popular black movie, "We ask you to do the one just and right thing: to return verdicts of guilty on all counts.''

At 3:40 P.M. Kenneth Mundy stood up to speak. Since court was adjourning an hour early that day, he had just 20 minutes to try to dispel Retchin's powerful, damning impression.

''May it please the court,'' said Mundy, as he stepped up to the podium. He nodded to the prosecutors who sat at a table to his left, then turned to the jury box.

''In this trial Mr. Barry has had his life opened up like a book to you,'' Mundy began. ''He has been under a microscopic glass for purposes of your examination and consideration. There are no saints among us, and none of us can fare well with that type of close introspection [sic].''

Having quickly established the defendant's imperfection and vulnerability, Mundy finally unveiled the first of the ''surprises'' he promised. ''Ladies and gentlemen,'' he said, ''I will start right from the beginning by telling you that we do not intend to indicate or claim that Mr. Barry did not use cocaine. We do not mean for one moment to give you the impression that there was not a use of cocaine, occasional use of cocaine, by Mr. Barry during the period in time that we have evidence about.''

The jurors appeared stunned by Mundy's revelation. Could they have heard him right? Was he really admitting, after putting all those witnesses on the stand to say otherwise, that the mayor was an ''occasional'' user of cocaine? Would such an admission mean Barry was probably guilty of the 11 misdemeanor charges of cocaine possession and drug conspiracy the government had brought against him?

''I also want to tell you,'' Mundy declared, ''that [Barry's ''occasional'' cocaine use] is not what the case is about.'' Nor was Barry being tried, Mundy asserted, ''because of what you might consider sexual improprieties or sexual promiscuity.''

''Except for the conspiracy charge,'' Mundy further asserted, ''he is being tried for specific instances of alleged misconduct and, in order to convict him you must be satisfied beyond a reasonable doubt of his misconduct as alleged specifically by the government in the indictment.''

Mundy knew he couldn't outslug the government, so he was trying to outfox it by recasting the argument: he was forcing the government to prove every single instance of alleged drug use by Barry. In many instances it was Barry's word against that of a single witness, and Mundy intended to remind the jurors of that fact so often as to plant a seed of doubt. If he could nurture that seed, make it grow, his client would reap the benefits.

"Nor do we mean to indicate that there was not some type of conduct that was not popular or not appropriate," Mundy continued, reinforcing his the-mayor-is-only-human theme. "But ladies and gentlemen, you sit in a jury box, you don't sit in a ballot box. You are performing a service now as jurors, not as voters, and it is not whether you like Mr. Barry, whether you like Mr. Barry's lifestyle, or whether you like things that have been paraded here about Mr. Barry. The question is whether the government has proven guilt beyond a reasonable doubt."

Mundy's direction was easy to see. Not only did the government have the burden of proof, he was also suggesting that the prosecutors were "parading" unseemly facts about the mayor in a public courtroom, that they were in effect, "out to get" the mayor. Mundy was keeping his promise to put the government on trial: *David v. Goliath.*

Citing Retchin's metaphor of Barry as a wartime general, Mundy said, "I would like to carry that example a step further. Mustard gas was long ago outlawed even among the nations that were fighting at war, but it is like, in order to stop misdemeanor charges, which are the principal charges, the cocaine use, minor charges, the powers that be, that govern and control in these situations, call in a battery of persons to inflict mustard gas. And the problem with that is mustard gas cannot be contained to one person. Mustard gas affects many around it, and it is a way of saying that the end justifies the means, but in our society that is not so."

As Mundy got his argument rolling, he began to prance around the well of the courtroom, inveigling the jurors with his words, gestures, and expressions. Barry watched him as attentively as any juror. This was a man at the top of his game, a consummate ring dancer, an orator with a marvelous command of the language and a voice he used like a musical instrument, modulating tone, pitch, and volume, to drive home each point. If anyone could get Barry out of his dreadful corner, it was Kenneth Mundy.

"Our society is a society of laws," asserted Mundy, "and even those who seek to enforce the laws are governed by certain responsibilities. And the danger with the mustard gas, which is the sting that was conducted at the Vista Hotel, is that it cuts at the very fabric of our entire society. It might be Mr. Barry today and somebody else tomorrow."

Denied the opportunity to portray the Vista operation as government "entrapment," Mundy was doing the next best thing—implying that the Vista sting was only the first in a series of undercover operations to be mounted against those whom the government didn't like. If he could convince even a single juror that Barry had been unfairly targeted for prosecution, he could render the government's awesome accumulation of evidence against Barry irrelevant. A desperate and cynical strategy, it capitalized on racial fears and suspicions. But, considering the facts in the case and how effectively the government had mustered them, a deadlocked jury, producing a mistrial, represented Barry's best, perhaps only hope to walk out of the courtroom a free man.

"One of the things that the government did deal with that I want to share with you now," said Kenneth Mundy, zeroing in on count three as Retchin knew he would, "is the matter of Lydia Pearson and her alleged visit to the Reeves Center on September 7, 1988.

"What Miss Pearson said was that she arrived after 10. Say she arrived at 10:10 or 10:15, and then she says she waited 15 minutes. That makes it about 10:30; so, if you accept any part of Miss Pearson's testimony, it seems that this would put her in contact with Mr. Barry at about 10:30."

"Now, the government took Mr. Bracey to task, but they didn't say one thing about Ola Ruth Jones, who didn't even know Mr. Barry, who has no reason to fabricate. Ola Ruth

Jones was the assistant manager of the Safeway, you will recall, that was being opened, and she said that Mr. Barry didn't leave there until about 10:30.''

Actually, Jones had testified that she thought Barry had left the Safeway about 45 minutes after he arrived, which she estimated was around 9:30. That would make his departure around 10:15, not 10:30 as Mundy claimed. Such a discrepancy would have given the mayor time to stop by the Reeves Center, pick up the drugs from Pearson, and still make the fire department meeting at around 10:45—the time the government, citing a 10:42 phone call made from the mayor's limousine, estimated Barry had arrived. But how could jurors be expected to remember such minute details? They had, after all, heard from 45 witnesses and seen nearly 150 exhibits introduced during seven long weeks of testimony. Plant a seed of doubt. Water it with clever wording. Watch it grow.

"Darcell Walker," said Mundy, of the secretary in defense witness Clifton Roberson's office who had typed an AWOL slip for Roberson, "couldn't explain who crossed out the time 4:30 to 6:30 P.M. [on the AWOL slip]. She said, 'It wasn't like that when he gave it back to me.' Do you remember her testimony?

"Ladies and gentlemen of the jury, why did we concentrate so much on September 7, 1988?" Mundy asked rhetorically. "The significance of the Lydia Pearson count is that when we were presented with [a] precise date and time we were able to go out and bring in Mr. Barry's official schedule. We were able to bring in witnesses [to refute the testimony of government witnesses]. We were able to contradict and defeat the charge, because we knew what the charge was."

Then Mundy blasted his opponents for using their superior resources and power to compel Pearson and other witnesses who "had something to gain by dealing with the government" to testify.

"The defense can't go out and make deals with people it wants as witnesses," he complained, by offering them a plea-bargain agreement or immunity from prosecution for testifying. Nor can it subpoena people. In fact, said Mundy, "We can't offer anybody anything. We are not playing on a level field."

David v. Goliath.

After charging that the government's use of "on or about" to describe the dates of the alleged offenses had left the defense playing a game of "pin the tail on the donkey"—"It's the hardest thing in the world when you are faced with the entire calendar," he said sarcastically—Mundy revealed the third and final prong of his strategy: to paint the government witnesses as a vengeful and unprincipled band of rascals, liars, and whores.

"Ladies and gentlemen of the jury, tomorrow morning I am going to start with each and every one of the government witnesses. I am going to take you to passages in the transcript, but perhaps most important of all is what Charles Lewis said when Charles Lewis was on the witness stand: Charles Lewis said self-preservation is the most important consideration."

By the time Jackson called a halt at 4 P.M., Mundy had subtly accused the government of selectively targeting Barry for prosecution, of basing its prosecution on the vaguest of testimony, and of using a pathetic cast of characters motivated principally by an understandable but not particularly noble desire to save their own skins. Not bad for 20 minutes.

On Thursday, August 2, the final day of trial arguments, Mundy topped the previous day's effort with a spectacular performance. Nursing a cold, putting so much into his delivery that he temporarily lost his voice near the end of his summary, the defense attorney still managed to cast doubt on the fairness and legitimacy of the Vista sting and to tar the prosecution witnesses as a "bag" of "facile liars" singing the government's tune.

"Yesterday Miss Retchin said that our government cannot function well if the mayor of the city is using drugs," conceded Mundy, who on the last day of trial arguments wore a grey suit, white shirt, and a burgundy-white-and-gold-striped tie, the colors of Washington's beloved Redskins football team. No detail ignored. Nothing left to chance. "That coin has a reverse side," Mundy continued. "Our government doesn't function at all when it stoops to the entrapment and the lure and the enticement that you have seen here today. If, as the government would have you believe, and if, as the government would indicate to you through its witnesses, Mr. Barry's drug use was so rampant and widespread and so blatant, then he could have been caught or he could have been discovered by more standard means."

This assertion was debatable, first, because, whatever else they were, Barry's drug-sharing "friends" were not, until they were pressured by the government, snitches. Secondly, Barry himself had devised a plethora of sophisticated methods, including coded language, to keep investigators at bay. Thus, if federal investigators were determined to bust Barry they probably would have to resort to unconventional methods, as they did.

"The government went to great lengths, great lengths, to catch Mr. Barry in a misdemeanor, a misdemeanor!" jeered Mundy, his voice rising in indignation. "The mildest form of crime known in our set of laws. The government, in effect, used a sledgehammer to kill a fly."

David v. Goliath.

"It is very much like using acid to get a spot out of your clothing," Mundy continued. "The cure is manyfold times worse than the ailment."

Turning to the sting operation, Mundy charged that the government had "provided the accommodations and the arrangements, the bait and the booze, the pipe and the crack, the light and the know-how."

As his proxy pressed his attack on the federal prosecutors, Barry, chin in hand and a bemused expression on his face, watched from the defense table. He wore a grey double-breasted suit, white shirt, red paisley tie. On his lapel were two tiny sweetheart roses, which, Barry told reporters, symbolized "the purple rose of power."

Mundy returned to Retchin's metaphor that Barry was a traitorous general. If you have a general like that, he said, "the proper thing is to cancel his commission. The proper thing is to recall him.

"Using Miss Retchin's parable, the proper thing would be to vote him out of office. Moreover, by that statement, Miss

Retchin in effect was saying he is being prosecuted because he is the mayor.''

Soon the judge would instruct the jury, Mundy continued, that Barry ''is being tried as a man, not as a mayor. Don't convict him because he is the mayor and don't acquit him because he is the mayor. The government has indicated that were he any other common man he wouldn't be here for these offenses.''

In fact, the government had indicated no such thing. Jay Stephens's entire thrust was to make Barry accountable for his actions like any other citizen. At this critical juncture, however, Mundy was throwing everything he had at the jury. He next attacked the government for the videotapes it had shown to the jurors of Barry at public rallies or functions exhorting residents not to use drugs and denying that he himself ever had used them.

''Despite all the protests and the denials,'' Mundy once more admitted, ''Mr. Barry was an occasional user of cocaine. It may be something you can understand, and it is difficult for a proud person who draws his strength from the office he fills to stand up and say, 'I use cocaine.' ''

Mundy claimed the government had shown Barry's anti-drug efforts simply ''to hold him up for scorn and ridicule for his apparent hypocrisy.''

Reminding jurors that Barry had advised Rasheeda Moore, Lydia Pearson, and Bettye Smith many times to cut back on their drug use, Mundy beseeched them not to ''hate the message because you disrespect the messenger.'' He added: ''Was this really an act of a consciousness of guilt, trying to cover up, trying to deceive and mislead? Or was it someone trying in his own frailty to at least say it [illegal drug use] is wrong?''

''The government tells you that Mr. Barry has been proven guilty beyond a reasonable doubt by a parade of witnesses,'' said Mundy, once more turning his indignation on Barry's accusers.

''Bettye Smith,'' said Mundy, focusing on one of them, ''told you she doesn't even know whether it's the last two weeks of December or when it was [that she last used cocaine with Barry]. Aren't we entitled to have a better shot from the government instead of spreading us all over the months of December and January, when they say he did something on a precise period of time?''

Then Mundy took his own shot at the man whom he accurately had dubbed the ''linchpin'' of the government's case against Barry.

''I want to show you that it all started with Charles Lewis,'' he said.

Mundy unveiled a new defense exhibit, a chart showing Lewis at the center surrounded by his four female Virgin Island friends: Dixie Lee Hedrington, Jonetta Vincent, Zenna Mathias, and Linda Maynard. Pointing to their names on the chart, Mundy said Lewis had recruited the women, in his words, ''as additional choir members in the FBI's glee club.''

As for Maynard's tearful tale of being sexually accosted by Barry, Mundy scoffed, ''She could sit here in front of you two-and-a-half years after the incident and cry about it, and the night that she says it happened, she walked out [of the hotel] and there wasn't a ruffled hair on her. There wasn't a tear in her eye. In fact, she kissed Mr. Barry goodbye.'' He paused a moment for effect. ''Was that, I respectfully submit to you, not contrived? Was that not intended [by the government] to throw a little more mud, a little more dirt on Mr. Barry?'' he demanded.

In fact, Judith Retchin had told the judge that Maynard's testimony was aimed at showing a pattern of drug abuse in Barry, not sexual aggression, and the defense had practically forced the government to elicit the seemingly irrelevant tale of Barry's alleged sexual assault. But Mundy had a point: in her quest to win every legal confrontation with the defense, Retchin may have gone too far; she may have alienated some of the jurors, turned them against the government.

Mundy unveiled a second new defense chart, illustrating the 21 times Charles Lewis allegedly had met with investigators after turning state's evidence in August 1989. Mundy counted up the hours that, according to police records, Lewis had spent with investigators; he reminded the jurors that during cross-examination Lewis had been unable to recall three meetings that took place only a week before the trial started.

Mundy suggested that the government spent over a hundred hours prepping Lewis for the stand.

"Charles Lewis also got a pretty good deal," Mundy jeered. "Charles Lewis was tried in the Virgin Islands, and in April of 1989 he was convicted, and then he got a 'wake-up call,' he says. "I guess people get 'wake-up calls' from the strangest places," Mundy said, sarcastically evoking Charles Lewis's testimony. "Charles Lewis got his when he was sitting in a prison in the Virgin Islands. Rasheeda Moore got hers when she was sitting in a shelter home in California. These are the principal witnesses. These are the two survivors. These, Rasheeda Moore and Charles Lewis, are the persons, the beginning and the end. And both of them got the strangest wake-up calls."

Moreover, Mundy continued, "Isn't the government still holding the sword over his [Lewis's] head? He is still facing whatever time he has in the Virgin Islands." Mundy held up a portion of the nearly 6,000-page trial transcript. "Self-preservation is first on anyone's mind," Mundy read from Lewis's earlier testimony. "And, ladies and gentlemen," He continued, looking directly at the jurors, "he [Lewis] stands for the rest of the government's witnesses."

Mundy picked up another transcript segment, flipped through the pages, found the right spot. "Can you believe that Charles Lewis says his reasons for running around town offering people cocaine is because they are 'human beings'?" Mundy mocked, reading the explanation Lewis had given for offering drugs to a maid at the Ramada Inn.

Several jurors smiled. Mundy had scored again.

"The government knows," said Mundy, "that Charles Lewis is a survivor and the government knows Charles Lewis will tell any tale and sing any song as long as his own fat may be in the fire."

Moving on to Rasheeda Moore, Mundy said, "she said she had an awakening in August of last year in California. At that time she was really down, down low economically, job, drug use, and everything else, and she just made the decision to turn her life around. Well, she made a half-turn if you believe her testimony, because she kept using drugs. She used drugs after the sting, was using government money she was getting in the witness protection program to buy her drugs. She got a real good deal. She not only gets herself and her three children taken care of at government expense, taxpayers' expense, but her boyfriend goes along with it. She gets him taken care of. They are getting $1,700 a month. She didn't say when it was going to end. It could be a lifetime for her contribution to this case.''

Mundy derided Moore's claim that she could not remember who had sent her the death-threat letter. ''Ladies and gentlemen,'' he said, ''if someone had threatened your life and it was serious, if you took it serious, you would know it [the name].'' He called the death threat claim ''a subterfuge to dine at the public trough.''

Having dissolved the character, if not the testimony, of the government's two chief witnesses with his sarcasm, Mundy turned to the sting videotape.

'' 'Have you been good lately?' is not a code for drugs,'' he insisted, of Barry's comment to Rasheeda Moore right after entering the hotel room, ''it's a sexual discussion. Agent Stern got up here and told you that Rasheeda did not invite Mr. Barry up to the room and Mr. Barry declined to come up to the room. You heard the tape [of Barry's phone call to Moore from his limousine]. Where was he [Stern]? He was in the next room!

''Ladies and gentlemen,'' Mundy entreated, ''even Agent Stern said that Rasheeda Moore exceeded his instructions with respect to how far to go in the sting. Mr. Barry said 'no' seven times. If you offer me drugs seven times and I say 'no,' I say 'No, I don't use it,' 'No, I don't use it,' 'No, I don't want any,' 'No, not tonight,' is that a predisposition?''

Mundy then cast the FBI and D.C. police as the Keystone Kops, bumbling yet menacing clowns who had used a great deal of time, energy, and, by implication, money, to bust the mayor on a misdemeanor charge. First they couldn't find the crack pipe for an hour and a half, he claimed, then they couldn't find the crack until a week later and finally they couldn't find cocaine on business cards till after the trial started.

A government witness had explained that the lab tests of the card had followed the investigators' realization that Barry habitually used the cards as makeshift coke spoons, but Mundy obviously hoped the jurors would have forgotten that detail. Plant a seed.

Even though Jackson had admitted the cards as evidence, Mundy urged the jurors to view them—and all other prosecution evidence—with skepticism.

"Ladies and gentlemen, except for the Vista [sting] and that one rock of cocaine that was allegedly found in his coat," Mundy asserted, "you haven't had put before you one smidgen of drugs. This is a [drug] case without drugs. All you have is the testimony of the witnesses." And the witnesses, he pointed out, all wanted to save their own skins.

Mundy also claimed, misleadingly, that "all the persons the government called were using drugs before they ever met Marion Barry." Jeffrey Mitchell and Hassan Mohammadi both had testified that Barry had introduced them to cocaine. Perhaps Mundy hoped the jurors wouldn't remember. Plant a seed.

"Jonetta Vincent," he quipped, about the Virgin Islands woman who had taken a sailboat ride with the mayor, "says she could catch the whif of a marijuana cigarette all of that distance [between the bow and the stern of the boat] on the open seas with [a] sinus [condition]—she beats radar!"

Several jurors laughed. As he drew the panelists further into his spell, Mundy reviewed the charges against Barry, attempting to refute each with a different argument.

"The government," Mundy stated flatly, "has failed to prove what it set out to prove" about count one, conspiracy to possess cocaine. The reason? The prosecutors had not tied Barry and all the other alleged co-conspirators together, Mundy asserted. In fact the government was not obliged to demonstrate such a network, only that Barry had conspired to possess drugs with any one of the alleged co-conspirators. But Mundy had nothing to lose by suggesting otherwise. Plant a seed.

For count two, Mundy attacked the credibility of Hassan Mohammadi. A resident alien, Mohammadi had cooperated with the government to avoid being deported to his native Iran.

Mundy said he "wouldn't even dignify" count three, the Lydia Pearson/Reeves Center count, "by responding to it." This was the count for which he had presented detailed alibi testimony.

Barry's chief defender also made quick work of counts four through seven, relating to Barry's visits to Charles Lewis at the Ramada, since these charges came out of the mouth of a "notorious drug dealer" and "liar."

Mundy lingered on the perjury charges—counts eight, nine, and 10—since they could bring his client serious prison time.

"I think it is very, very important," he counseled the panel, "for you to understand Mr. Barry is not charged with perjury about his own use of cocaine. None of the questions in the grand jury for which he is charged with perjury ask whether he has ever used cocaine. None of them."

Whose cocaine use Barry allegedly had lied about was irrelevant. He was charged with lying to a grand jury about his alleged knowledge of Charles Lewis's cocaine use. But that didn't stop Mundy from trying to tie the two charges—drug use and lying to a grand jury—together. Confuse the jurors. Plant seeds of doubt. Make them think the government was conspiring against the defendant, overzealous, trying to manufacture crimes, set Barry up, out to get him.

On count 11, alleging that Barry had used cocaine with Darrel Sabbs in 1989, Mundy reminded the jurors that "Mr. Sabbs couldn't remember whether he had moved back to Georgia in 1978 or 1985." He added, scornfully, "That is a memory you would scarcely want to trust about very minuscule matters, let alone a memory you would give much credence to beyond a reasonable doubt."

Mundy reminded the panel that Doris Crenshaw, on whose evidence count 12 was based, could not remember the exact date on which she had used cocaine with Barry at the Mayflower Hotel.

"If she was as uncertan about that as she was," posited Mundy, "then it could have taken place at another time, another place."

Plant a seed.

"Bettye Smith," Mundy asserted about the witness tied to count 13, "indicated that [Barry] never asked her for cocaine. Never."

Of course Barry wasn't charged with asking Smith for cocaine, he was charged with using it with Smith. Plant a seed. Watch it grow.

Mundy did not try to refute the final count, the one based upon the Vista sting, directly. How can you argue with a videotape? Instead he attacked Rasheeda Moore's credibility. "Do you believe for one minute," he demanded, "that Mr. Barry could have continued to function and run the city, a complex metropolis such as the District of Columbia, and the government of the District of Columbia, if he was as rampantly using drugs as Rasheeda Moore says?"

If the jurors believed the testimony of 32 government witnesses, the answer was yes. But Mundy was planting more seeds of doubt.

Mundy approached the jury box, took out a small brown matchbox from his pocket, laid it down on the edge of the nearby prosecution table, where the jurors could see it. It was the same matchbox Charles Lewis said Barry had used to bring him crack cocaine at the Ramada, the same one Judith Retchin had used a day earlier to accuse Barry of drug possession.

"Ladies and gentlemen," said Mundy, "supposing you had a cigarette to light and I asked you now what color the matchbox was that you used a year and a half ago, could you tell me?"

Several panelists smiled. Retchin and Roberts, by contrast, sat stiffly at the prosecution table, betraying no reaction to Mundy's obvious attempt to invade their territory, to taunt them before the jury. Their opponent had held the jury in his spell for nearly two-and-a-half hours; they were not about to give Mundy any more points by reacting to his ploy.

Mundy held the matchbox up. "This is not 'smoke,' " he said, mocking Retchin's swipe at him during her charge to the jury a day earlier, "this is not 'red herring.' This is shark, this is the real stuff, this is the record."

Mundy strode to the defense table, picked up a large, rounded light bulb with a short shaft, the kind one might see on a vanity mirror. He reminded the jurors that Charles Lewis had testified that the mayor unscrewed two such bulbs from the bathroom at the Ramada and put them in his pocket to take home to check for "bugs."

"Try to put this in your pocket," said Mundy, to the amusement of the jurors, as he tried unsuccessfully to force it into his right front jacket pocket. Then Mundy put down the bulb and quietly took the jurors into his confidence.

"This case is important," he said. "It is important to the community. It is important to Mr. Barry. It is important to all of us."

Mundy hardly needed to remind the jurors of how much was riding on their decision, how many Washingtonians of every race, color, and creed were anxious for a just verdict, and an end to the trial.

"Mr. Barry has made mistakes, and Mr. Barry has had his life held up, every seam opened up," said the attorney. "And this is the evidence that you have seen, a bunch of people just one step [ahead] of the law themselves as witnesses, a group of people that made deals.

"And I know the government is going to come back and say I stood up and told you that the government made deals with the devil. If they weren't full-grown devils, they were at least little Lucifers or small Satans because these were people that had their own problems and at any expense, at any cost, they were trying to help themselves.

"Ladies and gentlemen," said Mundy, "this case has been with us a long time, and it is now your job and your duty to resolve it. Whatever you do today, when you wake up tomorrow, you should be comfortable [with what you have done]."

Indeed, 12 ordinary Washingtonians had been stuck with the unappetizing task of chastising a man elected to lead them.

Their task was as much political as judicial, and Mundy knew it. He was playing to the jurors who understood that. Mundy ended his summary by urging the jurors to tell the government by their verdict: "This far and no further, this long and no longer, this much and no more."

Since the government carried the burden of proving its case beyond a reasonable doubt, it also had the last word. After the lunch break Richard Roberts, wearing a powder blue sport coat, dark grey slacks, white shirt, red-and-grey-striped tie, stood up to give the government rebuttal. A tall man, he stood behind the podium almost at attention. The job of finally unmasking Barry's deceptions and of deflating Mundy's masterful attempt to convince jurors that the government, not the defendant, had done wrong, had fallen to Roberts, a black man like the defendant.

"When Mr. Mundy addressed you beginning yesterday afternoon," said Roberts, "he alluded to how things sometimes get twisted, and then promptly treated you, perhaps unintentionally, to a twisting show that started then and carried through to today."

The first "twist" Roberts attempted to undo concerned Lewis.

"Now with respect to Mr. Lewis," said the prosecutor, "if Charles Lewis lied about the Ramada and drugs in the Ramada with Mr. Barry, and Charles Lewis lied about drugs and Mr. Barry outside the Ramada and elsewhere, then all of that corroboration that Judy Retchin outlined for you in excruciating detail, that overwhelming corroboration about all those other drug events, just doesn't exist."

As if to prove his point about Mundy's ability to "twist" the truth, Roberts reminded the jurors of Mundy's attempt to ridicule Lewis's testimony about the hotel light bulbs.

"Frankly," the prosecutor said as he stood with his right hand in his jacket pocket, facing the jury, "I've never seen a light bulb quite that big in a bathroom before. But I have seen one about this size." Roberts pulled out a bulb shaped identically to the one Mundy had displayed, only a quarter its size.

Everyone in the courtroom, including Barry and Mundy, laughed.

"Let's untwist another one," said Roberts, who had obtained the bulb from the Ramada Inn during the lunch break. "That couple, Ron and Lydia," he said, referring to Lydia Pearson and her boyfriend, who allegedly had sold crack to Barry, " 'They really came through good at times,'—do you think [Barry] was talking about milk and cookies?" he asked.

"Let's untwist a few other things, members of the jury," Roberts went on. "You heard Mr. Mundy say to you Rasheeda Moore said there was no cocaine in the Virgin Islands. You know better than that, and the transcripts will back up your recollection. Because what did Rasheeda Moore say? Rasheeda Moore told you she didn't recall whether there was cocaine there or not. Rasheeda Moore used cocaine so many times with Marion Barry she just didn't remember that time whether there was cocaine or not.

"Now, she could have come in here, the liar that they say she is, and gotten up there"—Roberts pointed to the witness stand—"and said there was plenty of cocaine, there was crack, we had everything down there. But she didn't. She just didn't remember, so she passed up that opportunity to lie about something."

Roberts debunked the alleged "sweet deal" Rasheeda Moore was given, calling her enrollment in the Federal Witness Protection Program "a life sentence." He charged that Marion Barry, rather than being a victim of an overzealous investigation, "lived above the law, lived one step ahead of anybody who was looking at his conduct." He said Barry had "snorted and smoked his way from 1988 right on into 1989." About Barry's decision to smoke crack at the Vista, despite his suspicions that he was being set up by Moore, Roberts said, "It's almost like he *wanted* to get caught."

Roberts tried to clear away the smoke and mirrors.

"Now, members of the jury, don't be distracted by the whining about precision on dates, particularly since a date is not a charge. The charge is possession, and there is no doubt about the defendant's underlying conduct of possession of cocaine or crack in the possession counts for which he is charged."

Then Roberts attacked the very heart of Mundy's strategy.

"The defense is, 'I didn't do it,' " Roberts said, " 'All the government's 25 or 30-some-odd witnesses are lying. But if I did do it, then the devil made me do it, and don't convict me because the government was out to get me. Out to get me.' Well, do you know what the sad fact is, members of the jury? Marion Barry was out to get himself."

He said Kenneth Mundy was "insulting your intelligence" by asking the jurors to believe that Barry was only an "occasional drug user."

"Can the defense look at you seriously and say there is no evidence that Marion Barry was predisposed to using a controlled substance?" Roberts demanded. "Can they seriously, seriously argue that to you? No predisposition? Members of the jury, look at all of these uses. Now, you remember the testimony of all the witnesses who took the stand and they talked about dozens and dozens and dozens of instances of crack possession, crack smoking, cocaine snorting, and other kind of drug possession.

"No predisposition? Ladies and gentlemen, it was Marion Barry that did all of that, and you know that. The government didn't cause the defendant to do anything. The government's investigation pulled the covers off this scam. The defendant was exposed, pure and simple, and there are no apologies for having conducted an investigation in which these crimes have been exposed and Marion Barry's conduct has been exposed. Case closed."

Roberts pointed at Barry, still sitting with his chin on his hand, a pose he held throughout much of the trial.

"He's asking you to help him continue his process of damage control," Roberts charged. He turned to directly face the jurors. "We all have jobs here to do. And your job, members of the jury, without favor or fear—is to speak the truth. That's what a verdict is." Knowing what a political and racial tightrope the government was walking in terms of some jurors' sentiments, Roberts then tried to soften his message slightly by adding, "This doesn't have to diminish the good Mr. Barry has done in his lifetime. But Mr. Barry has broken the law, and you must tell Marion Barry that he must rise up to his responsibility and to accept responsibility [for his alleged crimes] before he can rise up again and reclaim his place in history. Members of the jury, speak the truth. That is all we ask you to do."

28

THE PEOPLE SPEAK

When Judge Jackson read aloud the names of the six Barry panelists—three black and three white women—who were to be excused, one of the 12 remaining jurors, white college student and courier service co-owner Joseph Deoudes, looked briefly over at the spectators, grimaced, and shook his head. His gesture of resigned disbelief seemed to speak for everyone left in the jury box, which now included, in addition to Deoudes, another white man, a black man, and nine black women. For the next hour Deoudes and the others listened to Jackson's instructions, which he read in an authoritative baritone, peering at them frequently over the top of his bifocals. At 4:07 P.M. on Thursday, August 2, the slimmed-down panel repaired to a small room directly behind the courtroom to choose a "foreperson."

The jurors took seats around a dark wooden table that dominates the cramped, windowless, neon-lit rectangle where they would spend some 37 hours over the next nine days. On one wall, covered in tacky gold-and-white floral wallpaper, was an electric clock, to remind them the world was still out there, anxiously awaiting their decision. On another wall someone had hung cardboard reproductions of French impressionist and early 20th-century American paintings—in a failed attempt to liven up the dour chamber. The only other furniture in federal jury room two was a gray metal coat rack and a small, scarred wooden table holding a plastic water pitcher and salt and pepper shakers.

In these drab confines, the jurors quickly got down to business, choosing—to the surprise of many observers, who had expected a black juror to be tapped—Edward P. "Ted" Eagles, 54, the white, prep school history teacher, to lead their deliberations. The short, gray-haired, bespectacled St. Albans

345

"master," described by one juror as the most "logical candidate for the job" because of his even temper and the respect with which he was regarded by most of his fellow jurors, received nine votes.

The only other candidate was Hilson Snow, the black United Parcel Service driver, who later would publicly criticize Eagle's performance.

Although they outnumbered the men three-to-one, no woman volunteered to captain this conscripted crew through racially troubled waters.

Snow received votes from HUD accounting assistant Harriedell Jones and D.C. Department of Corrections secretary Valerie Jackson-Warren. Throughout the deliberations this trio, along with Southeast Washington housewife Joyce Hines and former department store supervisor Johnnie Mae Hardeman, would vote consistently for acquittal.

"We're not going to get personal here," Eagles reportedly told his fellow jurors the first day of deliberations. "We keep our emotions out of it. We're here to do our jobs, our service to the government or the nation, and just keep it strictly professional."

During the next nine days most of the jurors heeded his call but several did not. Instead, they turned the deliberations into a racial showdown, eventually arriving at a verdict that, according to Hilson Snow, "sends a message" to the country. (When asked later what the message was, he said, simply, "The message is in the verdict.")

Eagles, who later described his experience as a chance to "get into the political process instead of turning your back on it," sent his first note to the judge at 4:45 P.M. In a request revealing the methodical approach he would take to the mountain of evidence the jurors faced, he asked for "multiple copies" of the 14-count indictment and of the judge's 32-page instructions. He also told Jackson the panelists wanted to wrap up their initial work day at 5 P.M.

Later that night, at the Sheraton Greenbelt Hotel in New Carrollton, Maryland, where the jurors were sequestered, two jurors were treated to some unscheduled entertainment.

Howard University Hospital education coordinator Patricia Chaires and Valerie Jackson-Warren saw federal lawmen and Prince George's County police stage an abortive drug sting in the hotel parking lot. The main target, suspected cocaine dealer Brian Tribble, had gained notoriety when he was acquitted of supplying a fatal dose of the drug to University of Maryland basketball star Len Bias in 1987. The two jurors saw Tribble speed away in his black sports car as the lawmen closed in on him. Tribble escaped after a high-speed chase in which his car collided with two FBI vehicles, but he surrendered to DEA agents in Baltimore four days later. (An alleged accomplice in the aborted $30,000 drug buy was arrested.)

"I saw it happen," Chaires told the *Washington Post* after the verdict. "We were sitting in a room watching television and I heard a bang. I ran over to the window and looked out and I saw this car being rammed and then take off. Then I saw a guy on the ground. Valerie saw it too. She said, 'He's being arrested.' Then I saw the jacket with the DEA on it, the FBI, P.G. Police, the helicopter starts flying around. I said, 'Oh, my.' I said, 'Valerie, this is a drug bust.' I instantly thought this is a setup. I said, 'I'm sure this has implications [for the trial].' We went to the front desk and the marshals were leaning out the window. They witnessed it [too]."

In court the next day a U.S. marshal responsible for guarding the jurors incorrectly informed Judge Jackson his charges all had been "oblivious" to the commotion outside the Sheraton Greenbelt, but Kenneth Mundy learned differently and so informed the judge. According to the *Post*, on the night of the sting Chaires and Jackson-Warren had "reported what they saw to the marshals out of concern someone might be trying to sabotage the deliberations." The paper said "other jurors said they were informed about the drug sting during breakfast the next morning." In any case, the jurors were moved to another hotel.

On Friday, August 3, their first full day of deliberations, the jurors asked for transcripts of the testimony of 10 trial witnesses and for the "big magnetic chart" with the names of Barry's 10 alleged co-conspirators. Zeroing in on one of them, the panelists also asked for a copy of the cooperation agreement between the government and Doris Crenshaw, the Montgomery, Alabama, financial consultant who had testified to using cocaine powder with Barry more than a dozen times since 1984. The government had granted Crenshaw "use immunity," meaning it would not prosecute her for any potential crimes she might admit to during testimony.

The jurors, who by now had been sequestered for eight weeks—during which time, one juror said, they had gotten along outside the courtroom at least "superficially"—also asked to deliberate for half a day on Saturday, August 4. They wanted to finish their onerous task. They spent half that day in the mercifully large courtroom, examining nearly 150 exhibits and 5,772 pages of trial testimony. It was at this early point that two jurors, one black and one white, abandoned their already thin hopes that the panel would reach an objective verdict based solely on the evidence.

"We went in there [courtroom two] and half of the people weren't looking at things," said 22-year-old D.C. public school clerk/typist Marsena Hall. She had believed the mayor innocent at the start of the trial but once she heard the evidence, she voted consistently for conviction. "And then when they did they would go so far outside of what went on [at the trial] to look for reasons [to acquit Barry]. For instance, Valerie [Jackson-Warren] said that [the crack from the Vista bust] might not have been cocaine. It could have been some 'wet sugar.' And I could not believe that! This package was admitted into evidence as being cocaine, not as being sugar, that's a known fact.

"And then Hilson [Snow] being a video expert: 'They cut the [Vista] tape. I know videotapes.' I'm like, 'Look, we've got lawyers out here, investigators, FBI, and you think these people don't have common sense to know that if they take something like that and bring that in the courtroom [as contrived evidence] how stupid they can look? I mean, that would just blow the whole thing.' Wet sugar. Videotapes. I just laughed."

"That's just a clear-cut example of how these deliberations went," recalled Joseph Deoudes, who also heard Jackson-

Warren's comment, "and just how much lack of logic was involved. I don't care what Jackson-Warren said, If Ken Mundy didn't question it, what gives you or me or her or anyone the right to question it?"

Nevertheless, several jurors did—Johnnie Mae Hardeman reportedly claimed the crack was "baking soda." They also questioned the out-of-state bank checks and cocaine-tainted business cards confiscated from Barry at the Vista—items that Kenneth Mundy had urged the panel to view with skepticism, despite their admission into evidence by the judge. According to one juror, Joyce Hines said she believed these items had been "planted" on the mayor by the FBI.

As the deliberations progressed, they became even more tense and problematic, especially around the race issue.

"People thought it was the white government trying to get the black mayor," said one juror. "And when you said something against the mayor, regardless if it was crystal clear or not, [even] if you gave an example, some people would get offended. It was very touchy."

Marsena Hall agreed with the juror but emphasized, "We were not *trying* to make it a racial thing. But personal things got into it, because people were saying, 'Well, if he wasn't black, they probably wouldn't have gone that far. And by him being the mayor *and* being black, that's what made them [federal investigators] go after him.'"

Johnnie Mae Hardeman seemed to confirm this observation when she told the *Post* on the day of the verdict that the case, in her view, came down to "the government against the mayor. Evidently, somebody wanted him out of there, or else they would not have brought all these charges for so long."

Tonna Norman, a records manager for the federal Defense Mapping Agency, had expressed a similar view during *voir dire*: "I question whether the government would have taken the same steps against a less public figure." But while Hardeman voted "not guilty" on 10 of 14 counts, Norman, obviously swayed by the government's case, voted "guilty" on 12.

Hall said jurors favoring acquittal also brought up the case of Iran-Contra defendant Lt. Col. Oliver North and other whites who had received suspended sentences or community service after being convicted of felonies.

Hall said Barry's role as the city's highest elected official also complicated their job, especially for the nine black jurors.

"In the instructions [the judge] was saying to try him just as a man, not as the mayor, or not because of his race," she said. "But, honestly, as least I felt, we could never get beyond that point. We couldn't get beyond the fact of who he was . . . what he's done for the city and for black people."

Tensions among the jurors were not limited to race, or to Barry's status. They also touched on social class. According to the *Post*, at one point Harriedell Jones told college-educated Patricia Chaires that she was "sick of you bourgeois blacks" and accused Chaires of being insensitive to people like Barry who, in Jones's words, "was always a street person." At another point, said one juror, Valerie Jackson-Warren snapped at a middle-class black juror, "What the hell do *you* know about crack?" as if only a less affluent black person would understand such things.

Even personality played a role. Marsena Hall admitted that once late in the deliberations she lost her temper at Hilson Snow. "He would never get to the point," she said, describing his rambling style of expressing himself. Hall said Snow quickly ended his discourse, but her outburst chilled their relationship, even outside the jury room.

Although Hall and Deoudes both agreed Edward Eagles was the most "logical" person to lead the deliberations, he may not have been the best. They said Eagles never tried to forge an overall consensus among the disparate voices in the room—arguably a jury foreman's most critical role. Rather, they said, he took a "laid back" approach, allowing everyone to hold the floor virtually as long as he or she wished. Although commendably democratic, the process slowed down discussions and allowed more assertive and outspoken jurors to dominate the deliberations.

Hall said Eagles also seemed acutely aware that "if he said the wrong thing, all these [militant black] attitudes were going to jump on him."

According to another juror, the more militant black jurors also used persuasion sometimes to get what they wanted. Marilyn Thomas was leaning toward conviction on most counts, the juror said, until she was approached by Snow at the hotel.

"He started talking to her," said the juror. "I was with [two other jurors] and we debated whether to go over there and just get in the middle of the conversation kind of naively, you know, just to break them up."

They didn't, and from that point on, the juror said, Thomas began voting with the pro-acquittal bloc of Hines, Hardeman, Jackson-Warren, and Snow.

In addition to the racial attitudes straining the deliberations, the difficulty of having to judge the city's chief elected official, and the lack of a strong guide, the jurors also faced evidence that was not only voluminous, but in some cases provocative or ambiguous.

Some jurors saw the Vista sting operation as entrapment and refused to weigh the videotape evidence objectively, while others saw the sting as legitimate and the tape as graphic proof that Barry had indeed smoked crack.

Deoudes, one of six jurors who voted "guilty" on the Vista count, nevertheless conceded: "You can't really blame people for that [asserting entrapment], because you have a whole city divided on that count. [There are even] attorneys I've [since] read about: some say it's entrapment, some say it's not entrapment." Deoudes added, however; "I think if you read the judge's instructions, I think everything that took place in terms of what Rasheeda Moore did, she was allowed to do. This is my perception of the judge's instructions to the jury."

Deoudes was equally clear that the government had proven its case on most other counts (he voted "not guilty" on only three charges); but, according to Marsena Hall, defense counsel Mundy had effectively raised doubts on some of those charges.

"The evidence that prosecutors gave was good," Hall said, "but then Mundy would bring something up, he would [raise] in your mind a reasonable doubt, one little thing that could switch things around. For instance, a time or something: 'He said 10 and she said 11.' So that will cause a problem."

The jurors also had to sort the truth-tellers from the liars among the nearly 50 witnesses who took the stand. "You had a lot of witnesses," said Marilyn Thomas, "but there wasn't a lot of concrete evidence. Not that everybody up there [on the witness stand] was a blatant liar—I never believed that— but I was just going on what concrete evidence they had. Besides the videotape, it was more or less hearsay."

Marsena Hall also was skeptical of many of the witnesses, whose testimony, she said, she weighed in the context of what they could gain and what they could not gain by cooperating with the government. What would be their reason to lie?

Several jurors apparently thought James McWilliams lied about seeing Barry and Lewis disappear into a bathroom at the Ramada Inn Central with a pipe in December 1988 and later seeing white, pungent-smelling smoke billowing over the bathroom door. They also apparently were not impressed by McWilliams's character—he admitted on the stand to supplying cocaine to a female employee he described as "like a daughter" to him. Mundy had suggested during cross-examination that the woman was more likely an illicit lover of McWilliams, who was married.

Apparently finding McWilliams an unreliable witness, Snow, Jones, Hines, Jackson-Warren, Hardeman, and Marilyn Thomas voted "not guilty" on count six, the cocaine possession charge tied to the testimony of McWilliams and Charles Lewis, another witness with a decided credibility problem (according to the *Post*, some jurors openly referred to him as a "scumbag").

Deoudes, on the other hand, voted to convict Barry on count six. He saw James McWilliams as no more, or less, tainted than any other witness at Barry's trial. "People on the jury were saying, 'McWilliams doesn't have good character.' " he recalled. " 'Well, hell, neither does Marion Barry. And that's why we're all here. So why are you going to hold that against McWilliams? Name me one person that walked into court that is of good character.' " He added: "People were throwing out anything just to justify their acquittal stance."

Despite the formidable obstacles to reaching a consensus on *any* of the counts, on Tuesday, August 7, the jurors perhaps surprised themselves by voting 12 to zero to convict Barry on count 12. It alleged that the mayor had used powder cocaine with his old friend Doris Crenshaw at the Mayflower Hotel in November 1989. According to several jurors, the decision came down to the credibility of Crenshaw, an old friend of Barry's and former civil rights worker with impressive political credentials who, in Deoudes' words, "wasn't going to compromise herself for the mayor."

However, when Deoudes and others tried to make a case for also convicting Barry on count one, which alleged that Barry had conspired with at least one other person to possess cocaine, several jurors balked. The problem, said Deoudes, was not that they did not understand the charge or believed that Barry had not conspired with Crenshaw to possess the drug. He said some jurors—despite the instructions to ignore such factors—were concerned that if they convicted Barry on count one, and it turned out to be a felony charge, Barry could be facing hard time.

"People were not sure if the conspiracy charge was a felony or a misdemeanor," said Deoudes. "Had they been certain it was a misdmeanor, he would have been convicted on that, too."

At 3:40 P.M. Tuesday, Eagles sent a note to Jackson informing him the panel had reached a verdict on count 12. The judge had given the jurors the option of announcing their verdicts piecemeal or all together. While awaiting the arrival of the defendant and the lawyers for the formal reading of the verdict, the jurors returned to count three, which charged Barry with buying crack from cocaine dealer Lydia Reid Pearson at the Reeves Municipal Center on September 7, 1988. They were nearing a not-guilty verdict, but Deoudes and Patricia Chaires were not fully convinced by Barry's alibi. They told the other jurors they were leaning strongly toward acquittal, but before making their final decision they first wanted to see the videotape of Barry giving a speech at fire department headquarters on the morning of the alleged drug purchase.

When they announced that, said one juror, "She [Harriedell Jones] said, 'Well, I want to change my mind, too, if you-all are going to change your minds.' That's when a knock came on the door, and the marshal said for us to line up."

Joseph Deoudes asked the marshal if they could have five more minutes. The answer was no. "In the meantime," said the juror, "we're asking her [Jones] where she was coming from. And I think Ed [Eagles] was trying to get to her."

As they filed out of the jury room, the juror said, Eagles confronted Jones, who "said she would let him know" what her verdict was by giving him "a signal" inside the courtroom.

"Do you have a verdict?" Judge Jackson asked.

"Your honor, are you going to poll the jury?" Eagles replied, stalling for time. He could not, after all, announce a verdict that did not exist.

Jackson refused to poll the jurors. He asked Eagles the same question again. Eagles, who by now was turning red, repeated his request. There was still no signal from Jones. The jurors were fidgeting in their seats as the defendant and scores of reporters and spectators looked on.

"Do you have a verdict?" Jackson asked again.

Finally, Hilson Snow answered: "Not at this time."

Jackson sent the jurors back into the room.

"I laughed because I was so embarrassed," said Hall. "We made ourselves look stupid," She said there were "a bunch of attitudes when we went back" into the jury room.

Their mutual mortification, she said, lit a fire under the jurors, who quickly reached a consensus on counts 12 ("guilty") and three ("not guilty"). But when they turned to the 12 remaining counts, deliberations again bogged down. At this point, said Hall, "Everybody was tired and everybody was just sticking to what they were saying. It was like, 'I say it's this way, that's how it is.' That's why we couldn't come up with any [more] conclusions."

Around noon on Thursday, August 9, 34-year-old Deborah Noel was rushed to Providence Hospital, where her private physician, Dr. Ashraf El Khodary, found her to be "deeply depressed, under great stress, and overwrought, and unable to continue deliberations."

The judge dismissed her shaken colleagues for the rest of the day. If both sides agreed, the 11 remaining panelists could legally complete their deliberations without Noel, who had been voting consistently for conviction. Barry's legendary luck might once again have come into play. Noel, however, returned the following morning. By midafternoon, Eagles decided the jury had done what it could. Aside from the two unanimous verdicts, the panelists had deadlocked six to six or seven to five on all but two of the remaining 12 charges. They voted nine to three to acquit on count four, one of the crack possession charges at the Ramada and 10 to two to convict on count 13, the Bettye Smith cocaine possession charge.

At 4:25 P.M. on Friday, August 10, the same day on which a white former top Justice Department official, Henry Barr, was indicted by a federal grand jury for cocaine possession, Eagles sent a note to Jackson asking, ''If on any count the jury is unable to reach a verdict, what are our instructions?''

Jackson responded with a question of his own: ''Has the jury reached a verdict on any of the counts?'' Eagles said yes. Jackson called the defendant and lawyers to the courthouse. The hour and a half it took for everyone to arrive ''seemed like forever,'' recalled Deoudes, who kept a diary during deliberations in which he recorded the disgust he felt at the actions of some of his fellow jurors: ''I am convinced that this jury has failed the system. It is clear, no matter what the outcome, that Marion Barry, in the true sense of justice, was not given a fair trial.''

As the exhausted-looking jurors filed into the courtroom and took their seats in the jury box around 6:00 P.M., the defendant, wearing a grey double-breasted suit, white shirt, and red paisley tie, stood at the defense table, hands folded, nervously pursing his lips. He remained standing as Eagles read the verdict on count three: ''Not guilty.'' Barry did not react. But when Eagles read ''Guilty'' on count 12, the mayor looked down at the table for a moment, then raised his head. He appeared disappointed.

When Eagles announced that the jury could not reach a verdict on the 12 remaining counts, Barry turned to Kenneth Mundy, shook his hand, then embraced him.

After polling the jurors on the two counts they had reached, Jackson read them a federal jury instruction known as an "Allen charge," which, in effect, urged them to try a little harder on the deadlocked counts. He then gave them all copies of a brief questionnaire and sent them back into the jury room.

"It took us about 30 seconds," said Deoudes, to fill out the forms asking the jurors five questions, including, most cogently, whether or not they felt further deliberations would prove fruitful and whether or not they wanted to come back on Monday to resume their work. Everyone just said no, recalled Deoudes, adding that if they had been forced to continue their deliberations, an already tense situation "would have gotten a lot worse."

At 6:10 P.M. Eagles sent his 14th and final note to the judge. "It is our unanimous judgment," he wrote, "that no further deliberation will result in a verdict."

Jackson called the jurors back into the courtroom.

"I will declare a mistrial" on the 12 remaining counts, the judge announced at 6:18 P.M. After setting a "status hearing" for September 17, on which date the government would have to decide whether or not to retry Barry, Jackson turned to the jurors, some of whom he later would castigate publicly for failing in their civic duty. "Ladies and gentlemen," he said, "you are excused."

A tearful Marion Barry walked to the courtroom railing where he hugged Anita Bonds, Lurma Rackley, and other well-wishers. Effi Barry was not in the courtroom. After wiping his eyes with a handkerchief, the mayor strode purposely past a stunned-looking Jay Stephens and shook hands with Albert Arrington, the black detective who had helped convict him.

"See you next go-round," he said, referring to a possible retrial.

"You never know," Arrington said, smiling pleasantly.

After a brief strategy session, Barry emerged from a side entrance of the courthouse, where he was mobbed by hundreds of supporters, camera operators, and reporters. He smiled and raised a clenched fist in the air. He had come out of his seven-month ordeal better than almost anyone could have predicted. Under the D.C. Code, regardless of what sentence he received on the misdemeanor conviction, he still could run and hold elected office in the District. He could even change his mind and run for mayor if he so desired. With Kenneth Mundy in tow, and his worried-looking bodyguards clearing a path through the excited throng, the triumphant mayor began walking around the building to the main entrance where more media types were waiting.

Kool-Aiders in the crowd chanted "Bar-ry, Bar-ry!" "Four more years!" and "Run, Barry, run!" Some reached over the phalanx of protectors to shake the grinning mayor's hand or just touch him.

When passing motorists saw the spontaneous victory parade, many honked their horns in sympathy. Several pulled to the side of the road and joined the celebration.

Pressed by reporters about his plans, the mayor would say only, "I'm going to get back to the business of running the city."

When he got to the Constitution Avenue entrance, Barry beamed and waved to supporters while press secretary Lurma Rackley spoke for him.

"He is relieved, obviously," Rackley said in answer to a reporter's question. She added, "This is his 202nd day chemical-free."

Rackley said the mayor would reserve official comment until 2:00 P.M. the following day, when he would give a speech at the Reeves Center. Deferring comment was a smart move, made well in advance of the verdict, giving Barry time to reflect on it.

Jay Stephens did not have such a luxury.

As Kool-Aiders booed and chanted loud enough to drown out his words to all but a few who stood nearby, Stephens, flanked by a subdued-looking Judith Retchin and Richard Roberts, as well as several Barry investigators, defended the government's actions in trying the mayor and declared a limited victory.

"Our job as professional prosecutors," said Stephens, "is to follow up allegations of criminal conduct without regard to professional status or any other irrelevant factor." Calling the Barry investigation and trial "a judicial process, not a political process," the U.S. attorney said his office had received repeated allegations of criminal conduct by the mayor. "To fail to make the tough decisions [to investigate those allegations]," Stephens said, "would have been irresponsible."

Then he deliverd the government's bottom line: "The verdict today says publicly and officially to the mayor, 'You must accept responsibility for your actions.'" He said the verdict also demonstrated that "the clutches of illegal drug use are beyond no one, and no one is above the law."

Not even Marion Barry.

29

RUN, BARRY, RUN!

Barry's mixed verdict made headlines around the world. Nowhere were they more vitriolic than in Colombia, where hundreds of people—including judges, journalists, politicians, and police—are killed each year by cocaine traffickers who had declared war against the government in August 1989, after then-president Virgilio Barco summarily renewed his government's suspended policy of extraditing drug suspects to the United States for trial. (Barco's successor, Cesar Gaviria, has since backed off that policy, offering traffickers who surrender and confess to at least one crime a reduced sentence and a guarantee that they will *not* be extradited. However, traffickers who are caught by police still face extradition.)

"It weakens all of our arguments [for extradition]," one senior government official told the *Washington Post* about Barry's verdict. "While we endure terrorism here, they give in to racial pressure there."

The story ran on the front page of Bogota's three largest newspapers, including *El Espectador*, which ran the headline "Guilty and Free" over a photo of Barry smiling. The caption read, "The Laugh of American Justice."

While Colombians were understandably angry at what they perceived as the failure of the American justice system to hold a prominent American cocaine abuser legally accountable for his actions, Washingtonians, black and white, were perhaps even angrier at a man who had betrayed his public trust. Barry showed that he was acutely aware of their feelings when he addressed a sweltering partisan crowd at the Reeves Municipal Center the day after the verdict.

"I ask all of you, young or old, black or white, Jew or gentile, rich or poor, Northwest or Northeast, Ward 3 or Ward 8," implored the mayor in a televised speech, "to forgive me for any hurt I may have caused."

"We forgive you!" shouted one supporter at a rally that began with Barry reciting the first verse of "Amazing Grace" and soon took on the tone and character of a fundamentalist revival.

Having acknowledged that he had brought disgrace upon himself, his family, and all Washingtonians by "going against my own grain, my religious upbringing, and my mother's teaching," Barry called on all D.C. residents to "let go of the past, let go of the hate" and "come together to begin to heal ourselves and our city.

"I know my trial has helped to expose deep divisions and racism in our community that are reflective of what is happening around the nation," Barry asserted. "But I believe that Washington, D.C. can be a model to the world of how people of divergent beliefs and opinions, of various races and religions can work together for the good of all."

If D.C. was going to be a model of racial and ethnic harmony, it would have to wait. In a *Post* poll of D.C. residents taken the day after the verdict, more than half the 603 randomly selected respondents felt the mayor's trial had increased tensions between black and white residents. More than four out of 10 Washingtonians felt Barry's investigation had been racially motivated, while two out of 10 believed the federal government was "out to get" the city's black mayor. Only half the respondents were "satisfied" with the outcome of Barry's trial.

The mayor seemed to aim his remarks at those who were not satisfied. "American citizens should not have to walk around in fear that their constitutional rights are being eroded and trampled," he contended, "and Big Brother is all-powerful and all-knowing."

Big Brother was just another name for the federal Goliath.

"Therefore, I call on our leadership of this nation and our government to work together to guard our rights and insist that the government guard against a tendency to overreach in its zeal and its zest just to make a point."

The "point," of course, was to show that no American, not even the mayor of the nation's capital is above the law. But Barry obviously hadn't gotten the point, despite his conviction, or he wasn't prepared to acknowledge it.

"I believe that the conscientious men and women who served on the jury explored this concern," said Barry, harping once again on the theme that Mundy had injected so skillfully into his trial: that Barry, at worst, was guilty of a minor indiscretion by his "occasional' use of cocaine, while the *real* villain of the sordid drama was the federal "Goliath." "Let's not forget that these are human beings, too, on the jury, [they] have their own emotions, [they] have their own feelings about this. No matter what their opinions were, they put forth great sacrifice and great work. And they have spoken. Let their judgment be our last judgment."

After blasting the media for allegedly "overexposing, over-reporting, overreaching in their zeal and zest to grab headlines and get ratings," Barry offered himself as a "beacon of hope" to those seeking recovery from the ravages of drug addiction.

"I hope that my experience can show you, a recovery community, that with strength, courage and belief in a higher power, you'll turn to solutions for mood-altering chemicals," he said. "You don't have to look for the answer somewhere else."

Now that he had won a surprisingly gentle verdict, the mayor called on all Washingtonians to "forget about this trial, stop talking about the pros and cons of it, the rightness and wrongs of it." He closed his remarks by paraphrasing from the New Testament.

"Judge not and you shall not be judged," Barry entreated. "Condemn not and you shall not be condemned. Forgive and you shall be forgiven."

In brief remarks following Barry's, Kenneth Mundy echoed the mayor's call for forgiveness and an end to interracial hostilities. He also asked the city's media to "join us in being responsible. Do not rekindle the fires between the U.S. attorney's office and the defense. Do not refresh the coals in the long 10 weeks of agony that we've been put through."

The journalists Mundy was imploring to act responsibly were the same ones he had used during the trial to spread a racially divisive message by alleging that an FBI "assault force" had targeted black officials across the country. "It is a time for each side to extend the olive branch rather than throw down the gauntlet," Mundy contended. "It is not time to reload our guns, or to prepare for further combat."

Mundy then asked Jay Stephens to back off, now that he'd nailed Barry on a misdemeanor charge.

"I would ask the government to be measured and careful in its thought about whether it wants to inflict upon this community a retrial or a regurgitation of all that we've been through this [past] 10 weeks.

"I ask the government to bear in mind that it owes a responsibility to the citizenry. It owes a responsibility to awaken to the fact that sometimes it is better to step back, to reflect, and to rebuild. And we are going to be about this business for the next several weeks, whatever the mayor's other plans are."

Effi Barry had the last word. Smiling stiffly, the mayor's spouse, who three months later would leave Barry, taking along their son, Christopher, said, "This is a time for great introspection. This is a time of prayerful humility. It is human to err. It is divine to forgive."

The following day, D.C.'s newly forgiven mayor appeared at a gospel music conference at the Washington Convention Center and again sounded a note of contrition. "My God, my magnificent, majestic and almighty God is a forgiving God, isn't He?" Barry demanded rhetorically of several thousand attendees from around the country. They responded with cheers and applause. "He came into this world not to save saints, but to save sinners," Barry reminded them.

But then the born-again mayor quickly changed his message from one of absolution to one of vigilance.

"All is not well in our land," he warned. "Satan and satanic forces are everywhere, trying to destroy all that which we've built up. Particularly if you're African American, you better watch out." Unless African Americans "band together spiritually, economically, socially and politically," Barry added, "we're not going to make it here in America."

Only a day after calling for an end to racial tensions and hostilities in the city, the mayor was once more stoking racial fears, encouraging a mentality of a black "us" against a white "them" he now apparently equated with the Devil himself.

On Monday Barry changed his party affiliation from Democratic to independent, "in order to keep my options open," he said. The move cleared the way for a bid at an at-large city council seat, or even mayor in the November 1990 race. He waited only one day to clear up that mystery, declaring for the council race on Tuesday, August 14. Barry had held such a seat for four years before being elected mayor in November 1978. If elected, Barry said, "I can achieve my goal of continuing to make a contribution to the political life of this city without keeping the debate alive about my leadership of the city."

The mayor said he was going to take his campaign to every ward of the city, including largely white, affluent Ward 3, whose residents had voted massively against him in the past two elections. "I think I can reach out and be sort of the healer, the love and unity candidate," he said, incredibly.

Ever the fighter, Barry told reporters that, had he chosen to reverse his decision and run for mayor instead, he would win reelection by a plurality. A *Post* poll taken three days earlier gave a different picture: three out of four respondents said Barry shouldn't run for mayor and half said he should resign from office immediately. Barry conceded he had opted for the council race rather that try for a fourth mayoral term because the latter "would further polarize attitudes and further alienate certain segments of the population from each other."

By throwing his hat in the ring for the already crowded at-large council race, Barry also alienated one of his new rivals, veteran at-large seat holder Hilda Mason, who had helped nurse Barry back to health after he was shot by Hanafi Muslims during their 1977 siege of the District Building, and who had adopted Barry as a political protégé shortly after he arrived in the city 12 years before that.

"I do feel very disappointed in my grandson, Marion Barry," said the 75-year-old Mason, who chaired the council's Education Committee. But she added, "I think I have done a lot for the District of Columbia. I'm going to win this struggle."

As Barry launched his campaign, a politician who eight months earlier was considered virtually unbeatable in his bid for an unprecedented fourth mayoral term acknowledged that his run for a comparatively humble council seat would be a steep uphill climb.

"I know there's a solid bloc of anti-Barry voters out there now who wouldn't vote for me for dogcatcher," Barry conceded.

Knowing this, he ran like he'd never run before, showing up before dawn at Metro subway stations to press the flesh of mostly black working-class commuters, then touring till dusk while standing in a car with an open sunroof, stopping to meet and greet potential voters at stores and beauty shops, senior citizen centers and video arcades.

Not everyone greeted his official caravan joyfully. In the ethnically mixed Northwest neighborhood of Adams-Morgan, two men pretended to snort cocaine as Barry's car waited at a red light. As it passed into the Mount Pleasant neighborhood, a woman waiting at a bus stop flashed an obscene hand gesture at the smiling mayor and a small boy ran behind his car, shouting, "You smoked crack, man!"

To add to Barry's troubles, two of his at-large opponents, Advisory Neighborhood Commissioner Ray Browne and D.C. school board member Linda Cropp, asked him to quit the council race. According to the *Post*, Browne and Cropp felt it was time to "let the city heal from the racially divisive effects of his trial." But Barry ignored them, and he also ignored a majority of D.C. Council members who endorsed Hilda Mason in the eight-way race for two at-large seats. But when Barry's old friend, the Reverend Jesse Jackson, joined the rush to judgment, endorsing Mason as well, Barry broke his silence.

"Jesse Jackson's support of another candidate is an indication of a problem he has," Barry said bitterly, "and that is of betraying and going against people who helped him over the years."

Although the ranks of his supporters and allies were dwindling daily, Barry would not quit. As his campaign wore on, it became clear the outgoing mayor was impelled by more than a desire to win an election. Marion Barry was struggling for no less a goal than redemption in the eyes of the electorate after his debacle at U.S. District Court. There were other, more practical reasons to run as well: If Barry were to win one of the two at-large council seats being contested in the November race, he would qualify at the end of his four-year term in 1994 for a full-blown pension, since he then would have served in city government the minimum 20 years required for such a benefit. (He dismissed speculation that he was running for financial reasons as ''insane'').

On September 4 the veteran campaigner used his incumbency to grab the limelight by staging a news conference to warn city council members and his successor in the mayor's office that the city was facing a projected $93 million deficit for the 1990 fiscal year, a figure that would more than triple by year's end.

''They [his critics on the council] can pass it off as mismanagement,'' he said defensively. ''They can say the Barry administration was neglectful, which is not true. But at some point next year the D.C. government, regardless of what you're trying to do, is going to run out of money.''

The projected deficit, the largest in a decade, was not entirely the mayor's or even the city council's fault—the primary culprit was the U.S. Congress, which had arbitrarily frozen the city's annual federal payment five years earlier—but it nevertheless would become an inescapable part of Barry's legacy.

On Tuesday, September 11, Sharon Pratt Dixon, an attractive, 46-year-old black lawyer, former utility company executive, and former treasurer of the Democratic National Committee, scored a stunning upset over front-runner John Ray, a lawyer and veteran city council member, in the Democratic primary election. Dixon, a third-generation Washingtonian who ran on a platform of radical reform, attributed her victory to profound voter dissatisfaction with the corrupt status quo.

Six days after the Democratic primary—the first in which Barry had not competed in a dozen years—the District's lame-duck mayor got some welcome news: at a status hearing before Judge Jackson at U.S. District Court, Barry learned that U.S. Attorney Jay Stephens would not "reload" his prosecutorial gun and come after Barry, as Kenneth Mundy had put it in his post-trial speech directed at the federal prosecutor. Instead, Assistant U.S. Attorney Judith Retchin announced, the government was dropping the remaining 12 charges against the mayor.

After the brief hearing Barry said only that he was "relieved that this phase of the legal proceedings is over."

Jay Stephens, however, appearing outside the federal courthouse with prosecutors Retchin and Roberts, waxed eloquent. Citing the revelations at Barry's trial, Stephens said, "That overwhelming evidence is now a matter of public record. Now the residents of this city, as well as citizens from across our nation, can themselves evaluate the truth concerning allegations of drug use that hung like a dark cloud over the chief executive of this city."

Asked why he had decided not to retry Barry, Stephens responded, "In the final analysis, a retrial of this case would achieve little more than what already has been accomplished. The ultimate fact is the chief executive officer of this city—charged with leading the fight against illegal drugs and violence—himself has been convicted of contributing to this human devastation." In doing so, said Stephens, Barry "has betrayed his public trust, and has done a grave injustice to those he claimed to serve. The evidence of his criminal actions is deeply etched in the minds of people around the globe."

The federal prosecutor said the maximum one-year jail sentence and $100,000 fine Barry could face for his misdemeanor conviction "provides an adequate basis for the court to reach an appropriate" punishment to mete out to Barry at the mayor's sentencing, which Jackson had set for October 26.

The mayor, meanwhile, was also taking his licks from the D.C. Council, which had sat on its hands for years while Barry did virtually as he pleased as the city's chief executive. On October 9, the council belatedly flexed its oversight muscle by passing an emergency resolution limiting for the next 90 days Barry's power to approve city contracts worth more than $1 million. The move, which the council would later make permanent, was understandable, considering Barry's attempt to commit the city in recent months to such pacts as a $216 million building lease with an investors' group that included a major Barry campaign contributor. The move was long overdue, but the council had acted only after Barry seemed powerless to retaliate.

On October 12, Kenneth Mundy, despite his earlier call for an end to racial and judicial hostilities, reloaded his gun and took another shot at the government.

Citing alleged "irregularities and contamination of the jurors" during their sequestration, Mundy asked Judge Jackson in a motion to throw out Barry's drug conviction and grant him a new trial. Mundy wrote that a deputy U.S. marshal guarding the sequestered jurors had told one of the jurors that an alternate juror had pronounced Barry "guilty, guilty, guilty" in a television interview. Mundy also said "at least several" jurors had witnessed the botched drug sting at the Sheraton Greenbelt Hotel.

Would the whole sad spectacle be played out again, with Stephens, perhaps, also reconsidering his decision not to seek a retrial?

Fortunately not. At an October 19 hearing on Barry's pre-sentence report (which details a defendant's family back-ground, health, educational and employment history, and any prior arrests), Mundy surprisingly dropped his request for a new trial, telling the judge that Barry himself had made the decision.

"He just said it is time to let the matter lie and be at rest," said Mundy.

However, when Mundy asked Jackson to postpone Barry's sentencing hearing, set for the following week, because the defense supposedly had not been given enough time to respond to the pre-sentence report, Jackson refused. Mundy also disagreed "wholeheartedly" with D.C. probation officer Arthur Carrington's conclusion that the mayor deserved a stiffer sentence because he had obstructed justice and failed to accept responsibility for his wrongdoing.

Under federal sentencing guidelines, Barry's misdemeanor offense was rated a six on a scale that goes up to 43, for treason. A level six offense brings zero to six months in jail. Carrington, who had interviewed Barry and prepared the report, reportedly assessed the mayor two extra points for obstructing justice and refused to subtract two points for a show of contrition, an option he could have exercised had he believed Barry remorseful. That made Barry's offense a level eight, which brings a mandatory two to eight months in jail without parole.

Finally, on the eve of his sentencing, Barry repented. Sort of. In one of nine letters submitted to the judge in the convicted mayor's behalf on October 24, Barry acknowledged that he was a "recovering alcoholic and a drug addict" who had committed acts that were "degrading and outrageous" while "under the ravages" of addiction, an "insidious disease that afflicts millions of Americans." He asked Jackson to sentence him to community service, so he could help other recovering addicts "whose pain, while not as public, is just as deeply rooted."

"I have been embarrassed and ashamed to see and remember myself in those circumstances," Barry wrote, implying that he'd recently awakened from a nightmare of addiction over which he had no control at the time. "That behavior went against my basic value system and my upbringing," he asserted. "It has caused me, my family and the citizens of my city shame and enormous pain. For these actions, I am deeply sorry.

"One of my greatest shames is that my behavior hurt, confused and disappointed young people, the very youth I have fought so hard to help and uplift. I was once one of those aspiring youth proud of my heritage. When my disease and the behavior I engaged in took over me and became public, I lost much of the respect and support I had struggled so long to gain in the black and white communities; and I had to give up my quest for a fourth term as mayor of the District of Columbia.

"I had hoped to leave only a legacy of leadership in human and civil rights," Barry wrote. "Instead, because of my actions,

I must live with a personal pain and shame that cannot be erased. When I sat in your courtroom each day, hearing things about myself that I had not wanted to face, I may have appeared to be calm and unmoved, but on the inside I was suffering nearly unbearable humiliation and deepest regret.

"What I want to do now is use my experience to help, perhaps even save, others. . . . I respectfully ask the court to decide that the best way for me to be punished for my crime is through service to the community."

Mundy also wrote to Jackson, recommending that, as an alternative sentence, the judge sentence Barry to perform eight to 10 hours of volunteer work per week for a year tutoring disadvantaged or incarcerated youths.

In making his case, Mundy reminded Jackson that other public officials convicted of more serious crimes had not been sent to jail. He mentioned in particular Michael Deaver, the former Reagan White House deputy chief of staff, convicted two years earlier in Jackson's courtroom of lying to Congress and to a federal grand jury probing his lobbying activities. Both crimes are felonies. Jackson had fined Deaver $100,000, placed him on probation for three years, and ordered him to serve 1,500 hours of community service. However, federal sentencing guidelines, which give judges very little leeway in determining a sentence, were not yet in effect at the time.

Jackson received additional letters in Barry's behalf from city administrator Carol Thompson, NAACP executive director Benjamin Hooks, several black ministers, longtime friend Ella McCall-Haygan, and Effi Barry, who wrote: "I beseech you to search your humanity. What further punishment does this man deserve? For certain, there can be no greater sentence than to have the whole world tune into your day in court as you are publicly castrated.

"Must there be further abuse of a man who, because of his medically diagnosed alcoholism, became a pawn of those whom he mistakenly accepted as his close friends or confidantes and became vulnerable to the temptations they provided?"

Even Barry's wife wanted to blame something else (alcohol) and someone else (his "close friends or confidantes") for her husband's troubles. And she wanted the judge to know that Barry wasn't the only one who would suffer if he were sent to jail.

"For certain, it would only serve as a further stab to the heart of a little boy [their son, Christopher] who has so valiantly stood tall through all of this ordeal, and has constantly said, 'My Daddy is a good man,' as so many around him have laughed and called his father bad.'"

Jay Stephens was far less sentimental but no less articulate in giving Jackson the government's view.

"[Barry's] conviction for possession of illegal drugs was only one episode in an extended pattern of illegal drug use and attempts to cover it up that caused great harm to the community," the city's chief federal prosecutor wrote in asking Jackson to sentence Barry to the maximum one-year prison term permitted by law. "Because he was the highest-ranking municipal official in the nation's capital, it is near impossible to overstate the gravity of his conduct. His brazen disregard for the law conveyed a particularly devastating message to a number of people" and "had a devastating effect on our bid to convince youth that their future rests with their rejection of drugs."

Once more, the argument had been cast in highly emotional, evan moralistic terms by both sides. And while there were pundits and critics aplenty of both races offering their advice on how he should go about his job, few would have likely offered to switch places with white federal judge Thomas Penfield Jackson the day he had to sentence the black mayor of the nation's capital.

30

EXIT THE KING

O n Friday, October 26, the final act in Marion Barry's legal
drama was staged in the same courtroom where he had
been convicted 10 weeks earlier by a jury of his peers.
The mayor showed up in a black, double-breasted suit to face
his most difficult hour. For decades the bodies had been falling
around him, starting with his father's sudden death in Itta Bena
when he was only four. They had fallen elsewhere in
Mississippi when Barry was in his mid-twenties and saw
friends and fellow civil rights workers sent to an early grave
by white bigots. When he got to Washington in the mid-1960s
the bodies had kept on falling, literally and figuratively—
dozens dead in the 1968 riot, thousands in the crack wars of
the 1980s, murders and scandals at Youth Pride, Incorporated,
and scandals in the top ranks of his administration. Barry
himself had been felled by a shotgun blast in 1977, but he
quickly rebounded from what turned out to be a superficial
injury. Finally, in January 1990, after dodging numerous
investigative bullets over the years, the mayor had fatally
wounded himself at the Vista Hotel.

Kenneth Mundy spoke first, citing his client's "lifetime of
good deeds" and his unfortunate "Achilles heel" of addiction
in asking Jackson to sentence Barry to community service,
rather than prison. "Mr. Barry wants to give something back
to the city," he stressed.

Judith Retchin, speaking for the government, attacked Barry
for his refusal to "own up" to his misdeeds and asked Jackson
to impose the maximum penalty under the law. The mayor,
she said, had "caused far wider harm than any ordinary
citizen." She added, "It would not be grandiose to say that
what he has done has affected the whole nation."

Then Barry spoke. "If I appear nervous," he told Judge Jackson, resting one hand on the dark wooden lectern, "I am. My stomach is in knots. I have written you a personal and comprehensive statement about my conduct. It indicates I'm prepared and have been prepared to take personal responsibility for all my actions."

Regarding the allegations of his long-term drug use, Barry said, after glancing briefly at the spectator benches, "My mother, who is in this courtroom, didn't raise me that way. My wife, who married me over 12 years ago, wouldn't have married someone with those kinds of character defects and values." He added, "I've asked the community for forgiveness."

Reminding the court that he was now "279 days" free from the ravages of alcohol, Xanax [an antidepressant], Valium, and cocaine, all of which he had admitted abusing at one time or another, Barry said, "I could have continued down that road."

Finally, after asking Jackson to sentence him to community service, Barry said, "I stand before you truly remorseful."

Barry's belated show of contrition failed to quell the wrath of the court.

"Of greatest significance to me in sentencing this defendant," Jackson announced sternly, "is the high public office he has at all relevant times occupied. He was at the time of his offense, the time of his conviction, and is now at time of his sentencing, the elected head of government, as Mayor the chief public official and personage of the City of Washington, D.C., the capital of the United States.

"His breach of public trust alone warrants an enhanced sentence. By his own unlawful conduct the defendant rendered himself beholden to, and thus vulnerable to influence from, anyone who had first-hand knowledge of it. . . . Moreover, the prevalance of the public rumors of defendant's frequent and conspicuous drug use—never dispelled, and now unfortunately shown to have been true—has given aid, comfort, and encouragement to the drug culture at large, and contributed to the anguish that illegal drugs have inflicted on this city in so many ways for so long.

"His prominence inspired others to emulate him and to behave as they believed he did. Having failed as the good example he might have been to the citizens of Washington, D.C.—and, in particular, to the young who are so much more likely to respond to example than to admonition—the defendant must now become an example of another kind."

After chastising the mayor for his moral and exemplary failures, Jackson noted two aggravating factors, Barry's long-term drug use and his "willful attempt at obstruction" of justice by lying to a federal grand jury.

Then he said things could have been even worse for Barry.

"I am ignoring, for purposes of sentencing, what I perceive to have been the defendant's efforts, once prosecution had commenced, to induce the jury to disregard the law and the evidence."

Apparently, Jackson had not appreciated Barry's rather successful attempt to put the federal government on trial. Nor did he seem to appreciate how some of the jurors had responded.

"The jurors," Jackson scolded, "will have to answer to their fellow citizens for the way in which they discharged their duty."

(Four days later, at a Harvard University Law School forum, Jackson would come down even harder on some of the panelists, whom he accused of misleading the court about their true feelings about the defendant and the government during *voir dire*: "Some people on the jury ... had their own agendas," he charged in a speech at his alma mater. "They would not convict under any circumstances." He told the aspiring lawyers that he had "never seen a stronger government case" than the one mounted against Barry.)

After his rare public swipe at a jury, Jackson cited the cases of two unfortunate young men in the city who recently had been given multiyear sentences in the same courthouse for selling drugs.

"There would be no people like them—and also no drug crisis," Jackson said, "if there were no consumers to make a market for their illicit drugs. The defendant was such a consumer, not only in November of 1989 [the date of the count on which Barry was convicted], but on numerous occasions before and since. Proportionate justice would seem to call for some fairly comparable penalty for him.''

Finally, Jackson tempered his remarks by noting some ''mitigating circumstances operating in the defendant's favor,'' namely, Barry's admission to being an alcoholic and his ''significant and sustained progress at self-rehabilitation.''

Then he formally imposed sentence on the mayor.

''It is, therefore, this 26th day of October, 1990, ordered,'' he intoned, ''that the defendant Marion S. Barry, Jr., is hereby committed to the custody of the U.S. Bureau of Prisons for a term of six months, with a recommendation for drug treatment during his confinement, and fined the sum of $5,000, payable to the United States.''

When Jackson pronounced those words the mayor gripped the podium with both hands and bowed his head. It was clear he had not expected to do time. Despite his numerous scrapes with the law over the years—most of them related to protest activities—Marion Barry had never been locked up for more than a day or two. He had in effect led a charmed existence and perhaps come to believe, as many a doomed leader before him, that he was special, ''invincible,'' as he once had put it, and that the protective spell would somehow last forever. Of course, it would not, and could not.

As Barry stood in the well of the court, frozen with shame and anger, deputy U.S. marshal Albert Crew slipped quietly into position behind him, ready to take custody of his prisoner. Crew stopped, however, when Jackson ordered that ''the defendant may remain at liberty on his personal recognizance until his place of confinement is designated.''

The judge further ordered that Barry would under federal law have to pay the estimated $10,000 cost of his confinement and would be placed on supervised probation for one year following his release, during which time he would be subject to random drug tests, drug treatment, ''and/or aftercare when and as directed by the Probation Office.'' Jackson stayed the execution of the sentence pending an appeal.

As the stunned mayor stood, seemingly glued to the podium, Kenneth Mundy came up and patted him gently on the back.

Barry released his death grip, then looked at his wife and mother, still sitting on a bench near the front of the courtroom. But the faithful duo, whom he had trotted out on all appropriate occasions to act as symbols of his goodness and decency, couldn't help him now. A moment later the mayor disappeared with his lawyers through a side door of the courtroom.

Kenneth Mundy reappeared a few minutes later at the main entrance, his hat atypically askew. As a trio of black women on the steps behind him sang, "We Shall Overcome," he told reporters how "disappointed" he was with the sentence, which he said he would appeal, along with Barry's conviction.

The mayor himself slipped quietly out the building's 3rd Street door where his limousine waited. His mother got into the Lincoln Town Car, but Effi, who had come out separately, smiled and shook her head when Barry offered her a ride. He watched as she walked to another car farther down the courthouse driveway.

"Mr. Barry, do you have anything you want to say?" asked a white reporter who had followed the mayor out of the building. Barry just smiled at the newsman, ducked his head, and got into the limousine, next to his mother.

The Town Car moved quickly down the courthouse driveway with a blue Ford Crown Victoria LTD carrying the mayor's bodyguards in pursuit. Sirens whooped and red lights flashed as the cars sped down Constitution Avenue toward the District Building, mournfully signaling the end of Marion Barry's long and controversial reign in the nation's capital. He had come a long, long way from Itta Bena and a South Memphis ghetto, but, even by his own admission, he still had a very long way to go.

EPILOGUE

O n November 6, 11 days after being sentenced, Marion Barry lost his final claim to political power in the District when the voters decisively defeated his bid for an at-large council seat, a position he had won easily four years before becoming mayor. The D.C. Council subsequently awarded Barry a $45,000 readjustment allowance and sent him on his way. Friends of the outgoing mayor, led by D.C. Council member H. R. Crawford, softened his fall from grace by presenting him with a new $25,000 Chrysler New Yorker automobile.

In the same election that marked Barry's apparent political demise, Democrat Sharon Pratt Dixon, who had promised to end corruption and inefficiency in city government, rode her "clean house" platform to a stunning victory in the mayoral race, winning a record 86 percent of the vote. "We have lived through a decade of national excess," Dixon proclaimed two months later in her January 2, 1991, inaugural address, "ignoring all the while the fundamental truth of our condition. There has been a corruption of the public estate, a disregard by those on top for those fundamental values that would hold us together."

She could have been talking about Ronald Reagan, Oliver North, Michael Millken, Neil Bush, Ivan Boesky, Jim Bakker, Donald Trump, or some members of the U.S. Senate. But everyone in the crowd gathered in front of the District Building knew she was talking primarily about the man who stood near her on the podium: Marion Barry. In part because of the political spoils he had handed to his cronies and constituents, and the corruption and mismanagement in his administration, the outgoing mayor had left his successor with a projected $300 million budget deficit.

Yet regardless of how Dixon fares in her attempts to tackle this and other daunting problems, her most important challenge cannot be measured in programmatic terms. She will need to start healing the rift her predecessor only exacerbated, a rift that mutual fear, distrust, and prejudice have caused and continue to cause not just in Washington, but everywhere that black and white inheritors of America's post-Civil War century reside together. Clearly sensitive to this problem, Dixon reached out—not just to these two groups, but to *all* Washingtonians—in her inaugural address: ''We are rich with many hues and many cultures. We are African American and Latino, Irish American and Italian, Ethiopian and Vietnamese. We hail from San Salvador, Managua, Asmara, and Lagos. We speak Spanish, Korean, Hebrew, and Farsi. We dance the Electric Slide and sing in the Gay Men's Chorus. We worship in synagogues and storefronts, in great cathedrals of Christianity and mosques dedicated to Allah. We are a community reflecting the new diversity that is America. We come from every region of the country and every nation of the globe— yet all of us call Washington, D.C., home.''

Creating a harmonious community out of the ''new diversity that is America'' is a challenge Dixon's successor, no doubt, also will face, one that Americans, as well as others, will wrestle with year after year—perhaps with increasing rancor and futility—until the day arrives, if it ever does, when Dr. King's prophetic dream finally becomes a reality, when people of every race, ethnic background, and religious persuasion find in themselves the courage and faith to join together and ''transform the jangling discords of our nation into a beautiful symphony of brotherhood.''

ACKNOWLEDGEMENTS

Writing a book about a complex and controversial political leader in just eight months would have been impossible without the help and encouragement of some very special people. Bonnie Fitdpatrick, an adolescent counselor by trade, adopted the equally daunting role of cheerleader/editor to this writer. Chuck Crawford appeared out of nowhere to put me in touch with British American, which quickly commissioned the book. Paul Mahon, my lawyer/agent, fought for a better contract and coached me through an exhausting journey. Rich LaDieu taught me how to use the laptop computer, which became, in effect, my portable ball and chain. Lisa Ritchie and Margaret Roberts helped me shape the manuscript. Margaret Mirabelli, my editor at British American, skillfully polished my prose and through her encouragement made me *want* to work hard. My father, Martin, helped me focus my theme, kept the buzzards at bay while I finished the book, and, most important, set in his long and remarkable career a standard of journalistic excellence to which I shall always aspire. My siblings, Marcia, David, Julie, and Rachel cheered me on, but also kept me from taking either the project or myself too seriously. Linda Tressa steered me to unexpected sources, turned dozens of tapes into transcripts and mountains of newspapers into a valuable research tool. Fred Pearson gave me two great contacts and kept me laughing. Ravi Khanna taught me to meditate, Edith Bennett untied the psychic knots, Mark Petty wrestled the monkey. Vernon Richards traveled with me to Itta Bena, Barry's birthplace, when my scheduled guide fell through. Leslie Sorg, Jonathan Ebinger, Robert Riccio, and Mary Rozell Hopkins helped me find facts that mattered. John McCaslin generously made the *Washington Time*'s copy of the trial transcript available. Mark Feldstein, Bruce Johnson, Aretha King, Patricia LaPointe, Judy Peiser, Nancy Hart, Vasco Smith, Taylor Branch, Clayborne Carson, Allen Hammond, Rich Adams, Ronald Roach, Rep. John Lewis (D-Ga.), Calvin

Lockridge, Stuart Long, Geraldine Storm, Stephen Romansky, Thomas Rose, Louise Rucker, Robert Moses, Zora Lee Davis, Matthew Gilmore, James Forman, Ron Johnson, Jim Money, Jack Chaillet, Steve Allen, Al Arrington, Mike Folks, Jerry Washington, Joe and Sarah Favara, James and Mary Coffey, Joseph Deoudes, Tina Hall, Jon Hilsenrath, Jack Speer, Carl Stern, Bob West, and J. J. Green gave me key contacts or information. LeeAnn Flynn Hall gave me a pass to the trial. I am also indebted to Mark Feldstein, Juan Williams, Arthur Brisbane, Milton Coleman, Leon Dash, Richard Prince, William Raspberry, Courtland Milloy, Dan Morgan, John Fialka, Stephen Lynton, Barry Kalb, Robert Pear, Ronald Sarro, Fred Barnes, Bernard Garnett, Elizabeth Hickey, Mike Folks, Jerry Seper, Bella Stumbo, Bart Gellman, Michael York, Elsa Walsh, Edward Sargent, and other fine journalists who went before me in seeking an understanding of the elusive topic of my book; and to Taylor Branch, Clayborne Carson, Howard Zinn, Willie Morris, Robert Weisbrot, Howell Raines, Juan Williams, David Garrow, Thomas Battle, Donald Doyle, Alan Westin, and Doug McAdam for their enlightening nonfiction books on Barry, the civil rights movement, or the South. Thanks and blessings to you all, and to everyone else who was kind enough to help.